FISHING
AND
HUNTING
GUIDE TO
UTAH

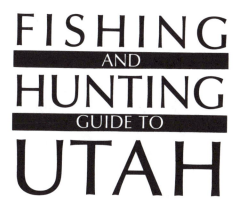

By Hartt Wixom

Wasatch Publishers
4460 Ashford Drive   Salt Lake City, Utah 84124

ISBN: 0-915272-33-4

Library of Congress: 90-070575

Editorial Correspondence: Wasatch Publishers, 4460 Ashford Drive,
Salt Lake City, Utah 84124

Trade Distribution by: Wasatch Book Distribution, P.O. Box 1108,
Salt Lake City, Utah 84110 (801) 575-6735

The North Fork of the Provo River. The esthetics are wonderful and the brook trout fishing can be great too.

ABOUT THE AUTHOR

Born in the center of the greatest outdoor recreation area of the United States, Hartt Wixom is well qualified to write about the country he loves so well. Having explored virtually every nook and cranny in the State of Utah, he can write about fishing and hunting as no one else can. In another era, he might have been a perfect guide for a wagon train enroute to the Unknown West.

He was fortunate in his youth to spend much time in the comparatively little known mountains and deserts of Utah with experienced experts. This served as a perfect background for his many years as

Hartt landing a respectable brown trout.

an outdoor writer and later as an environmental editor. Here he again enhanced his knowledge of the state's wildlife with the help of willing conservation officers, Ute Indian guides, and game wardens.

No one has fought harder to protect our dwindling fish and game areas than Hartt. In over half a century of hunting and fishing, I have never met anyone so well prepared to write this guide.

Hartt has been Rocky Mountain field editor for Field and Stream magazine, Utah editor for Western Outdoors, and published his own Utah Outdoors. He was an early member of the Outdoor Writers Assn. of America. He served as chairman of the Fish Committee (campaigning for the first legislation ever to protect Utah fishing streams) and the Information-Education Committee of the Utah Wildlife Federation. He was founder and first president of the Utah Chapter of Trout Unlimited, signing the letter requesting the first fly-fishing only stream in Utah. (It was granted with the Wild Strawberry River, still a fly-only water ever since 1965 along with others in the state.) While with the Salt Lake City Deseret News, he received several state and national awards for " . . . unbiased writing about fishing and hunting resources of Utah." He has written many magazine articles about fishing and hunting in Utah, with the purpose of getting beyond the surface veneer to discover the many vital fishing and hunting details described in this guide.

Dave Freed
Salt Lake City

Dedicated to Judene —
who encouraged this book be written for the enjoyment
and wise use of Utah's outdoor resources.

In memory of a superb outdoorsman,
J.L. "Casey" Bown:
no one knew Utah's outdoor resources better, loved them more,
nor did more to preserve them for us who follow.

CONTENTS

PREFACE

"Where's a nice trout stream around here to take the kids fishing?" a caller asks. Someone else inquires about a "good" bass or walleye lake. A non-resident businessman seeks a duck hunting marsh to share with a client. And there is always the question, "Where do I find a respectable buck this year?"

This book answers such challenging and interesting questions. Many states have published guides to hunting and/or fishing. But prior to this guide book, Utah has published little on the subject. Many Utahns also drive out of state for their outdoor recreation — when excellent fishing and hunting are nearby. Here, then, is a book geared to provide tips about where and how to better enjoy the Beehive State's many beckoning natural resources.

This guide recognizes many *levels* of fishing and hunting. One person may desire to know where the kids can almost certainly catch some small fish (any size, any fish, just so long as they catch something). Likewise, a parent seeking a first small buck for a teenager wants to know where deer abound. Another type of enthusiast may be on a vigilant quest for a trophy, willing to put in extra scrutiny. All of this will be addressed.

The reader should also be aware there is more to success than geography alone. Other vital factors to outdoor success include timing, weather, special techniques, careful scouting ahead etc. How-to can sometimes be even more important than where-to.

From the beginning, I also pledged this guide wouldn't be a mere chamber of commerce promotion. I'm trying to put myself in your place. No blanket phrases like "paradise for fishing and hunting" . . . unless that's the way you, the reader, could experience it. I take most seriously a national outdoor writing award received for "telling it like it is."

I have included advertisements because I believe they can provide helpful information to serious outdoor enthusiasts — in pursuit of quality fishing and hunting — about needed services and equipment. I have personally benefitted greatly from such information in guide books used when driving to other states.

The author assumes responsibility for many value judgments about best fishing and hunting areas and techniques. It is based on some four decades of outdoor exploration in this, my native state. That experience includes 13 years as a Utah-based newspaper outdoor writer-environmental editor, eight years publishing the magazine Utah *Outdoors*, four years as regional editor with *Field and Stream* magazine (assisting with that publication's New Standard Fishing Encyclopedia section on Utah), authoring the book *Utah*, another titled *Elk and Elk Hunting.*

Where personal successes afield are mentioned, it is with the idea of sharing short-cuts, and hopefully motivating enterprising readers to personally discover their own valuable outdoor wisdom. Since the Beehive State comprises some 84,000 square miles, the author is also grateful for the expertise of many outdoor enthusiasts willing to share personal secrets and refined techniques. This includes Utah Division of Wildlife Resources personnel who live almost daily with the state's trout, bass, ducks, deer, and other natural resources.

In some cases, I might not agree with the way a governmental agency manages fishing and hunting resources; but I will try to give both points of view so readers can come to their own conclusions.

This is a third printing, indicating the popularity of fishing and hunting in Utah. Yet, so many new developments have occurred in the past few years (trophy trout of the Green River for one example, more warm water fisheries, growth of elk and moose populations) that nearly every sentence from earlier editions has been revised and updated. In some cases, fishing has actually become better than ever. It was with pride in the state that my brother, Douglas, and I fished several small streams in Utah during the summer of 1989 specifically for the purpose of updating this guide. We were able to catch and release some 80 lbs. of trout total in three days. Yes, the Beehive State still produces excellent outdoor opportunities . . . with the right where-to, how-to. Of course, it helps to get off the beaten path, a thing the author learned even when driving his van 7,200 round trip miles to Alaska in June-July of 1988.

In summary, I gratefully acknowledge the assistance of many people, too many to name, who helped make this third edition as complete and up-to-date as humanly possible.

Hartt Wixom
Provo, Utah

Introduction

While emphasis in this guide is on successful fishing and hunting, it is hoped the esthetics which should be part of any outdoor experience are not missing. Rarely is an outing of full value without taking time to see a swooping Swainson's hawk, or to hear the Clark's nutcrackers on a mountain hunt. It should be reason enough to protect this non-game wildlife. The sportsman also has a right to view an unlittered landscape with blue skies and clean water. It is hoped the user will keep it that way for those who follow. Everyone can assist in protection of the environment.

In this regard, there is the matter of resource renewal. It is hoped that those who catch fish in excess of needs will release fish to be caught again, even if local regulations do not so specify. Think of it: an 18-inch stream cutthroat may require six years to attain that size. It is then caught and killed in minutes. It may then be tossed in the refrigerator and later thrown away! Trout Unlimited says that a trout is "too valuable to be caught only once." The idea has considerable merit.

Sportsmen also need to learn how to release a fish without injury. Many anglers use a landing net to assist in containing a fish long enough to release carefully. Here's how: hold the fish upside down to minimize squirming, then grasp the *lower* jaw between thumb and forefinger. Avoid touching the gills. Remove the hook carefully without undue squeezing. If the hook will not come out readily, consider snipping the leader. (The fish's stomach acids will dissolve bait hook metal given time, with no injury to the fish.) Rotate the fish gently in the water to revive, and release in a quiet place. Show the youngsters how to do it.

There are some exceptions to the releasing philosophy, such as stunted brook trout in a high lake. Here, thinning out may actually be beneficial by providing more food for fish which remain. Keeping a very large brown trout, which eats many pansize (6-10 inches) fish a day, might also be beneficial to the remaining ecosystem.

In the same manner, many veteran hunters won't shoot just any buck or bull. They seek one larger than their past best. Of course, in designated areas, particularly on depredation (agricultural damage) permits, the state may *seek your help* in reducing antlerless deer *et al.* to maintain game populations within carrying capacity of the rangeland feed.

If you see streams being dewatered, lakes polluted, lands littered, gates left open, untended fires left burning, molesting of livestock, poaching of deer when vulnerable on winter range, *etc.*, it is hoped you will accept this invitation as a citizen sportsman to become a part of the solution rather than the problem. In addition, you can help the landowner on public, as well as private land. If we can teach our youngsters to do the same. Utah — and all of us — will be better for it.

NOTICE

Regulations

References in this book to specific fishing and hunting regulations are current at the time of printing. But, these regulations change annually.

The current regulations are detailed in the annual proclamations issued by the Utah Division of Wildlife Resources. These include the **Fishing Proclamation, Big Game Hunting Proclamation, Small Game Hunting Proclamation, Waterfowl Hunting Proclamation,** and **Bear-Lion Hunting Proclamation.** The documents are free and are available at most sporting goods stores or from the UDWR. Always check the current proclamation for seasons, limits, open and closed areas, and other rules.

Private Property

Although most of Utah is public land, some of the best fishing and hunting locations in Utah are on or adjacent to private land. Know the land ownership status of the places where you fish and hunt and always ask permission before fishing or hunting on private land.

Landmarks

The free highway map produced by the Utah Department of Transportation is an excellent reference for exploring Utah. Wherever possible, locations and directions are described in terms of landmarks shown on this map.

Fishing and Hunting in Utah stacks up very favorably. A 34-pound striped bass from Lake Powell.

CHAPTER ONE

How Does Utah Stack Up?

The Bonneville Salt Flats . . . Canyonland cliffs . . . Great Basin . . . High Uintas . . . Great Salt Lake . . . all describe Utah.

People around the world have a well-defined but narrow picture of Utah. Yet, very little is known about much of the state with its high, green mountains and red-rock canyons. And even those tourists who travel miles of sage and cedar flats on U.S. 89 or I-15 often fail to realize there is excellent fishing and hunting tucked out of sight just half an hour away. Such is Utah!

So, let's take a closer look at the fishing and hunting opportunities. Many are unknown even to life-long Utah residents.

Utah stacks up very favorably with other western states in total resources. In his *New Standard Fishing Encyclopedia*, A.J. McClane says: "Utah harbors some of the West's best fishing and has also supplied many pounds of prize-winning brown trout to *Field and Stream's* annual fishing contests. And few states can surpass Utah's Uinta Mountain fishing." McClane is also amazed at the many 6-7 lb. brook trout hailing from Boulder Mountain. It should be added that the well-traveled McLane has seen about everything the planet Earth has to offer icthyologically. Erwin Bauer, Outdoor Life's highly-respected world wanderer, has also called a certain place in eastern Carbon County, "The greatest mule deer hunting to be found anywhere."

Utah's Green River below Flaming Gorge Dam, with its tens of thousands of well-fed trout per crystal-clear mile is considered by many cosmopolitan anglers to be the best fly fishing trout stream in the continental United States. I know of none with more "seeable" lunkers, not even Idaho's famed Henrys Fork.

In 1989 I caught a 4-lb.plus brown from a small central Utah creek . . . while standing with one foot alongside pavement, a roadside trout catch I didn't duplicate in a 7200 mile drive from Montana to Alaska. And this stream is scarcely known among Wasatch Front anglers. Other waters such as the Lower Provo River, Logan and Blacksmith Fork, and Weber River, do not yield the 2-4 pounder as often as, say, Montana's Madision. But then, these Utah streams have all produced brown trout over 18 lbs. — something the world-famous Madison has never done. Include an incredible 37 3/4-lb. brown from the Logan's First Dam Reservoir, a 33 1/2-lb. brown from tributary Blacksmith Fork (electro-shocked by a Utah State University biology class and returned unharmed to the water), a 20 1/2-lb. brown from the Lower Provo (*Salmo trutta* from the Provo at one time dominated the annual Field and Stream fishing contests) and an 18 1/2-lb. brown, caught as recently as 1988, from the Weber River just above Echo Reservoir. A brown estimated at 19-20 lbs. was caught and released about four miles below Deer Creek Reserovir using a Size 14 hare's ear nymph in May 1989. Regulations required returning all trout over 15 inches, for spawning purposes, in this section of the Lower Provo River.

But of course, no water in Utah can touch Flaming Gorge Reservoir for sheer number of oversized game fish. The 33 lb-10 oz. brown trout caught by Californian Robert Bringhurst from the Gorge in the early 1980s stood, until relatively recently, as the world record. The Gorge has given up hundreds of browns over 15 lbs. It now produces giant lake trout instead of browns, with Curt Bilbey, Vernal, holding the Gorge and state record at 51 1/2-lbs. This leviathan lake trout is the largest fish of any species ever landed in Utah, and the third largest lake trout legally caught anywhere in the world! Shortly after Bilbey's giant, a 50-1/2 lb. laker was also dredged from the Gorge.

Then, there's Fish Lake. With all the decades this water has been plied by man's fishing lines, it was in 1989 that one angler subdued record-breaking 37-and 38-lb. lake trout — within one week of each other.

Many warm water fish species are beginning to catch on with Utah anglers, especially black bass and walleye (called by that name herein, since they are not a true pike). Some Utah Lake and Green River channel catfish are even getting notice from "trout purists" who once turned up their noses at anything without a Latin name beginning "*Salmo*" or "*Salvelinus*." This edition features a completely new chapter on warm-water fishing.

MULE DEER

Utah has the number two Boone-Crockett world record non-typical buck and many other high entries, including archery trophies. Other bucks which didn't score well in B-C competition (one with a rack spread of 47-1/2 inches, now hanging in the First National Bank, Morgan, taken north of Francis Canyon) would make anyone proud. Huge bucks from the Paunsaugunt Plateau north of Kanab seem commonplace. Some of these giant bucks were displayed in the 1989 Mule Deer Expo in the Salt Palace, Salt Lake City, with plans announced to show them again in future years.

Many Utahns have bagged racks large enough to make the record books, yet have not recognized them as such in a state with so many large deer. Taxidermists like Merlin Anderson, Sandy, have discovered for amazed owners many antlers that made the record books. In the 1988 Rocky Mountain Elk Foundation Expo in Salt Lake City, several hunters also brought wapiti racks out of attics and garages to enter Utah for the first time in Boone-Crockett elk annals. Moose, of course, have begun to proliferate in northern Utah. No one is really sure why. But northern Utah is now beginning to rival Wyoming for abundance of the Shiras (or Wyoming) moose.

Those are the hunting highlights. But back to *Odocoileus hemionus*. Let's see how Utah deer stack up. Below are listed Utah's top places in Boone-Crockett typical (four tines per antler), and non-typical records as of 1988.

Boone-Crockett (rifle)

Typical		Non-typical	
position	location taken	position	location taken
6th	San Juan Mountains	2nd	Box Elder County
13th	La Sal Mountains	19th	Duchesne County
16th	Rich County	20th	Provo River area
40th	Kanab area	21st	Morgan County
42nd	Weber Canyon	33rd	Morgan County
56th	Garfield County	40th	Beaver County
		42nd	Kane County
		46th	Morgan County
		52nd	East Canyon

(also many others in book)

Pope and Young world archery records show the following for Utah:

Typical		Non-typical	
3rd	Beaver County	6th	Juab County
10th	Utah County	9th	Lambs Canyon, S.L.County
11th	Cedar Mountain	11th	Iron County
13th	Oquirrh Mtns	12th	Manti Mountain
		18th	Manti Canyon

Other typical world-wide archery trophies were taken in the Parowan area, Fishlake Forest, Strawberry, Cache with non-typical trophies from Blanding area, and Uintah County. A new scoring method of measuring bow-harvested muleys in the velvet include several top scores for Utah: typical, the number 1 buck from Garfield County, 8th from Sevier County, 13th from Box Elder County, 18th from San Juan County. Non-typical, 4th from Kane County, 5th from Box Elder County, and 6th, Sanpete County. The reader can see that Utah produces large bucks from many counties. Utah's deer compare well with any state or province

Note: Precise locations where trophies were taken have not been more accurately pin-pointed by the hunter than shown above.

Boone-Crockett records also show the world's number 1 black bear from Utah's Sanpete County, number 4 from Sevier County, number 5 from Sanpete County, and number 9, Uintah County. The world number 2 cougar is from Utah's Garfield County, losing out to a British Columbia mountain lion by 4/8th of an inch. (All B-C and P-Y points are shown to the nearest 1/8th.) Utah also has two Carbon County cougars tied for 14th best in the world.

Utah's 6000-10,000 foot high bitterbrush and mountain mahogany slopes are ideal for mule deer. Utah elk have been on the increase for years and are now found in many regions where pioneers did not see them. The Utah terrain does not harbor the high bear populations of Washington, nor is it as likely to ever hold as many bighorn sheep and goats as Idaho. When it comes to antelope, Utah lacks the high plains habitat of New Mexico or Wyoming. But there are growing pronghorn populations throughout the state. Utah's Colorado River canyons have always had desert bighorn sheep and game biologists have transplanted more. Cougars have always liked Utah's rimrock country. Probably only Arizona has as many mountain lions. Other big game, like mountain sheep, have been introduced and are taking root in some half a dozen areas. The same is true of mountain goats along higher peaks of Wasatch, Tushar and Uinta Mountains. Conversely, Utah pheasant hunting is not on a par with big game. It is partly a problem of geography. There are too many people along the thinly-cultivated Wasatch Strip, and ringnecks' cropland habitat is limited to 2 to 3 percent of the state. With much of that habitat on private land, gunners compete in a limited area for every rooster. Farmers now leave less cover for pheasants as they utilize more "efficient" farming practices.

With so much uncultivated land, the game biologists have introduced a welcome newcomer, the chukar partridge, which fills an upland gap left by the pheasant. More Hungarian partridges are being planted in northern counties. Blue, ruffed and even sharp-tailed grouse have always been plentiful in Utah, inhabiting the same general lands as the mule deer. Sage grouse have never been numerous across the Beehive State, but there is some hunting for them. Mourning doves are plentiful. Turkeys and quail are fair game. Utah now has a hunt on ptarmigan and sandhill cranes. Cottontail rabbits are found statewide. Farmers need help cutting back jack rabbit populations. Many hunters seek coyotes in Utah.

As for waterfowl, Utah takes a back seat to no one. The Rocky Mountain Flyway funnels birds from the Canadian potholes into Great Salt Lake and Utah Lake, southward to Bicknell Bottoms, and the upper Sevier River Valley. Goose shooting has few hotter moments than along the Green River of eastern Utah. Pintails, gadwalls, mallards, and three species of teal are frequent nesters along the eastern shore of Great Salt Lake only 20 minutes from downtown Temple Square. The 1983-86 floods washed out Great Salt Lake waterfowl nesting, particularly marshes in Bear River Bay and those near Salt Lake City. But excellent duck hunting is expected to return as those waters recede in the 1990s. Canada geese and whistling swans are numerous in Utah.

What is the answer, then, to the question, "How does Utah stack up in the fishing and hunting picture?" The answer is, "Very favorably."

CHAPTER TWO

Fishing in the Beehive State

Utah has a reputation of being only a desert state but Utah has many streams, natural lakes and reservoirs, from Clear Creek on the Idaho boundary to Lake Powell shared with Arizona

Much of the fishing water will not be seen from the highways running parallel with the north-south mountain ranges. It is when you travel east-west in Utah that you come across the most streams-lakes, and for that matter, big game forests. You'll be better able to decide where you want to fish if you have a general idea of the state's geography. So, let's look at Utah (see map) by region.

NORTH: From Salt Lake County north to Idaho much of the area is high and mountainous, similar to nearby western Wyoming and southern Idaho. Rainfall is relatively heavy. Water is mostly clear and cold. The region has many small lakes and creeks, most harboring a permanent trout population. Pollution is minimal, so that the Ogden River has given up brown trout over 12 lbs. even within the city . The Logan River, Blacksmith Fork, and Little Bear River have been some of the state's greatest brown trout producers. Major trout waters which have yielded giant trout include Bear Lake, with the largest cutthroat an 18-pounder. There are some bass waters such as Mantua Reservoir and walleye-channel catfish Valhallas such as Willard Bay. Ditto for Pineview Reservoir east of Ogden. But most of northern Utah is trout water. There are even some small trout creeks around Salt Lake City, as well as alpine trout lakes in the Big and Little Cottonwood Canyon areas between ski resorts. Most of the waters in this region drain to the Great Salt Lake . But northern Box Elder County has Raft River tributaries which flow to the Snake River and the Pacfic Ocean.

CENTRAL: From Salt Lake City to the Richfield-Fillmore area, Utah is divided by high mountains rising abruptly from the eastern edge of the Great Basin. With elevations frequently over 10,000 feet, they draw much moisture from passing clouds. However, the drainage is such that most of it courses downward in small streams, or is stored in relatively minor reservoirs. The one exception is Utah Lake, the "best warm-water fishery in the West." It has ample white bass, walleyes, channel and mud cats, with some black bass, and near the stream mouths, an occasional trout. Most of the higher waters, like Scofield Reservoir, have trout populations. The Central Region also has several warm-water lakes with many species, like Yuba and for contrast, the nearby 100-mile long Manti Mountains' many small lakes and canyon creeks carrying a variety of trout. Then, there is the Provo River which topped the nation a few decades ago in the annual Field and Stream contest with a 20-1/2-pound brown trout.

EAST: From the Wyoming border to Grand County are some of Utah's highest mountains and best trout fishing. This includes Strawberry Reservoir, once labeled as Utah's "bread and butter" fishery, now plagued with chubs and scehduled for chemical treatment in 1990. Many middle-sized trout streams cascade from both the north and south slopes of the Uinta Mountains. This range includes many peaks over 13,000 feet, including the state's highest in King's Peak (13,528 feet) and two national forests, Wasatch and Ashley. Utah's and perhaps the continental United States's top trout stream, the Green River, is found here. Rainbows in the 16-20 inch class are in view almost anywhere, challenging anglers from around the world. The region also boasts numerous oversized lake trout from Flaming Gorge Reservoir which produced the state record lake trout in July 1988 at 51 1/2 lbs. The fishing hole once produced brown trout to 33 lbs. 10 ozs., but the Mackinaw have clearly taken over since the middle 1980s. Pelican Lake is renowned for outsized bluegills. Starvation Reservoir offers giant walleyes. Then there is Hill Creek on the Utes' Uintah-Ouray Indian Reservation with remote Towave and Weaver Reservoir trout fisheries. Most of the waters in this region drain to the Colorado River and Gulf of Mexico.

SOUTH: Utah's most varied geography and fishing are found in this region. You can select largemouth and smallmouth black bass, plus walleye and striped bass fishing below the orange-hued cliffs of Lake Powell, or hike into the brook trout lakes atop the 11,400-foot high pine-studded Boulder Plateau. The upper Sevier River, with East Fork Sevier, has large browns, or you can troll for lunker rainbows and browns in Otter Creek Reservoir . . . Then, there is Fish Lake, an 8,800 foot high natural lake (one of the highest large lakes in the country) with, Mackinaw (lake) trout to 38 lbs., and browns to 21 lbs. Most Fish Lake anglers these days are on a quest for splake (hybrid brook or speckled trout crossed with lake trout) averaging 2-3 lbs. This region also has a number of unsung waters like Piute which can produce 2-5 lb. trout. This region includes the Fremont River, with pockets of nice brown trout. Cedar Mountain has many air-clear lakes, along with Mammoth Creek and Duck Creek Springs. Many new reservoirs such as Gunlock and Quail Creek Reservoirs near St. George provide good late spring black bass fishing. This region receives less fishing pressure than the remainder of the state.

WEST: The western sector ranges from semi-desert to 12,101 foot high Haystack Peak in the Deep Creek Mountains along the Nevada border. There are some quality outdoor experiences in store for those rugged enough to explore this remote region. The few trout streams it does have are almost wholly neglected. Trout Creek in the Deep Creeks possesses one of the few remaining pure strains of native cutthroat (no hybridization from hatchery trout). There are largemouth bass in Rush Lake and Blue Lake (a favorite Scuba diving water along the Nevada border) and brown trout in Vernon Reservoir, all in Tooele County. You might call it Utah's "Forgotten Corner."

SPECIES

Utah is predominantly a trout state, although warm-water species are gaining popularity. This is particularly true as people move into Utah, bringing their fishing habits with them.

Trout include cutthroat, the only *Salmo* species native to Utah, plus browns and rainbows which have been introduced; brook trout and lake trout (technically charr which closely resemble trout) have been transplanted. The golden trout has been planted into the higher waters of the Uintas, but has not flourished in competition with other species. Albino rainbows (a flourescent orange color) are stocked in 9-12 inch sizes to numerous small roadside lakes and streams in the western Uintas. Arctic grayling are stocked as 2-3 inch fry via airplanes, mostly in the upper Weber and North Fork of Provo River lake basins. Grayling are usually limited to waters not accessible by vehicle. Some lakes like Fish, Round and Sand in the upper Weber drainage are reproducing grayling so rapidly that no further stocking is anticipated.

Other major Utah game fish include the (land-locked) kokanee salmon which seldom grows beyond four pounds, before spawning and dying. Large-mouth bass proliferate in Lake Powell plus a few Washington County waters; smallmouth bass are catching on in Flaming Gorge, Powell and Starvation and some smaller waters. White bass are found primarily in Utah Lake. Introduced striped bass took Lake Powell by storm in the mid 1980s, with myriad 2-6 pounders caught, and some whoppers to 40 lbs. Large bluegill are usually found in Lake Powell, and in Pelican Lake in eastern Utah. Walleyes are becoming more popular, with greater stocking possible in lowland waters. The state record walleye is from Starvation Reservoir near Duchesne. Walleye were not stocked in Powell, but are mushrooming there anyway. The state has Northern pike in Sevier County's Redmond Lake, Yuba Lake, and Lake Powell. Pike specimens over 20 lbs. have been taken. Channel catfish are important in Utah Lake, Willard Bay, Bear River below Cutler Dam in Box Elder County and the Green River below Dinosaur National Monument. Crappie are caught primarily in Pineview Reservoir, with some in Willard and Powell. Tiger musekellunge, especially adaptive to cold waters, have been stocked in Pineview. Some hybrids like splake (brook trout and lake trout) are flourishing in Fish Lake and alpine waters. "Wipers" (white bass x striped bass) are contemplated for future planting. Mountain whitefish are native to most Utah streams, and were in abundance when pioneers arrived.

The Bonneville cisco, unique to Bear Lake, is so small it is caught by dip-netting, but is a favorite food fish of some anglers. Bear Lake is also home to the Bonneville and Bear Lake whitefish. Both are unique to this water.

A species of the future may be the Chinook salmon. Since it has done so well in the inland Great Lakes, it is being contemplated for Bear Lake on the Utah-Idaho border.

General Seasons — Utah's general fishing season is open year-around, 24 hours a day. Regulations, including special openings and catch limits, are found in the official Division of Wildlife Resources angling proclamation each year. A copy can be obtained by writing to the UDWR information officer, 1596 West North Temple, Salt Lake City, 84116, or from most sporting goods stores.

Angling with live fish or parts of game fish are not allowed in Utah, although dead minnows (non-game fish) are legal. Corn is banned. All chumming is illegal. The trout limit is usually eight. Beehive State anglers will have many waters to themselves after Labor Day. Yet, many of the state's largest fish are caught in the cool weather months. This is certainly true on the brown trout streams when fish are more active in the fall and spring. But, plan on bringing your overcoat! It is cold in Utah after late September in the higher elevations.

Special seasons — In order to protect spawning fish and sometimes due to agreements with landowners, Utah does have some limited seasons, many of them opening July 1. This includes the lower (Wild) Strawberry River, and all inlets to both Strawberry and Scofield reservoirs. Limits and keeper sizes are different in these areas so check the proclamation closely.

Quality fishing — Various fishing waters within Utah may be designated from time to time as "quality fishing waters" with different (usually lower) limits, minimum sizes, flies or lures only. Fishing is for natural trout only (no hatchery trout are planted). This requires more astute and refined angling skills, but fish are usually larger and you have a chance to become a more proficient angler. Examples of "quality" waters are upper Blacksmith Fork, Lower Provo River from Deer Creek Dam down to the Olmstead Dam, Wild Strawberry, etc. On such streams you often have the opportunity of catching 12-15 inch browns and cutthroats, and a few lunkers, which haven't been removed by baiters.

It is to the credit of the state's fisheries managers that they have been far-sighted enough to provide for this type of recreation angler who is on the increase nowadays over the old "meat- hunters." Managers are realizing you can't hope to supply enough fish to feed hundreds of thousands of anglers daily. A quality experience is now being encouraged.

Timing — The importance of timing cannot be overemphasized. When you go fishing can be as important as where. For example, several days after ice goes out on any high lake is probably the best time of the year to be there (and perhaps the only time). Thus, late June is probably the "hottest" period to take youngsters for brook trout in Mirror Lake or one of the Uinta Mountain waters. Just after ice-out may be about the only time a shoreline angler has a reasonable hope of taking fish, particularly lake trout, from a large reservoir. By mid-summer, most lake fish will move to the very bottom to escape warmish water. Bass and walleyes are best caught by most anglers when spawning fish are active in shallow water near shore in the late spring. Stream fish will be most readily caught when warm spring temperatures trigger hunger — but just before heavy snowmelt runoff. An excellent time to be on hand is when the stream drops and clears, probably in late June-early July. Late September-early October cool weather usually activates spawning brown trout which grow especially hungry just before and after spawning.

Stream fish *can be caught* in mid-summer, of course, but usually only during the coolest part of the day. This is especially true if dry fly fishing on the surface. In spring and fall, fish are often more prone to feed in the warmest part of the afternoon. Remember that air temperatures are not the critical thing . . . it is the water temperatures which count. I once caught nice browns in a bitterly cold April blizzard . . . but the preceding week had been sunny, making the water temperature just right to precipitate a hearty appetite after winter feeding doldrums.

The only waters little affected by season are the spring-fed or reservoir-release streams where temperatures are fairly constant at all times. Such is the Green River below Flaming Gorge Dam. It is also more likely to be good fishing throughout the year because it is less adversely affected with high spring runoff or late fall droughts.

Methods — The best methods of bait angling in the smaller Beehive State streams include: small baits like fresh-water shrimp, rock rollers (caddis larvae which wrap in shells of pebbles or sticks on the underside of stream rocks); thinnish grey or red angleworms in the early summer; grasshoppers in late summer. As a youngster, I also discovered that little white serviceberries found along Utah streams, fished with barb hooked through the skin, will excite trout. As with other offerings, get it down deep. If necesssary, attach splitshot a foot above the hook. Winter fishermen favor something easy to store and to handle, like waxworms and /or salmon eggs. If spinners are used in small streams, best sizes are 0 to 2. Large lures may spook fish in small streams.

Best fly patterns on Utah creeks include renegade, the grey hackle series, Adams, gingerquill, black barberpole, etc. in relatively small sizes 10-16. In Utah streams there are three basic types of insects to match: caddis flies, or *Trichoptera*, which appear as "rock rollers in the immature underwater stage; *Plecoptera* or stone flies, two-tailed and two-clawed, "hellgramites" and *Ephemeroptera* (three-tailed may flies). Just turn over a few of the flatter, darker rocks in the stream to view them for yourself. Any fly which imitates one of these insect types should bring attention from trout in Utah. Check a professional fly-tyer's shop. Best hues for all waters seem to be black, grey, brown and yellow, natural colors in the fish's natural world. White, green and blue work at times. Purple, red and orange patterns are used less often, except for the latter color simulating a fish egg. Beginning fly tyers should focus on size 4-6 bucktails and streamers which require no wings and little hackle or tail; even though being more easily tied, these "bugs" catch large fish. (Also see fly fishing techniques.)

For rivers with oversized trout, try a size 3 spinner (I prefer a Mepps), a size 7 Rapala, or similar-sized flatfish or plugs. Whether you use bait, lures, or flies, larger fish will be attracted to larger offerings in high water. In late season low water, fish seem to feed on smaller tidbits.

For flat water, many Utahns will wait out trout with a hunk of nightcrawler (often tipped with a small marshmallow to lift the crawler up out of bottom moss) or cheese. With natural bait, remember: a fresh, lively offering usually works best. Oft-times, a bait suspended below a floating bubble works well on lakes because it reaches between moss lanes where fish visibility is much better than on the very bottom. In some of the Boulder Mountain high lakes, veteran anglers also like to get out on a raft and probe with a leadhead jig down between moss lanes.

One of the most deadly lures I have ever found for large stream trout in Utah — and it will work at times on lake fish also — is a size 3 Mepps spinner. The beauty of a number three is that no casting sinker is necessary, and without additional weight, the blades turn more readily at a desirable, slower speed. A no. 2 will work with a couple of splitshot about one yard up the leader, where they will provide weight without stifling the action of the lure. If there are chubs or other silver-ish fish around, I use the silver Mepps. If the bullhead or sculpin, brown trout favorites, are seen frequently in the water, I use a brass Mepps. Fish it just as slowly as the blades will continue to turn, along the bottom. To achieve the desired, slow-moving, fluttering effect, cast UP, then retrieve DOWN stream. This is the best technique, for it makes the spinner appear to be a half-alive baitfish of some kind being washed downstream. What a tempting combination it is to a "killer" trout lying in wait if the offering is still alive, yet appears so vulnerable and helpless that it is washing downstream!

If you have difficulty reeling straight downstream, and keeping it off the bottom, retrieve slightly cross-stream. Then, you will not have to reel as fast as the current to keep the offering from fouling. The object is to keep the offering as close to the bottom as possible — without snagging. Reel no faster than absolutely necessary. Keep the rod tip low in order to keep the lure low. Minnow-feeding fish usually remain deep. Of course, fish will often strike a spinner out of territorial irritation if you can get the action near them. Be ready, because a fish mouthing hard metal instead of expected flesh will probably be fooled only once.

A spinner is far more effective when retrieved downstream. For some reason, big browns will often let the flashing blades proceed down-current past them, then turn around to the attack. Watch for the fish to turn his head and then, be ready! The "slow" minnow ploy works almost anywhere for all game fish. Predator fish like black bass and walleye also smash such a retrieve with vengeance.

When it comes to lure casting on lakes, I prefer a small but heavy spoon like the "Indian Joe," or a red-white Daredevle. If the water is extremely shallow, as are many of the hotspots in alpine lakes, then cast the lure with a water-filled plastic casting bubble to keep you off the bottom moss. Of course, best lunker lure at Flaming Gorge is frequently a size 11 sinking Rapala plug, a magnum flatfish or a white lead-head jig. The latter is not trolled, but "fluttered" just off bottom. (An electronic fish-finder is most helpful to get you over specific fish.) These methods have accounted for many brown trout over 20 lbs. and more recently, 30-lb. plus pound lake trout.

Techniques can be extremely important even after you have found the correct place to fish. Many anglers know about the presence of crappie in the shallow eastern bays of Pineview Reservoir. They even have the timing down to late May. They know these fish will hit a yellow jig. However, I once witnessed a fisherman with 11 crappie to his belt, a companion with none. I noted that the successful angler eye-droppered his yellow jig down the submerged willow stalks, while the empty-handed friend merely tossed his yellow jig close to the willows. Likewise, I have seen bass fishermen at Powell work only the shadowed areas with full stringers, while others fished vainly in the sunshine. Some note *underwater* structure harboring good fish, while others see only what lies above the surface. Some anglers will experiment, turning to green Rebel plugs for example, when spinners aren't working. Don't be a conformist. If one offering doesn't work for some reason, keep trying.

Just about everything is tried by the large lake trollers, from big spoons and spinners to plugs. Fish in lakes often prefer a heftier meal than the stream trout. So use half or more nightcrawler on the lakes, less on a stream. Dig your worms near the stream if you can. Some trout prefer the bankside greyish worms which fish see more often than the "city" nightcrawlers. On some waters (such as Summit County's Chalk Creek) try the little red worms. Do not hook the "crawler" around the bend of the hook. How many worms have you ever seen tumbling down the current bent around in a ball? Very few. It is important to cover the hook-leader knot, but let a little piece of the bait dangle beyond the end of the hook. (Do not try to cover the bend, or barb of the hook. itself. Fish are rarely bothered by the visible barb, contrary to popular belief.)

Remember that it is usually best to go "light" if you want more strikes. That is, if you are fishing a creek where it is not likely you'll ever encounter a 10-lb. fish, why fish with easy-to-see 10-lb. test leader? Use say, 4 lb.-test, and invite more strikes. You will have plenty of strength there to land the pan-sized fish you hook. It's just a matter of playing the best percentages.

Talk with local people. When you buy groceries, or anything for that matter, in most small Utah towns there is "scuttlebut" you can pick up; like so and so's kid caught a six-pounder on a stone fly larva. (The larval form is often termed "hellgramite" in the West, atlhough not a true hellgramite.) It pays to talk to other fishermen.

MODERN FLY FISHING TECHNIQUES

Fly fishing is growing in popularity for good reasons: more challenge, especially for those bored with conventional sit-and-wait limitations, and the fact that any fish can put up more fight on lighter tackle. "It's fun just to wave the fly out there," as one beginning angler puts it, "and there is nothing in the outdoors to compare with watching a large fish take your fly right in front of your own eyes." The science of fly selection and correct casting technique can, indeed, become so fascinating that other methods are forgotten. In some shallow or mossy waters, a fly will even catch more fish, properly presented, because heavier bait or lure fouls in moss or "kerplunks" noisily enough to spook fish out of their wits.

Pattern selection — The right fly? It depends on the particular water. Veteran flycasters at Strawberry Reservoir have known for years that the Wasatch County lake swarmed with a strange insect containing white bands around a black body. That fly, the black barberpole, accounts for many good trout in Strawberry; yet, I've never had any success with it on the Green River. The Siberian wood-ant with jointed yellow body is my favorite pattern for high lakes, but it is a dud on the Wild Strawberry, where the best fly is easily a mosier (bulbous-bodied captain) . This pattern was apparently first tied in the Uintah Basin near the Wild Strawberry and possibly for this specific water. But if I was restricted to one fly I could use on all Utah waters, I would select a double renegade. Even in large sizes like 2 and 4, it resembles a stone fly nymph frequently irresistable to stream trout. I also like it on large lake inlets. A friend of mine, Bill George of Salt Lake City, has a different favorite for Utah's reservoirs: a "muskrat" pattern with light-hued body.

When fly fishing, be observant! Are there smallish black beetles in the water? Match them in appearance and retrieve! Are there fresh-water shrimp, those tiny, greenish (sometimes pink creatures) found in the stomachs of fish you have caught? Then try a similar artificial. And if there are grasshoppers on the water, try simulating one with bucktail, humpy, or sofa pillow patterns. Of course, if you are an expert in the little things, you might also try to match a minute gnat or midge. Some anglers have found that a small green pattern (probably mistaken for a fresh-water shrimp or scud) entices trout on Rockport and Deer Creek when nothing else will.

Presentation — Of course, much depends on presentation. Traditional technique on a streams "calls" for a dead drift, with line carefully "mended" to avoid drag. But ever since I was a 12-year old casting to specific fish I could see in the water before me (browns in the Logan River, cutthroats in Salt Lake County's Parleys Creek) I observed that trout often preferred a moving, or live insect to one dead drifted. Skipping upcurrent attracted many fish. The main thing is to find what the fish want and get it to them while walking softly and keeping your shadow off the water.

At times, in order to convince the fish a hatch was on, when it wasn't, I dobbed a fly out in front perhaps 60 to a 100 times, or until fish decided it was worthwhile to focus their attention to the surface. In another 20 casts, recalcitrant trout might decide the "hatch" provided more calories taken in than to be expended . . . thus worth their effort. It is this factor, conservation of energy in a fish, vital to putting on weight, which often requires that the angler place his fly directly in the path of a feeding fish. Many lunkers get that way by concentrating on sipping the hatch of the moment, and even at that, will not move more than a few inches for the target fly.

Casting techniques — For beginning fly casters, practice will teach you to bring the rod tip back sharply, as you begin the cast, to about the one o'clock position. Be in no hurry for the forward cast until you have straightened out the line behind you. A common mistake of most beginners is to force the forward thrust too quickly, the line falling in a heap at your feet. Cast forward by thrusting your wrist ahead in such a way as to bring the butt forward first, followed by a whipping rod tip. LET THE ROD TIP DO THE WORK FOR YOU. Strip line from the reel as you feel you can handle it. Be sure you have clearance for the length of line you are working. The nice thing about fly casting is that the rudiments can be learned in a session or two, much faster than golf or skiing!

Setting the hook — When setting the hook on a taking fish, let the rod tip (not your hands) do the work. Merely hold the line tight in your free hand, and

"Buggy Patterns" like these are favorites for large trout.
Upper: muddler minnow imitations.
Lower: nymphs resembling below-surface insects.

raise the rod tip AFTER you see or sense that the fish has your fly. In other words, DO NOT MAKE A CONSCIOUS ATTEMPT TO JERK the fly into the fish's mouth. If you make certain the fish has the fly (in moving water, the fish will frequently turn with the pattern), then simply tighten the line by raising your wrist holding the rod. As the fish strains away from you, all to the good, for it embeds the artificial more deeply. Keep a fly line tight in order to feel striking fish. Never allow slack in the line. One way to do this is keep the fly moving ever so slightly toward you, a technique I employ especially when using a below-surface fly such as a nymph and cannot see the leader.

　　Correct equipment—If surface fishing in clear water, I use up to 12-13 feet of leader. I've tried short and long leaders, and the latter definitely entices more trout. I also prefer overcast or cloudy days which muffle leader shadow and keep fish from getting edgy everytime an overhead sparrow flashes a shadow over the fishing hole. For below-surface nymph fishing, I use a short leader because a shorter leader sinks much better than a long one. Fish are also less likely to see a leader below than atop the surface. In addition, the sub-surface leader does not cast a shadow as does one floating overhead. Also, for casting distance and control, use only tapered leaders, or build your own using a few feet of 15-lb. test tied to 12-lb. test, then 10, 8, 6 etc. Also use tapered lines; for long distance casting, use rocket (weight forward) types. Level lines and leaders (without taper) are not for fly casting. Let a fishing tackle salesman allow you to feel the difference in casting *acumen* with tapered lines and leaders.

Special procedures — As for enticing strikes, some fish will jump for a fly pattern caroming overhead, or one lying still; but more will follow your slightly-moving artificial. With a little wind and gentle ripples, a fly will move on its own. Or you may have to gently move the artificial by raising the rod tip and taking in the slack with a free hand. However, when a trout shows absolutely no interest in your offering, you may have to attract him with special techniques. One I find highly successful is to very rapidly raise the rod tip and then lower it, with the effect of "skipping" the fly, then "letting it die." The fish will often move in and strike as the artificial "dies."

Experienced fly anglers usually go with nymphs, or immature insect imitations, early in the season, fished deep; they move to "dries" on top when the water warms. Note: cool nights in Utah's early autumn can often be good because cool nights cause heavy insect kills. Trout soon sip at the insects as they wash into the shoreline shallows. This is a good time to use dry patterns. I like middle September in the high lakes and late September-early October on the lower waters.

To learn fly fishing procedure, including proper knots, check with an angling shop for one of the instructional videos. I have seen one how-to video of superior quality, covering Mountain West fundamentals, put out by Gean Snow and Mel Hardman, 2292 So. Highland Dr., Salt Lake City. This video is offered in several national mail-order catalogues. There are other videos available on how to fish specific waters like Flaming Gorge.

Of course, all this pre-supposes the angler understands the basics. Recently, I was asked by a fisherman why he couldn't get any casting distance on a Uinta lake. He was using non-tapered line and leader. The wrong line, say a heavy 10-lb. test mono seated deep on the reel, can even prevent reasonable spin casting. These are little matters which need attention just as much as refined techniques. You can't catch fish if you are not casting where the fish are.

FISHING PRESSURES

The areas near larger cities, particularly along the Wasatch Front from Logan to Payson will usually have many roadside anglers on weekends. Fewer people get out Tuesday to Thursday. Some popular waters like the Provo River yield good trout in spite of the load. But if you want to get away from the competition, get away from roads. Hike even a half mile off the road in the Uinta Mountains, and you'll find the lakes there have more solitude and better fishing. Explore out of sight from pavement. There are usually some secrets there even the locals won't tell you about!

FIRST AID FOR BIG FISH

If you catch a trophy fish — one you want to mount later — here are some simple steps to follow in order that the taxidermist can give you the most beautiful wall mount possible:

1. Either do not clean it at all, or clean one side only. Do not clean on the stomach, or the cut will show later. Select the side you feel is most presentable, and make cut to clean fish on OPPOSITE side, which won't show against den wall. Important: if you can freeze your fish within 24 hours after catching, deliver it to the taxidermist UNCUT, UNDRESSED AND WHOLE.

2. Make sure during this time that nothing (or as little as possible) touches the side you want to show. This means you should see that no sticks, rags, boat chairs, or fly rods touch the fish. If anything does, the spot will lose color.

3. Never place a cold-water fish species, including trout, back in the water after it is dead. The color will fade. (Warm-water fish such as bass and walleyes do not seem to lose color in this manner, but cold-water fish species always do.)

4. Get fish into your freezer as soon as possible. You can wrap something around the fish AFTER it is frozen without danger of losing color. Wrapping is wise to avoid, "freezer burn."

5. Transport from there to taxidermist as soon as possible. If you must ship it, make sure it is packed so it will remain frozen. Dry ice may be necessary if it will require more than approximately 36 hours to reach its destination.

Fish taxidermists say that an angler who follows these steps should be able to look at a naturally-colored mount some four-six months later which resembles almost perfectly the one beheld at water's edge. Cost of mounting fish (price is usually by the inch) rarely comes cheap; so if it is worth taking to a taxidermist, it's worth making certain it arrives in the kind of condition you can be proud of later.

Names of reputable taxidermists can be obtained from local fish-game officers and sporting goods dealers. But before contracting for a fish mount, be certain to see a sample of previous work. After all, it's your money — and your memory you want to treasure.

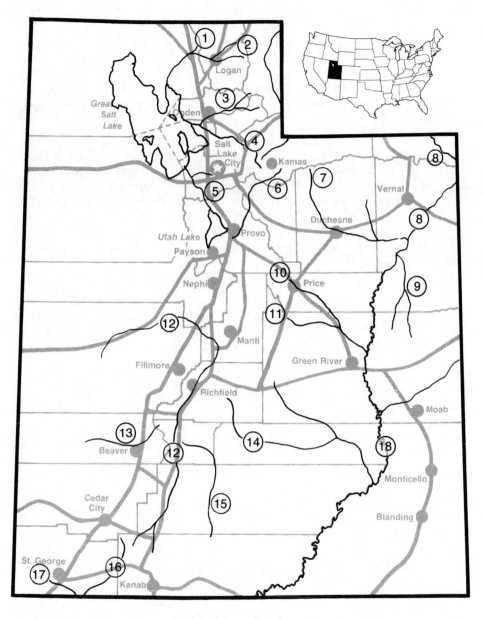

Major River Drainages

1. Bear
2. Logan-Blacksmith
3. Ogden
4. Weber
5. Jordan
6. Provo
7. Duchesne
8. Green
9. Hill-Willow
10. Fish-Price
11. Huntington
12. Sevier
13. Beaver
14. Fremont
15. East Fork Sevier
16. Virgin
17. Santa Clara
18. Colorado

CHAPTER THREE

The Top Streams

If you want to catch "lunker" trout on a large stream in Utah, your best bets would be the **Green River** below Flaming Gorge Dam; the **Weber River** above and below Rockport Reservoir; the **Blacksmith Fork River**, the unaltered portions of the **Logan**; the **Provo River** where it has not been channeled; a small section of the main **Ogden River** and the **South Fork of the Ogden**; plus **Rock Creek, Lake Fork River, Uinta** and **Whiterocks Rivers**, and sectors of the **Duchesne River**, all on the south slope of the Uinta Mountains; the **upper Sevier River** drainage including the entire **East Fork**, the **lower Beaver River** and a few remaining miles of the **Fremont River.**

Some streams like the Fremont, once considered Utah's premiere brown trout stream prior to flood-damage silting, will be also discussed in the chapter on Utah's Fishing Future. Numerous lunker trout creeks will be covered under the chapter on "Little Waters and Big Trout."

The word "lunker" is a relative term. It could be 12 inches on a tiny brook. But for Utah rivers, let's settle on 17 inches or more. The better you get to know those waters, the better your chances at a larger fish. Obviously, you could be lucky; but more often it is a matter of doing the right things at the right time. If pure luck alone did it, oversized fish could vanish quickly.

My list of top streams does not compare precisely with the "Blue Ribbon" list compiled by the Division of Wildlife Resources for a simple reason. The offical state list has given high priority to "accessibility" and "past use." I'm much more interested here in big fish wherever they might be. It is assumed you will put forth extra effort to reach larger fish (thus making that water "accessible") even if you have to hike, horse pack, or drive another 40 miles.

The **Green River** below Flaming Gorge Dam in northeastern Utah has been adjudged by many well-traveled anglers as the *top fly fishing trout stream* in the Lower 48, and for sheer number of large trout, I'd agree. Anyone can see them in air-clear riffles from the dam to Red Creek Rapids. Electro-shock sampling (trout are returned unharmed) has indicated thousands of trout even in the raft-launching ramp area immediately below Flaming Gorge Dam. Many 16-18 inch rainbows can be seen morning and evening nipping nymphs or dry flies near the banks, with only a short cast required. However, the trout often zero in on one particular insect and it can be singularly frustrating if you are not offering it at the moment.

The Green is reached via Utah 44 north of Vernal in Uintah County, or from Salt Lake City northward, via I-80 to Utah 43, through Mountain Home and McKinnon, Wyo. to Manila Utah, then across Utah 44 to Dutch John. The road to the launching ramp is just north of the Flaming Gorge Dam.

In this pine and meadow-mirrored stream, I have witnessed torpedeo-shaped fish go several feet out of their way for one artificial fly pattern, and move as far to avoid another. But week in and out, the pale pink or green scud, fresh-water shrimp imitation, sizes 10-18 is excellent. The caddis fly nymph (rock roller or trichoptera larvae still attached to black case) pattern is another excellent choice. The oversized crane fly nymph (sizes 4-8) fetch attention in spring-early summer. Grasshopper simulations in muddler minnow or sofa pillow work well late in the summer. Large trout may go wild over black cricket imitations, a natural thing considering the number of crickets and cicada which float down this stream in a given day, especially from Red Creek Rapids area (some five miles below Little Hole — be careful if floating) down into Brown's Park. The cicada is a favorite Green River pattern of David Freed, Salt Lake City angler, who has spent some 70 years fly fishing, with a focus on the Green.

Double humpies often attract oversized brown trout from Little Hole downstream. But if they don't work on any particular day, pattern switching is often the hourly ritual. On one float to Little Hole, my angling companions and I could entice nothing in the cold, drizzling rain of mid-July. When it warmed up in the early afternoon, trout began to gorge on something rather minsicule, a size 16-18 pale morning dun. To tie on such a minute fly may require a 5x leader or smaller, so bring a magnifying glass if your eyes strain easily. Then, of course, a rainstorm or hatch may dictate an entirely new fly.

It is a not an easy challenge to hold a 3-lb. rainbow in swift water even with a 3-lb. test leader. Poor knots, like a straight overhand, will reduce leader strength up to 50 per cent, so you may unknowingly be fishing with only 1 1/2 lb. test. Lighter leaders do have their virtues in that they are less easily seen. But gossamer ultra-lights will not hold a bucking trout on this stream's swift riffles. I prefer to use at least 4-5 lb. test on the Green, and the larger size 4-8 fly patterns if in rough water because they are more visible. When fish demand smaller fare, especially nymphs, many veterans here use a red yarn or plastic bead strike-indicator at juncture of line and leader. The bead is particularly helpful in determining strikes in swift riffles.

But the first rule of the Green with its fastidious feeders is that you must give the fish what they want. You can sometimes witness this at work just routinely wading shallow water. Trout congregate at your feet as immature insects are knocked loose. (But it is illegal in Utah to deliberately scuff up the bottom, the "San Juan Shuffle," to chum for feeding fish.) Yet, finding feeding fish is not particularly difficult on the Green.

Trout in the Green River are not as easily spooked as in many other waters, probably because of the numerous recreational rafts and daily summer fishing pressure. Fish seem to have adjusted to the confusion, remaining in place, particularly between the boat launch ramp and Little Hole, seven miles below the dam. In this sector, I've seen trout continue to rise rhythmically even as several rafts pass by a few feet away. However, it doesn't mean you can be careless. The trout may tolerate routine rafts, yet still spook from a waving rod tip overhead. Incidentally, if you want to avoid most of the competition for space with raft traffic, don't fish mid-day or weekends from late June through August. Angling before Memorial Day and after Labor Day eliminates some 80 per cent of the river traffic.

By early afternoon on any given day, water releases from the dam can also raise stream flow several feet, not the best time to be wading or fishing. Trout may also be bothered with overhead leader shadow on a bright afternoon in shallow water. It points out the value of casting dawn and dusk, or at least leaning toward cloudy days. Some anglers I know fish after dark in mid-summer when there is so much confusion on the river. Incidentally, most trout in the Green seem to lie at the edge of riffles, often where quiet water allows maintaining feeding position without extra effort. This is often very near the bank. Walk the shoreline with light steps.

If you prefer to spin-fish and are a master at the black leadhead jig, by all means cast out, let it settle near bottom, retrieve in little up and down motions, and rest again. The trick is to give it an exaggerated swimming motion. Spinners do not seem to work particularly well on this stream, probably because trout are so totally tuned to insects. Best lure, if you prefer spin gear, has frequently proven to be a size 7 dark-hued Rapala plug. Take pliers to remove barbs from hooked fish, as all between 13 and 20 inches must be released on the Green. I once witnessed a 15-year old boy arrested here for keeping an 18 1/2 inch trout kept after failing to sucessfully remove a treble hook. Another strategy is to clip hooks from trebles to leave a single hook. Check the proclamation or local signs prominently posted for fishing regulations.

One good thing about the Green from dam to Red Creek Rapids is that it does not run roily with spring runoff. Not only is outflow controlled by the dam, but water 50-55 degree temperatures are constant. The Green was once colder, but the U.S. Bureau of Reclamation installed an outlet high on Flaming Gorge Dam to emit the lake's upper and warmer upper layer. The result has been a faster growing trout.

In May and early June when many streams are high and too muddy to locate fish, the Green is still clear and wadable. At least until mud pours in after a storm at Red Creek. It is unfortunate no one has found a way to construct a check dam here to hold back mud coming from Red Creek. In the murky water there, most anglers go to large flies. The Green holds trout generally as far downstream as Swallow Canyon, almost to the Gates of Ladore. However, mud and catfish begin to take over near the Colorado border

Even when mid-winter, air temperatures are below freezing, water temperatures remain high enough in most of the river for trout metabolism to remain active. Trout feel hunger and continue feeding in the "warmish" flows even while the angler must wear an overcoat.

When you feel a strike while fishing the Green, chances are very good it's a nice rainbow. However, it could also be a brown or cutthroat, as a few have been planted here and are doing well. Some brook trout are found, especially in the first quarter mile below the dam. While the average rainbow will run about 13-18 inches, they could go as high as 15 lbs. A 14 1/2 lb. brown was taken above Little Hole by a fly fisherman in 1988. The pattern: a grasshopper imitation.

In getting around to the better hot spots along the Green, rubber or neoprene rafts can be rented at Dutch John. (Since this region is administered by the U.S. Forest Service, only one lease is allowed to provide motel-fuel-cafe-fishing tackle services. It is the Flaming Gorge Lodge, or its affiiliate service station on the west side of Dutch John.) The lodge tackle shop offers several hundred fly patterns to choose from and has become a gathering point to discuss best daily fly patterns.

As for floating the river, it does not contain any high waterfalls or Grand Canyon type rapids from dam downstream some 30 miles to the Colorado border. It does have boulder-strewn currents. Several people have also drowned in the stretch from dam to Little Hole. Most people use rubber or neoprene rafts because they sustain less damage bouncing around the rocks. Wooden or other non-flexible craft require careful negotiation. Running through the heavier cascades (on the right side of the flow in most cases) generally does little more than temporarily halt you on partially-submerged boulders. Take a patching kit if you plan on several runs. At confluence with Red Creek, some five miles below Little Hole, rafters should take time to study the rocks and rapids before proceeding.

Guides can float you (and help with fly pattern selection) for an agreed fee, or pick you up at Little Hole, or at the Taylor Flat Bridge in Brown's Park, about four miles below Red Creek Rapids. (The ride around by vehicle from Dutch John to this bridge is a rather lengthy round trip of 45 miles.) The USFS allows only a limited number of approved guides to be licensed here, with major contact via sporting goods stores or hotels along the Wasatch Front, or at Dutch John.

An acquaintance fished the Green extensively in June, 1988, and hooked into several four-pound browns below Little Hole on a number 4 humpy fly pattern. He found the browns would rise to the surface for an oversized humpy as long as the water was reasonably clear. In fast water five-six miles below the Taylor Flat Bridge, my friend found brown trout still liked the humpy but he could not hold them on anything less than 6-lb test leader.

If it rains, a four-wheel drive is an advantage, particularly in the clay-based side roads around Browns Park. A paved road has been discussed. But, if it happens, angling competition is bound to increase. For further information on the Green River, contact the Utah Div. Wildlife Resources (UDWR) Eastern regional office in Vernal. Also, contact sporting goods store employees who have either fished the stream recently, or likely talked to someone who has.

The **Weber, Provo, Blacksmith, and Logan Rivers** are examples of excellent trout habitat which have been subjected to heavy weekend fishing pressures near roads. However, during midweek, if you walk far enough from trampled trails, you may even find yourself alone. All are capable of producing respectable browns away from roadside access.

The Blacksmith Fork, along Utah 101 east of Hyrum, Cache County, is not fished as frequently as the nearby Logan alongside U.S. 89. Blacksmith's artificials-only angling sector above the confluence of Rock Creek receives very little pressure much of the summer, and less in spring and fall. The Blacksmith, and to a lesser extent the Logan, have a special challenge: their beautiful air-clear riffles punish a slightly clumsy angler who doesn't wade ultra-carefully and avoid all rod shadow. But good browns can reward the cautious, lightly-treading fisherman.

Blacksmith Fork. Fly fisherman trying for a big brown trout.

All these streams have produced monster trout. The Weber just above Echo Reservoir in Summit County, near I-80, yielded an 18-1/2 lb. brown trout as recently as 1988. Minnows or minnow imitations can be productive here. The Provo River has yielded behemoth browns in the past . The Blacksmith coughed up a 33-1/2 lb. brown to a biologist's net (Dr. Gar Workman, Utah State University) in the early 1980s. It was returned unharmed. No one has yet bragged about subduing this giant *Salmo trutta*. Dr. Workman estimated that the Gargantuan brown feasted on two or three hatchery rainbows a day, and many UDWR workers expressed a hope the predator could be (legally) caught and removed.

Channelization and water diversions have hurt fishing on some sectors of these streams. Hardest hit is the Provo River above Deer Creek Reservoir in Wasatch County. The Logan has also been gouged out below Logan to the 6th West bridge. Don't bother fishing for large trout in waters with recent heavy equipment scars.

Not too many years ago an angling companion tossed a number 10 royal coachman into the darkish currents of the Weber near Wanship. The fly had been chewed down, was watersoaked, and so bedraggled it appeared "ready to crawl away." When the fly slipped below the surface in a swift glide near bankside willows, the leader suddenly stopped. The fish took my friend through three deep holes, but he waded on, wet to his armpits. Like many browns, it doggedly sought every snag. Then, five minutes later, with what appeared to be a 6-7 lb. brown nearly beached, the fisherman became excited in seeing size of the fish. He tried to net him before the fish was played out. Balking in the shallow water, the trout twisted quickly, and broke off the 4 lb.-test leader, finally disappearing in heavy current. Such is fishing the Weber!

You never know, either, when a 13-1/2 pounder might suck in your little fly, as happened to one Weber angler on a cold Nov. 30 several years ago. I haven't hooked any that big, but have taken rainbows to four pounds on the Weber by drifting a double renegade. Many 15-17 inch browns have been landed on brass spinners, which likely simulate the local sculpin, a trout favorite. Since other anglers have probably walked the banks before you, try to envision a little pocket or undercut bank where angling competition hasn't yet focused. Look for natural holes and riffles, a gnarled root or undercut bank, where it is difficult to fish. If it is tough for you to get a line in there, then it was tough for others, too! Here, you just might "troubleshoot" your way to a good trout.

The upper Weber can be reached south of Wanship in Summit County, or in the Peoa Meadows area, via U.S. 189. Around Oakley, much of the Weber has been drained into irrigation canals, with mostly put-and-take rainbow fishing. It regains more flow south of Peoa with spring water and the addition of Beaver Creek. The lower Weber, below Echo Reservoir, is visible alongside I-80 in Morgan County near Henefer and the community of Morgan. Look for areas where the stream channel has been left intact. Downstream near Peterson there is a chance of a decent brown — until you get in the "canalized" sector near the mouth of Weber Canyon.

There are some cutthroats left on the Weber above Rockport, but the day of the "easy" 16-inch cutt is gone. You'll have to work hard under the heavy brush for smaller cutthroats. Again, avoid channeled or canal-like sectors where cover and bottom food have been altered. An occasional 2-4 lb. whitefish is not uncommon. In mid-June you could also run into spawning suckers in the deeper pools above Rockport. They can be so numerous that lures will snag the creatures; to avoid them, you may want to use flies, or stay in the riffles.

The good thing about most of the Weber from Rockport to Oakley is that it's within an hour of Salt Lake City, and untouched by heavy equipment. When local fish hatcheries have 4-7 lb. rainbow spawners no longer egg-or spawn-productive, just below Echo is often a favored place to stock them. A tip: in very hot summer weather, Echo Reservoir rainbows often escape torpid temperatures by gathering upstream in the first few riffles of the Weber River. A hot mile's walk through the mud flats with hip boots may be necessary; but if the fish are there, the hike is worth it. Above Oakley, much of the river is closed to trespass all the way to Holiday Park. (See section on fee waters.) There are a few places at Holiday Park, where the various forks of the Weber gather from the Uinta Mountains, that an angler can fish near the road. You can also find upstream wilderness fishing, with small cutts, on the Wasatch National Forest.

Best bait by far for the Logan and Blacksmith (Cache County) are rock rollers, or nymphal (larvae) imitations in size 8-16. Stone fly nymphs often work well in the high murky water of early summer, when such large fare is washed down with frequency. The Logan has potential lunkers below or immediately above three reservoirs in Logan Canyon (U.S. 89), away from the highway in brushy sectors, or below Sixth West west of Logan where the brush-lined stream deepens all the way into the sloughs above Cutler Reservoir. Water is often diverted for a short distance below these canyon impoundments to generate power. Electro-shocking studies show nice browns in the marshes between Logan River and Cutler, but you need a canoe or floating device to reach them.

After early summer, the Logan and Blacksmith are often running crystal-clear and should be fished where shadows darken the water. Wary browns are much bolder on these streams then. This is especially true on the Blacksmith (Utah 101 above Hyrum). After the road departs Blacksmith in the upper canyon, you can hike to pansized brown trout for several miles in emerald meadow-surrounded waterfall holes. Esthetics are excellent on the entire Blacksmith, even where near pavement. The road is not a major through-highway and stopping places are easy to find. A brass spinner or muddler streamer works well for browns feeding on sculpin along the entire river. Grasshopper imitations are a good bet in late summer. The Blacksmith is biologically capable of growing large trout, especially in the deep channels with undercut banks just above the two reservoirs. (For these reservoirs, see "Small Waters, Big Trout, Cache County.")

Best lunker areas of the Provo are a short distance above Deer Creek Reservoir, during the brown trout fall spawning period; the difficult-to-reach riffles below the dam; and especially the unchanneled sectors alongside U.S. 189 all the way to the mouth of Provo Canyon. Below Murdock Diversion Dam, there is intermittent flow with put-and-take rainbow fishing and a few pockets holding wary, but respectable browns. The dry fly fishing is better with warm weather and lower water flows of July through autumn.

Use nymphs or lures in the high water of spring and early summer. Get absolutely *on the bottom* with nymphs, either by casting upstream, or using splitshot, or both. The lower Provo insect hatches became less frequent after copper sulfate was used to treat culinary water on Deer Creek Reservoir. Fortunately, this practice has been discontinued and myriad large stoneflies hatching may once again mean rapid trout growth on the Provo.

When the trout are on top, a light-hued may fly will often work, as will a caddis. Like the Green, many of the Provo trout subsist almost entirely on insect hatches. Big browns will often ignore even a spinner (or other minnow imitations) when insects are plentiful. Watch for the first consistently rising trout of summer in mid-June on the little dam behind Olmstead Diversion, some four miles upstream from Bridal Veil Falls. Other hatches of snow flies may appear year-around. Gean Snow, Salt Lake City, who has fished the Provo often, advocates many of the same precise patterns for the Provo as the Green: gold-ribbed hare's ear, chamois caddis, prince nymph, pheasant tail, scud. Brent Beck, Sundance, fishes this stream frequently and has settled on a small caddis imitation when fish are working the surface. Both anglers emphasize "mending" or taking in slack line to keep the fly drifting at natural current speed.

A few monster browns are caught every year on the Lower Provo, albeit not as many on the highway side where construction has removed brush and undercuts. The Utah Dept. of Transportation has installed some so-called "fish condos" as mitigations for loss of habitat, but the best bet is to stick with natural ecology where there have been no channel changes at all.

The Upper Provo (above Hailstone in Wasatch and Summit Counties) was channeled and all but methodically destroyed 30 years ago by the U.S. Bureau of Reclamation. For some 20 years, sizable brown trout were absent. In the early 1980s, the author succeeded in taking a 20 1/2-inch brown and several 17-inchers in the channeled area, the first sign to him that respectable brown trout fishing had returned. Chad Hardman of Francis showed me the large caddis imitation he used in July of 1989 to catch a 21-inch brown from the Provo near his home. I went down the very next evening to convince myself the upper Provo habitat was beginning to finally return by catching a healthy cutthroat of just under 18 inches.

The Upper Provo's once-ubiquitous 2-lb. brown, with myriad cuts and large whitefish, have not returned in former abundance; but respectable browns do show up on occasion now in deep riffles away from the road above Hailstone through the old Lemon's Grove to Pine Valley above Woodland. A 10-lb. rainbow was caught in 1988, probably a spawner from Deer Creek. Above Kamas, along Utah 150, a scenic, spruce-lined stream, with many forest service campgrounds, parallels Utah 150 to Trial Lake. The stream here runs extremely low in the late fall and is mostly put-and-take rainbow trout, with a few small cutthroats. Some brook trout may be present from upstream lakes.

The Provo from Hailstone upstream for some six miles will be inundated with construction of Jordanelle Reservoir by about 1993-94. A plus could be spawning browns above the lake in the fall and rainbows in the spring.

The Provo has been diverted and dredged so much from the Jordanelle area down to Deer Creek that a constant flow of dam-released water-should now benefit fishing. But there is concern that heavy flows from Jordanelle could scour the Provo below both Jordanelle and Deer Creek via additional irrigation season high water releases. In 1988, the stream bed west of Heber City was allowed to go nearly dry. Hopefully, Jordanelle will forever change that. Until then, the only prospect for big trout between Deer Creek and Jordanelle are with spawning fish out of Deer Creek. The resident fishery there is all but gone.

Fair-sized browns have been taken within the community of Provo. I took a 19-inch brown below the Provo City entrance bridge one April morning a few years ago. But it is difficult for such a fish to subsist here anymore due to late summer water drawdown, both in 1988 and 1989. Some 12-17 inch browns were electro-shocked and returned to the stream from Riverside Golf Course above Provo to the canyon mouth in 1989.

A few nice browns are also caught at times in the Provo River inlet currents to Utah Lake, especially in spring high water. Unfortunately, carp from the lake inundate the river in early summer as flows drop and water warms. As one angler put it, "I didn't see any trout just above Utah Lake but I could walk across the stream on the backs of the carp."

The **South Fork of the Ogden River**, above Pineview Reservoir, has probably been fished at one time or another by every rod-toting citizen of Weber County, and then some. It is not recommended for the angler who wants solitude, unless willing to hike upstream from the point where Utah 39 and the creek separate. However, a two-pound cutthroat or brown and some nice brook trout are also ocasionally taken from the South Fork above Pineview Reservoir. Also, the main **Ogden River** has yielded browns to over 12 lbs. below Pineview right through the Ogden City limits. Some of the deeper pools are within the city limits west of Washington Blvd. Fishing potential is very good if industrial pollution is kept out of the stream.

Rock Creek, the Lake Fork, and Uinta River on the scenic south slope of the Uinta Mountains, in northern Duchesne and Uintah Counties (reached via a network of county roads north of U.S. 40) have in the past few years each given up browns over 10 lbs. More likely is a 10-13 inch cutthroat or rainbow. The Lower Stillwater sector of Rock Creek gives you the feeling a moose is going to appear any second — and one sometimes does.

Much of the best, least-pressured fishing is on the Ute Reservation (see Ute Reservation in the chapter on "Fee Fishing-Hunting.")

You can fish Rock Creek for pan-sized rainbows almost anywhere above confluence with the Duchesne River. But best fishing is well upstream, reached by driving up from Utah 35 on the Duchesne River over the Ute reservation. Or come in to upper Rock Creek via Utah 87 north from Duchesne, then 15 miles of pavement west from Mountain Home. A 12-lb. brown was caught on a Lower

Stillwater beaver dam a few years ago, and one nearly that large was hauled out of the Duchesne-Rock Creek confluence hole. Four- to eight-pounders have been taken in the deep meadow holes of the Lower Stillwater's green meadows. Much of the latter is on the Ute Reservation, with the special tribal license required.

Upper Stillwater Reservoir inundated much productive stream habitat on Rock Creek. Wilderness stream fishing still exists above the lake; but it is a long way around to reach the pack-in trailhead.

Lake Fork owes most of its reputation for large trout to Moon Lake. Big browns occasionally find their way through the dam into the stream below. Some respectable browns can be found in deep and brushy holes in the stream east of Mountain Home, as attested in the community's Country Store picture gallery. Fish these Uinta streams above major canal diversions. Only intermittent flows are found below. Browns to 13 lbs. have been taken on both Lake Fork, and the Uinta River, but fish are more often nowadays 10-14 inches. Some side streams with beaver dams along the Uinta south slope abound with brook trout, particularly the Frog Ponds on the Moon Lake road.

Upper Rock Creek, Lake Fork and the Uinta River on both the Ute Reservation and Ashley National Forest are remote and beautiful. The Uinta, in particular, should be fished above the U-Bar Ranch by every serious dry fly stream enthusiast. Here two-pound cutts rise to such dry patterns as Adam or gingerquill in a pine-rimmed setting. I have seen brook trout to three pounds in the gorge sector. Some steep (yet not lengthy) and careful climbing is required to get in and out of the Uinta as you head northward. The trail above U-Bar is good, but a 3-4 mile hike is required to get into the best fishing. Below U-Bar, the white water riffles include stocked rainbows, with some small cutts.

The **Whiterocks River**, east of the Uinta River, is really a creek. Fish are not big. But the stream is listed with the "heavyweights" because trout are plentiful and bids anglers with wilderness-type fly fishing. Walk up from end of road for a feeling of solitude and a look at wild brookies and cutts ready to belt almost any Adams, black barberpole, or ginger quill. These trout are rarely fussy if you can avoid spooking them in the shallow, clear water. Movie actor Robert Redford liked the Whiterocks Canyon so much he insisted that much of his mountain man film, "Jeremiah Johnson," be filmed there. While there is no road up the canyon bottom, a Jeep "cut" does connect to the upper Whiterocks canyon. Access is northwest of the community of Whiterocks.

The **Duchesne River** is located on the Uinta south slope along Utah 35. From the confluence of North and West Forks above Hanna down almost to the town of Duchesne, it is capable of producing respectable brown trout when running clear. However, the stream flows through red clay banks which turn the stream into a muddy onslaught in a rainstorm. Most trout fishing is several miles up from the diversion dam above Duchesne. A small Rapala or spinner can often work wonders. Don't bypass the bridge abutments along the road because some respectable browns may live beneath them. The Duchesne also has rainbows, cutts, and a multitude of oversized whitefish wherever they can find cover. The stream does not always display a high pool-to-riffle ratio as it nears Duchesne, so an angler may have to do more walking on the lower river. Whitefish make for fast action in the Tabiona area on any stone fly imitation. Watch for signs, since a few sectors of the Duchesne below Tabiona cross Indian land.

The upper **Sevier River** is a prime trout fishery from headwaters to Hatch (just south of Panguitch on Utah 89) and in "pockets" to Piute Reservoir and again in brush-lined riffles down through the canyon near Big Rock Candy Mountain in Sevier County. I've taken browns to three pounds above Panguitch. My brother Douglas (a dedicated sort who once fished Vancouver, B.C. streams for 37 consecutive days) has taken rainbows and cutthroats above Panguitch to five pounds. He focused on deeper holes with a size three Mepps spinner.

Work the deeper cutbank holes, especially those with current. If shadowed, so much the better. Note: Since flows are intermittent from the little diversion dam a few miles above Panguitch into the Circleville area, look for any infusion of spring water which could supply year-round flows.

One angler who has found the Sevier's big trout is Richard Spencer of Orderville. In July of 1989, I looked at two browns in the seven-pound class he coaxed from deep holes between Panguitch and Hatch. These were deep-bellied, beautifully chocolate-splotched fish which fell for a live grasshopper kicking overhead.

Also, try for some of those 2-5 lb. trout in the **East Fork of the Sevier** near Antimony, south of Otter Creek Reservoir, within a shout of Utah 22, and again, downstream in Kingston Canyon (Utah 62) upstream from Junction. A spinner is great medicine here, especially in April before heavy runoff hits. The East Fork is probably Utah's least known roadside fishery. Best trout, however, are in the meadowy bends, and cutbank pockets away from easy access. Some sectors seem fishless, but you never know when you might latch into a slab-sided brown. I hooked into a 22-incher a few autumns ago in a deep riffle where I'd drawn a blank two months earlier. Best fly patterns seem to be the larger ones, muddler minnow imitation, grasshopper-like sofa pillow or humpies. Largest trout feed near the bottom and you will need to get into deepest pockets with pin-point casting alongside cutbanks, moss and other structure.

One potential problem on the East Fork is that high water can be released any time during the irrigation season, making fish difficult to find. It can also roil quickly in a clay stream bed. However, if you reach the stream when clear, you should find some cooperative trout. There are a few camping spots in the canyon, or two recreational vehicle campgrounds near Otter Creek Reservoir, one a state park, the other privately owned. There are also primitive camping spots about seven miles south of Antimony.

The **Lower Beaver River**, flowing from Minersville Reservoir in Beaver County, alongside Utah 21 right down into the town of Minersville, is a "sleeper" with relatively little-pressured brown and cutthroat trout. It has about 10 miles of meadow-lined riffles with food-rich moss banks, and ample back-casting room, excellent for fly fishing. Deep pools are probed successfully with spinner and lures. There is some posted private property.

The stream also had a mysterious fish die-off a few years ago, thought to be a toxic agricultural chemical poisoning. It has left fisheries biologists guardedly optimistic over the stream's future. Browns to seven pounds and cutts to 20 inches have nevertheless been caught in recent years. The stream received a heavy infusion of cutts in the mid-summer of 1988 when many trout washed from the newly-stocked Minersville Reservoir into the stream below. The large pool below the dam has become a favorite for both sit-and-wait cheese fishermen and nymph anglers. Average trout sizes ran about 13 -14 inches in 1988; fish will be bigger in 1990s. Say biologists, "We expect this to be a fine trout fishery in the years ahead if we can locate the cause of the chemical poisoning and prevent it from re-occurring in the future."

One of my favorite streams over the years has been Utah's **Fremont River** in Wayne County, via Utah 24. Many 2-7 lb. browns have been enticed from this stream each spring and fall. Milt Taft of Bicknell once caught them in the marshy Fremont to nearly 13 lbs. The problem is that heavy flooding during 1983-86 silted in most of the Fremont pools in Bicknell Bottoms. The stream in many areas now courses dozens of feet wide and a few (fishless) inches deep. That now includes the Fremont-Pine Creek confluence "hole," and the "narrows" some five miles east of Bicknell. Fortunately, the current below hastens sufficiently to maintain a natural channel. Brushy pockets for about five miles below Utah 24 still hold respectable browns.

My best trout from the Fremont was a 6-lb. female brown. It came only after dozens of casts in the same riffles with a weighted spinner. After observing an 18-inch rainbow chase bouncy minnows into a nearby spring, I realized my spinner did not simulate those minnows. So I removed the weight. Suddenly, both the rainbow and the 6-lb. brown found my unweighted offering to their liking. The brown crashed into the lure almost at my feet. Such fish may yet exist in the Bottoms marshes, but an angler would need to do considerable walking to find unsilted and neglected lairs.

A different set of problems seem to halt trout as the Fremont nears Torrey. The stream levels out with less oxygenated water. But while fishing is tradtionally poor here, it picks up when the stream spills down into the roadless canyon below Utah 12 (Grover-Boulder highway). Your best bet is to walk several miles into the canyon, or the total ll roadless miles to the Fruita campground. You can be dropped off at the top and have someone pick you up at the campground at day's end. Pick a day with little chance of muddy side runoff. All but the last two of this ll miles have trout, the latter sector apparently being too mud-choked and too warm. Tip: avoid long, straight sections as they seem to have been hit hard with flood runoff. Best bets are the bends, especially those with cutbanks. Note: The canyon trek is an all-day challenge and should be attempted only by someone in good health. Take hip boots and plan to wade the stream between sheer canyon walls.

The upper Fremont, just below Johnson Reservoir, is primarily stocked rainbow fishing. But an occasional large cutt often drifts down into these brushy holes from Johnson. My largest has been a 3-1/2 pounder, with some in the 15-18 inch category. These trout have grown wary with fishing pressure, especially around Zedds Meadow. Things will get more crowded with a face- lifting of the narrow, gravel road from Utah 72 to Johnson Reservoir, earmarked for pavement in 1990. From the deep canyon below Zedds to Mill Meadow Reservoir, the stream is less crowded. Below Mill Meadow, some nice rainbows are taken during spring months in quieter stretches of the Fremont. By late summer there may be no flow. There is no or very little Fremont River left near Loa, but natural springs and accretion flows refill the stream bed year-around just upstream from Bicknell.

Near Capitol Reef, this little river loses altitude quickly and is no longer cold enough for trout. The map labels it the "Dirty Devil River," so named by Maj. John Wesley Powell.

A new fish hatchery on Pine Creek, a Fremont tributary, could mean heavier emphasis on rainbow trout in this area. Pine Creek and nearby Spring Creek will be covered under Wayne County.

The Green River at Little Hole is a world famous trout fishery.

CHAPTER FOUR

Lake and Reservoir Hot Spots

Few states have more lakes and reservoirs with excellent fishing than Utah. Below are listed the larger ones, those which are in the daily angling spotlight. Chapter six has county-by-county information on smaller angling waters, including both flat water and creeks.

FLAMING GORGE — This world-famous reservoir straddling the Utah-Wyoming state line has in the last decade produced more lake trout over 30 lbs. than any other fishing hole in the United States, and possibly the world. Some 10 years ago, the 91-mile long artificial lake (dammed on the Green River over a quarter of a century ago) had yielded more brown trout over 20 lbs. than any other known water. That included the 33-lb. 10-oz. brown trout which stood for years at the top of the *Salmo trutta* heap in the Freshwater Fishing Hall of Fame. Other brown trout in mammoth sizes of 31, 30, and 29-1/2 lbs. had been battled to boat in the past. Most browns were enticed at that magic half-hour when the world awakens to the first purple signs of dawn. .

By the late 1980s, lake trout or Mackinaw began to take-over Flaming Gorge and the battle is nearly complete. Ironically, while browns were stocked some 20 years ago, no lake trout were ever formally introduced to the lake. Some came down the Green River from Fontennelle Reservoir, and then began flourishing on chubs and kokanee salmon in a grand style that is still amazing fishery biologists. A 37-pounder caught at the Gorge some seven years ago only lasted as the state record until 1988. Many larger than that have now been dredged up.

The state record 51-1/2-lb. laker comes from the Gorge's Lucerne Bay area. That fish, caught by Curt Bilbey, Vernal, in July of 1988, was first listed at 53 lbs, but when officially weighed tallied 51-1/2. It taped 46-1/2 inches long, and has been hailed as the third largest lake trout ever taken anywhere in the world. The fish was adjudged to be 35-40 years old. Yet, in a water with unlimited superlatives, a 50-1/2 lb. lake trout was was also taken in Lucerne Bay in late September, 1989, and on 12-lb. test monafilament, not steel or lead line. The angler said that "It was the only the large fish I've ever caught." (This bay is sometimes listed as "Linwood Bay," after the old community of Linwood, and also "Henrys Fork Bay" because Henrys Fork enters the upper arm.)

As for 25 to over 35- pounders, they have almost reached a ho-hum status in nearby Manila taxidermist Dewey Erlich's front room . . . and his bedrooms and bathrooms and basement. The last time I looked, he had more whopper lake trout in his home than I have ever seen at one time even in the lodges of Great Slave Lake, Northwest Territories, Canada. One was a 42-pounder and it hadn't even made the Wasatch Front news. The 30-pounders barely raise eyebrows anymore.

This is not to say that just anyone trolling a large frog flatfish or jigging a white leadhead (doll) fly for a few hours in the lake is going to catch a whopper. The lake has its productive and slow times like any other fishing hole. However, there are guides, available only through one of the marinas on this 6,000 foot high reservoir, who have gotten clients into 20-plus pounders in a few hours' angling. A few knowledgable anglers do it on their own. In May, 1988, Bilbey's father-in-law caught a 39-pounder. Anglers who have studied the lake latch onto 16-18 pounders often enough that they don't even bother to keep them anymore.

How do they do it? Most of the experts will do one of two things. Some use a sophisticated electronic fish-finder device, station overhead and then lower a large white leadhead to the bottom. They raise and lower the jig rhythmically. The strike frequently occurs when the jig begins to fall. Another method is to use steel or metal line to bounce a trolling model-sized flatfish or size ll Rapala off the bottom. If snagging up, as you might on the old channel brush, then simply tug it loose. Hooks will pull away before the steel or lead line breaks. Some anglers also use regular monofilament, especially in spring and fall when fish are not quite as deep. The lakers are usually closest to the surface just after ice-out in late spring, or in late fall when spawning. In the summer, you'll need to get deep, frequently 90 feet or more (in some places the old channel is over 200 feet down) to reach the 45-55 degree temperatures lake trout demand as their comfort zone.

Because the lake is so deep, few anglers tie into these giants from shore. In one respect, however, the lakers are easier to catch than were the giant brown trout. While the latter fed almost exclusively at night, or very early daylight, big lakers dine mostly during daylight hours. At the depth these fish dwell, they are seldom affected by sunlight. They likely know little about life near or above the surface.

Oversized lakers are caught year-around in the Gorge. Middle summer produces many good fish, probably because they are concentrated at rather predictable depths in precise locations. They are capable of ranging the open water, but certain underwater ledges and shoals also offer more opportunity to ambush smaller fish. Keep in mind where you caught one good laker and return to that precise lair again. A monster fish that puts on surplus weight, because food was easy to come by with little effort, will likely be replaced by another Gargantuan fish. Many oversized Gorge lakers are filled with chubs and other forage fish when caught.

The general Gorge hotspots seem to be right out from the Lucerne Valley Marina east of Manila, in all of Lucerne Bay eastward into Antelope Flat, north into Wyoming until shallow water is reached; also, downlake through the old Green River channel, including the mouth of Sheep Creek (where the world record brown was taken) and the many deep coves from Cedar Springs Marina to the dam. During the autumn spawning period, the giant fish seem to congregate in the middle of Lucerne Bay over old gravel beds. At times, a circle of boats slowly trolling around and around marks the spot. But fishing in late October-early November means cold weather. The thermometer may dip below zero. "Only the hardy need apply," as one fisherman puts it.

The Gorge is, of course, more than a Mackinaw lake. In the early spring, fishermen begin catching 2-4 lb. rainbows on lures or bait from the bank, with an

MAJOR FISHING LAKES AND RESERVOIRS

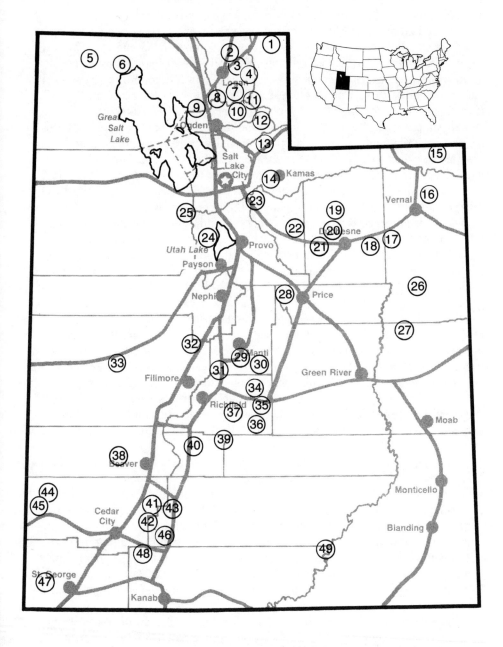

Key to Lakes and Reservoirs

1. Bear Lake
2. Logan River dams
3. Blacksmith Fork dams
4. Porcupine Reservoir
5. Lynn & Etna Reservoirs
6. Locomotive Springs
7. Hyrum Dam
8. Mantua Reservoirs
9. Willard Bay
10. Pineview Reservoir
11. Causey Reservoir
12. Lost Creek Reseroir
13. Echo Reservoir
14. Rockport (Wanship) Reservoir
15. Flaming Gorge Reservoir
16. Stanaker (Steinaker) Reservoir
14. Flaming Gorge Reservoir
17. Bottle Hollow Reservoir
18. Borham (Midview) Reservoir
19. Moon Lake
20. Twin Pots
21. Starvation Reservoir
22. Strawberry Reservoir
24. Utah Lake
25. Settlement Canyon Reservoir

26. Towave Reservoir
27. Weaver Reservoir
28. Scofield Reservoir
29. Nine Mile Reservoir
30. Palisade Reservoir
31. Gunnison Reservoir
32. Yuba Dam
33. DMAD Reservoir
34. Fish Lake
35. Johnson Reservoir
36. Mill Meadow Reservoir
37. Koosharem Reservoir
38. Minersville Reservoir
39. Otter Creek Reservoir
40. Piute Reservoir
41. Red Creek Reservoir
42. Yankee Meadows
43. Panguitch Lake
44. Escalante Reservoirs
45. Baker Reservoir
46. Navajo Lake
47. Gunlock Reservoir
48. Kolob Reservoir
49. Lake Powell

Note: check local maps for smaller lakes and reservoirs.

occasional cutthroat. Also see Chapter Five for smallmouth black bass fishing in the Gorge.

Kokanee salmon grow big here. The Gorge and state record stood in late 1989 as 5 lbs., 5 oz. and kokanees of six pounds are being predicted. Large kokanee are caught by jigging a small bait or lure in side bays. This species has a small mouth and is not attracted to large lures.

This salmon remains out of the spotlight much of the year, however, as it feeds on zooplankton and insect tidbits difficult for anglers to simulate. But in late September, the species gather in places like the inlet end of Sheep Creek Bay, turn a deep crimson like their close cousin, the Alaskan sockeye, and wend their way upstream in a most colorful display. Sheep Creek Bay, some eight miles south of Manila, is closed part of the autumn to protect spawning *Oncorhynchus nerka*. But the fish are worth seeing for kaleidoscopic reasons alone. The kokanee, a true salmon, dies after spawning in the third or fourth year. They can attain average weights of approximately four pounds in such a relatively short time, which is a testimony to the availability of feed in the Gorge. Kokanee are a bonus fish — they feed on minute insects and compete little with trout after the latter reach 10-12 inches.

As for general feed conditions in Flaming Gorge, I have examined dozens of huge game fish of all species from many waters, including Alaska and Canada, but I have never witnessed fish with any more depth and thickness in girth and breadth as those from the Gorge. The lake has few moss beds in comparison to, say, Strawberry or Fish Lake, but Gorge fish grow quickly from pansize to bathtub size on everything from beetles to crayfish to bait fish. This lake seems to have no gaps in the food chain. Biologists began to realize how rich the lake was in fish feed when they put out gill nets some 15 years ago and hauled in two brown trout just over 30 lbs. Chubs were found to provide much of the needed forage for oversized browns, and still do for lake trout. For that reason, any lure resembling a chub, like flatfish and Rapalas, is usually successful if you can get it in front of a hungry fish. After three weeks camping-fishing the Gorge one spring, I saw the remains of numerous large chub suddenly emerge to the surface. They were bitten part way through, an indication of the mayhem and violence occurring somewhere below.

Some of the huge lakers are also caught on strange offerings. The aforementioend 50 1/2 pounder was caught on a chartruese fatgitzit. The most attractive offering seems to be something bite-sized for a large mouth, with a trying-to-get-away action. The trolling model flatfish fill that bill.

An occasional brown is still caught at places like the "Bushes." This is a 180-degree bend in the old Green River Channel below Red Canyon Lodge where Ray Johnson of Salt Lake City caught numerous 20-plus brown trout years ago. Other hot spots are Lucerne Bay, near the dam, and Sheep Creek. It should be mentioned that uplake into Wyoming is also good for browns. Certainly the dedicated angling club of "brown baggers" are not likely to give up on the lake yet.

The browns, then or now, are rarely more than 20 feet down, usually feeding only in dim light, and when weather is cool. A lake trout, by contrast, simply goes deeper to find its comfort zone and continues to feed. Remember that with the lakers, in particular, depth is everything. Mackinaw, like brook trout (both being true chars) simply cannot stand warmish water. So if you are not finding lake trout, vary the depth before doing anything else different. That includes lures, time of day, surface location, or other adjustments. Be prepared to spend some time at it, too, since a trophy fish of 25-50 lbs. requires almost that many years to attain its weight. Catching a giant can happen in a few hours, but those who have scored big in the Gorge or anywhere else know that the more you know and the more time you put in, the "luckier" you are likely to be.

Fly fishing in general has not gained overwhelming popularity at Flaming Gorge, but the feats of some anglers cannot be ignored. Coloradoan Del Canty made the pattern "Grizzly Shrimp" (and the Gorge) famous by catching a world-record 26-lb., 2-oz. rainbow trout on that artificial one blustery spring day. To do it, he spent a grand total of only 45 minutes casting near the shoreline of Antelope Flat northwest of Dutch John. Other large rainbows have been hauled out of this region by flymen, often in float tubes. The grizzly shrimp has accounted for other large Gorge rainbows.

Given more time, a world record lake trout here is a distinct possibility. That would mean beating a 65-lb., 8-oz. laker from Great Slave Lake. But then given what the Gorge has done so far, no one would be too surprised.

The best way to reach the south end of Flaming Gorge is Utah 44 from Vernal to the Dutch John area. For the middle side, take Utah 43 from I-80 south to Mountain Home, McKinnon and to Manila. Another route is via Wyoming 55, from the town of Green River southward to the Utah line. There are several back roads also connecting various bays of the lake.

The Utah side of the lake is served by two marinas, Lucerne Valley, out of Manila and Cedar Springs near Dutch John. Both have launching ramps which can handle low or high water, as well as overnight slips for large or small boats. Cabin-type craft are recommended for extended excursions in wilderness-like areas of the lake. Flaming Gorge has many roadless bays where people are rarely seen, and the boater-angler should prepare accordingly. There are also several "boat camp-grounds" from Cedar Springs to Lucerne Valley, with tables, fire pits, latrines, etc.

The marinas also have tackle specifically geared to the Gorge. Take cold weather gear at all times of the year, plus your binoculars for wildlife watching. Such big game as mule deer, Rocky Mountain bighorn sheep, pronghorn antelope, possibly elk, black bear, bobcats, and even mountain lions have been spotted here. You'll also want a camera and color film.

LAKE POWELL — This fishery, featuring islands and cliffs of brilliant orange and crimson, has more than 1,800 miles of shoreline, most of it in southeastern Utah. Many oversized rainbow trout have been dredged out of deep water in the old Colorado River channel. When the dam was first built over Glen Canyon, I remember catching 2-lb. largemouth bass on one cast, 2-lb. rainbows on the next three. I also remember one spring day sight-seeing in the Rainbow Bridge Bay region when a trout of some six pounds swam lazily by .

But the trout are hardly the main reason an angler visits this 181-mile hunk of scenery. The lake is now being managed for warm water species like striped bass, largemouth and smallmouth black bass, walleyes, crappie, channel catfish, etc. (See the chapter on warm-water fishing.)

Access is from the north via Hanksville on U.S. to 95 to 276 and Bullfrog Marina. To reach Hite Marina, stay on 95 south of Hanksville. Powell can also be reached from Wahweep Marina west of Page, Ariz., then a short boat ride up-lake into Utah.

FISH LAKE — This is a conifer-surrounded, azure-hued natural lake, located in Sevier County at 8800 feet. Like Yellowstone and Crater lakes, this is a large rare gem for such a lofty altitude. To get there, take Utah 24 east of Sigurd then turn off onto Utah 25. The lake yielded 37 and 38 lb. lake trout in 1989 — subdued by the same angler!

Named by early Indians, this water became legendary over half a century ago with tales of giant fish. Stories were later spun in Bowery Haven and the Fish Lake Lodge about leg-long lakers hooked just out from the only conspicuous shoreline vegetation at "Joe Bush" on the north end, or from the deep "trough" a few hundred yards from the west bank, or in the late fall, along east side moss bed which attract spawning fish. Veteran anglers provided the proof. Whopping lakers of 20 to 25 pounds were taken within a week after ice-out to ice-in, come middle autumn. One of the farthest south Mackinaw fisheries, it became a popular place to beat the heat on a summer day.

With the warmer temperatures, trollers soon found fish were deep. Best lures were red-head Davis plugs, while others used spinners or cowbells with minnows attached. A few did it with flatfish, or Rapalas. As with most Mack lakes, the angler must be certain he is well down in water which extends nearly 200 feet below.

But as the lake grew in popularity in the middle 1950s-60s, it was also apparent that the lake had a problem. Many anglers came up empty on heavy hardware, finally settling for a 10-inch rainbow on light spin gear. There seemed no fish to fill the gap between 10 inches and 10 lbs. or more, except for an occasional oversized brown trout. I remember looking at one beached by Tom Spotten of Provo, an almost 21-lb. brown, at the mouth of Twin Creeks from shore near the Fish Lake Lodge.

But there were not enough of these oversized browns. And the lake trout seemed to be in shorter supply. A state fishery biologist named Arnold Bangerter spearheaded one of the early efforts to bring in an "opposum shrimp" or *Mysis relicta* , from Colorado lakes. The shrimp had a reputation for flourishing in deep, clean, cold lakes and fish which subsist on them attained impressive weights. Alas, it did not, at first, seem to work in Fish Lake. But by 1987 and 1988, the results of Mysis began to show. Fish Lake rainbow began putting on weight. So did the browns. And quite obviously, the lake trout.

Rapid growth is also expected for the newly-introduced splake, a cross between brook or speckled trout and lake trout. The fish retains much of the brookie's beauty and the laker's age-growth factors. But more about splake later.

The aforementioned angler who took 37 and 38-lb. lakers at Fish Lake in 1989, Gerald Colby of Salina, had set a Mackinaw record from the same lake with a 36 1/2-pounder in 1979. The local angling world had supposed this record would stand forever. They gasped at his 37-pounder, then again a few days later when he returned to subdue a 38-pounder.

This master angler has been asked many times to disclose his secrets. But Colby will say only that he has been fishing the lake for over a quarter century, that there are other monsters in Fish Lake and most people "don't fish right for them." He confides that he used dead minnows to catch the oversized lakers, and that he prefers a line board, which feeds out line from his hands, rather than a rod tip. He says he is able to impart "more sensitive" action to the line by holding it in his hand. Efforts to get him to disclose more have mostly failed, but then as he says, "I didn't learn my secrets overnight . . . "

Veteran Fish Lake guide Neil Garrett out of Bowery Haven, who has produced many lakers of 20 lbs and more for clients over the years, uses a Lowrance Fish Locator, with a downrigger on his boat to get deep quickly with a large flatfish. He likes the deep "trough" a few hundred yards off the west shoreline. He says middle July is a good time to be on the lake because fish are congregated in the known deepest pockets of the lake. When fish are shallow earlier in the year, they could be anywhere, Garrett points out. On one outing with him, I caught respectable rainbows on a black flatfish along west side moss beds.

Bob Poulson, Magna, has taken many oversized lakers on the north end of the lake, usually with a redhead Davis plug. However, "just in case," he also keeps a few thousand other plugs and lures on hand. Poulson adds that "spending a lot of time on the lake also seems to increase one's chances of being lucky." On this long and evenly-shaped water, with few inlets or irregular coves, an angler must apply special concentration to remember where the best dropoffs and deep areas are located. The consistently successful fishermen have them memorized. Frankly, catching rainbows is normally not that difficult, because they are scattered widely over the lake.

Fly fishing for rainbows seemed to be popular at the lake some time ago, but fewer respectable fish are being taken this way lately. Maybe the opposum shrimp have them feeding farther below the surface. In any event, when the trout are taking flies, it's often near the moss beds on the northeast corner and some areas of the westside algae lanes. Incidentally, Widgeon Bay on the far north end is too warm for trout and contains mostly trash fish from Pelican Point north.

The lake became a winter haven about 1988 when anglers discovered how easy it is to entice 2-3 lb. splake through the ice with lures "sweet-tipped" with sucker or other meat. Weather is cold, but jigging can bring a number of nice fish in a few hours. The sport has grown so popular that snow is now being cleared daily on paved roads along the entire lake. Cabins and recreational vehicle parks are also open year around at Fish Lake beginning in 1990. Bring the binoculars. You should also see considerable big game animals.

STRAWBERRY RESERVOIR (including combined Soldier Creek Reservoir) — As old-time faithful know, this Wasatch County lake has known some euphoric angling history. Strawberry was once considered the state's "bread and butter" flat water, attracting more anglers at any given time than any other fishing hole in Utah. Certainly, the rainbows and cutthroats in Strawberry, and introduced brook trout, kept fly anglers happy in past years at this 7500 foot high lake known for its myriad insect hatches. I remember one evening at the mouth of Trout Creek and another in Jake's Bay on the north end hooking many gyrating rainbows on a size 6 black barberpole and light tackle. Any cast with a lure between moss lanes would produce a 3-lb. rainbow. This was especially true two-three years after chemical treatment in the early 1970s.

However, it fell on tough times. Twice viewing the large reservoir from U.S. 40 in 1989, I didn't see a single boat — where I would normally view dozens. Trout catching was obviously no longer a sure thing. The problem was a massive take-over of chub and sucker populations in all but the coldest depths of the lake.

This lake fishery improved considerably with rotenone-spraying treatment to kill trash fish in 1971, and will almost certainly improve markedly again with the same treatment. Some of Utah's best lake fishing followed rotenone treatment. Trout grew quickly without competition from trash fish. The problem in getting the lake treated this time around, however, has been amassing enough rotenone in the South American countries to treat a lake of 14,000 surface acres. The UDWR says efforts to treat the lake in August 1990 would be the largest such attempt anywhere in the world.

Fish stocked as catchables in Fall 1990 would perhaps attain 1 1/2 lbs. by the following spring. I wouldn't be going out on too much of a limb in predicting 3-lb trout by late 1992.

Emphasis after treatment would be on promoting rapid growth of "Bear Lake" cutthroat which feast more readily on forage fish than other strains of cutt. However, it follows that this strain may not focus on surface insects as has the old Strawberry cutthroat. Veteran fishermen out of Clarks and Woodbury and Madsen "boat camps" remember hooking cutts two decades ago up to 12 lbs. on dry flies. One thing has improved for sure with the enlarged lake: Those old trash-littered, cabin-lined shorelines were replaced with a cleaner environment and unhampered access after the Uinta National Forest took over. The USFS now allows camping in designated areas only.

If the lake can be treated successfully — it carries four times more water now than before combining it with Soldier Creek — there is no sure way of knowing if the Bear Lake cutts in the deeper and larger lake will recall Strawberry's past *fly fishing* glory. For a time, with no forage fish to feast on, it would appear insect hatches will have to form the bulk of a trout's diet. The rainbows, which will be sterilized to avoid hybridizing with the cutts, may also turn out to be long-range fly feeders, even if the cutts are not. Ditto on brook trout, if introduced. Time will tell. A few returning forage fish would help speed up initial trout growth. But the trouble with chubs is that if one male and one female get together anywhere in the lake, there will soon be far too many of them for trout to compete with once again.

Flaming Gorge offers scenery and fishing. Utah Travel Council Photo.

It is a sure thing kokanee salmon will be added to the fishery, because this species did so well with only minimum planting efforts in Strawbery-Soldier Creek during the 1980s.

The combining of Strawberry-Soldier Creek, has forced old-time anglers to become completely re-acquainted with the new and deeper lake. New maps had to be drawn. Fish were found in new locations. But a significant change is this: fish can now survive better in the deeper water. It means more dissolved oxygen, winter and summer. Strawberry had been subject to periodic fish kills, especially in cold winters with thick ice and decreased dissolved oxygen supply.

The chemical kill in 1971 was so complete that I did not see, nor did I talk with anyone who did, even so much as a minnow or dace, let alone a chub, perch, or sucker, for nearly six years. Renewed campaigns to avoid using trash fish as live bait were apparently successful .Use of live bait is suspected of being the major cause of trash fish contamination which eventually "trashed" trout fishing in Strawberry in the 1980s. Heaven help anyone caught placing a live trash fish in Strawberry following chemical treatment .

Strawberry is reached some 20 miles southeast of Heber City, on U.S. 40. You can see the lake to the east after topping the summit at Daniels Canyon. A paved road circles around the west and south ends, and leads to the Strawberry Marina. Ten miles east of the turnoff to Strawberry Marina on U.S. 40 a marked exit road sign indicates Soldier Creek Marina .

SCOFIELD — This reservoir, located in northwestern Carbon County off U.S. 50-6 east of Soldier Summit, has been considered second only to Strawberry in use by trout fishermen. However, an algae bloom in the early summer of 1989 robbed some bays of dissolved oxygen, causing a fish kill estimated to be around 30-40 per cent of the lake's total trout.

Another problem for the future on Scofield is the illegal introduction of walleyes. Some large specimens caught in 1987 sent out a warning from fisheries biologists that the predatory walleyes will drastically reduce populations of small trout. Particularly upset with the appearance of walleyes in this traditional trout fishery is Bruce Schmidt, Utah fisheries chief. Schmidt expects the lake's cold water elevation to prevent it from being a great walleye fishery, "but walleyes will eat young trout and also prevent it from being a great trout fishery. Everyone loses," Schmidt concludes. The lake will be watched closely in the next few years to see if the walleyes begin rapid reproduction. In the meantime, heavy penalties are listed in the annual angling proclamations for anyone illegally introducing new fish species into any Utah water.

As for now, knowledgeable trollers and bankside baiters, particularly along the outlet area and east (U.S. 96) side, still fetch respectable rainbows and cutthroats from this huge lake which collects some three small clearwater creeks from the northeast Manti Mountain. Scenery above the lake is attractive at the edge of the Manti-LaSal National Forest, although the lake itself often has severe mud flat drawdown in late summer.

On one mid-October foray to the north side near the island, a friend and I caught so many 11-14 inch cutts and rainbows on surface-wobbled flatfish that we couldn't unhook them fast enough. Fall is the best time to fish Scofield, with fish concentrated and hungrier in the cool weather.

The directions to Scofield are somewhat confusing, with one sign off U.S. 50-6 saying "13 miles." My odometer said 9-1/2. The signs are indicative of several mysteries shrouding this lake, one of them being why there are so few truly large trout. It lacks the 3-6 pounders which thrust Strawberry or Minerville or Otter Creek Reservoirs into icthyological prominence. The feed does seem to be there. Crayfish, upon which most large game fish feed, are available in large supply. An angler can catch the crayfish with a small hunk of worm. .

Would rotenone treatment to kill trash fish improve Scofield? Maybe, since it does have heavy sucker and carp populations in the shallow bays. But there has been no serious discussion up through early 1990 to treat Scofield, one reason undoubtedly being that Strawberry was given a higher priority. Cost and scarcity of rotenone will likely prevent any other major treatment programs in Utah for several more years.

Boat launching ramps at Scofield are found in a state park near the outlet channel, southwest side, via U.S. 96, and just across the bay at a private facility.

OTTER CREEK RESERVOIR — This lake in Piute County (east from Junction via U.S. 62) was chemically treated in the fall of 1989. It was then restocked with pansized rainbows. Trout grow fast here and fishing will be possible for 2-3 lb. trout by autumn, 1990, with some lunkers expected a few years after that. Like Strawberry, this water became burdened with chubs. It has produced large trout and will again for several reasons: constant water supply from upstream Koosharem Reservoir, favorable cool water temperatures at 7000 feet elevation, ample feed in a relatively shallow lake with many sun-grown moss beds, sufficient dissolved oxygen supply, seemingly everything required by healthy trout. A 16 3/ 4 lb. brownie was beached in 1989 on a green wooley worm fly cast from shore. Rainbows to 15 lbs. have been caught on the locally sold troller's favorite, a bouncy, needle-nosed spoon (much like a triple-teaser but slightly heavier).

Fishing friends and I have caught many 2-3 lb. rainbows in this one. In addition, Robert Gleave, Antimony, picked up a dead rainbow, which may have died of old age, from the south shoreline in 1989 which was as long as his leg. Gleave is not a small man. So, the potential is very good for oversized trout on the lake by about 1992. I would predict some 10-lb. and better rainbows and/or browns by 1996.

Fly fishermen on the north end have hauled in rainbows from 2-4 lbs. with fair consistency. Any of the wooly worm patterns seem effective, especially in green and black. If wading, access to the Otter Creek inlet requires permission to cross private property.

Otter Creek Reservoir also has a pond just below its outlet, plus a large waterfall hole, which traditionally grow large trout. In the spring of 1989, a young boy landed an 8 1/2-lb. cutthroat in the outlet pond spillway inlet. Several rainbows nearly as large have been caught there. Apparently, fish wash through the dam outlets, then find the necessary food to attain size. April is a good time to go after them, as temperatures warm and trout go on a feeding binge. The most effective lure in the pond and Otter Creek below seems to be a size three spinner.

The lake has its moods, as do most waters with oversized fish. Trout can be tougher to catch here following searing heat, spring and fall's severe cold spells, and large insect hatches which leave fish satiated. Since feed is plentiful, it follows that your hook-disguised offering is often competing with the real thing. You'll need some time to connect with the ingrained feeding habits of the largest fish.

A launching ramp is found on the south end of the lake, along with a state park and developed campgrounds, as well as a nearby private recreational vehicle park. The nearest community is Antimony, some six miles to the south. Because there are no trees or grassy areas, you may want to bring your own shade. Most of Otter Creek's esthetics come in its quiet, remote location, away from pollution or crowds, with the possibility of viewing such wildlife as herons and eagles. Mule deer abound in the hills almost everywhere around the lake.

MINERSVILLE RESERVOIR — Located on the high sage plains about 20 miles west of Beaver, via Utah 21, this lake has produced many slab-sided rainbows over the years. It has also been chemically treated at times to eliminate trash fish, the last time in the early 1980s. Then it was restocked with rainbows, while both fishermen and fisheries biologists sat back to wait. But in successive drought years, many of the rainbows apparently gathered near deep water by the dam . . . and in mid-summer of 1989, the fish spilled into the Beaver River below. In fact, there were so many trout in the large pool directly below the dam that fisheries officials issued a temporary closing order to the stream at that point.

After initially losing many rainbows from the lake, biologists decided to restock with cutthroats. The fish were expected to be about 14-17 inches by early summer, 1990. Since the lake has comfortable water temperatures for trout, plus a plethora of insects and minnows, these cutts should put on weight rapidly. Expect some lunkers by 1991-92.

Minersville has ample public parking room around its treeless 6500 foot high shoreline, with some camping luxuries like tables, fire grills, and latrines. Most anglers here stay in recreational vehicles, as they do at Otter Creek. There is a well-marked state park boat ramp on the south shore. The lake has no commercial development, so purchases have to be made in Beaver .

Best offerings for what can be extremely temperamental fish seem to be bottom baits, with lures working for cruising fish. Minersville has not gained a reputation as a great fly fishing lake, although I have seen respectable trout rising on its surface. I've also trolled here with a veteran fisheries biologist who could not locate the trout in half a day of trying. "They must have just filled with a midge hatch," the biologist decided. On the other hand, I've seen women and little children catch good trout here on everything from Velveeta to liverwurst and marshmallows. The open and sandy banks make it a favorite place for wait-'em-out baiters. The new cutthroat trout stocking program might put more fish on the surface, but only time will tell.

Best times for fishing the lake seem to be in spring and fall. Fish go very deep in summer's warm temperatures. Unlike say Fish Lake, there is little shade around the lake. But esthetics skyrocket with the catching of a tradtionally deep-bellied Minersville trout. The lake has a potential for a trophy trout, so it is rarely neglected.

PANGUITCH LAKE — A natural lake bolstered with a dam, this scenic water has had good rainbow trout fishing. I remember one mid-May dawn when I could scarcely see through a wet blizzard and heavy fog, but caught three feisty 17-inchers in as many casts. I was near the outlet in deep water, casting a Mepps. Most of the trout were small-headed and deep-bodied, showing excellent feed con-ditions. Their stomachs yielded snails, nymphs, minnows and beetles.

With a pine-shrouded setting within the Dixie National Forest, the lake has plenty of nearby campgrounds. The lake can be reached via U.S. 143 west of Panguitch, or from Cedar City via U.S. 14 to U.S. 148 and 143, or directly from Parowan on 143. The weather is often cold here, even on summer evenings, so bring the coat and cap.

PIUTE RESERVOIR — This Piute County lake, north of Junction, visible from U.S. 89, attrracted little attention for half a century. Then, suddenly, it seemed to yield some of the fattest and most colorful cutthroats and rainbows in the West. Best shoreline fishing is near the deep coves by the dam, although the inlet end where the Sevier River enters offers fast fishing at times.

Boaters and shoreliners alike often have their best luck in late spring just after ice-out with a leadhead jig retrieved in short jerks. The strike could well be from a 4-5 pounder, fish which seemed to emerge in greater profusion about 1986, apparently the result of a stepped-up trout stocking campaign. The potential for a trout fishery was always there, but trash fish also thrived. In any event, the trout seem to be getting enough of an upper hand to make Piute a good bet. The cutthroats are beautifully golden-hued, despite Piute's slightly murky appearance.

The lake receives little attention in the fall, probably because deer hunting is so good in this region. But it is one lake, well removed from the heavily populated Wasatch Front, which could stand up to considerably more fishing pressure. There are few tree-shaded camping spots around the lake, but there is ample room just about any place you want to pull off and spend the night.

BEAR LAKE — Despite its 6000-foot-plus elevation evenly straddling the Utah-Idaho border, Bear Lake has gained the reputation as a South Sea Isle recreational resort. Water ranging from cobalt blue to emerald green, depending on how sunlight strikes the surface, and tropical-like white sand beaches beneath swaying cottonwoods makes Bear Lake almost akin to an ocean beach.

All of this sometimes makes it necessary for fishermen to compete with water skiers, pleasure boaters, and swimmers. Fortunately, the best seasons to toss a line in the water are on cool spring and fall days. In the summer, the lake trout and cutthroats are well off the shoreline, toward the 208-foot bottom and difficult to find. So anglers are usually able to keep themselves separated from other recreational users.

As living quarters for fish, Bear Lake has been called "all bedroom and no kitchen." The sandy, nearly glass-smooth lake bottom means little concentration of fish in one area — they range widely. I found this out for myself in catching three nice cutthroats in three consecutive Aprils: the first was a 7-1/2 lb. cutt while trolling a large green flatfish just south of the Idaho-Utah line about 300 yards off U.S. 89 near the west shoreline; the second was a 4-1/2 pounder taken from the east side of the state boating park harbor dike; the third was on the south end near Gus Rich Point, again from shore. I have never had a second strike in any of those previous "hot spots." The best concentration of fish I have found is 13-15 inch rainbows on the deeper, east side about mid-lake. At times, pansize cutts, usually due to recent heavy planting, can be taken in and around the boat harbor. The harbor is on the west side, just south of the Idaho boundary. Large Macks are also taken on the far north (Idaho) end by anglers casting from a pier which juts well out into deep water. Note: a Utah license is good anywhere on this water, as is an Idaho permit. Big lake trout are also caught on the deep east side, even with the North and South Eden Canyons. You'll need downriggers or heavy weights to reach the lake trout here in mid summer.

Incidentally, the second cutthroat I mentioned above was taken near a deep channel cut through the harbor dike, where boats enter and exit. Another fisherman had cast there for nearly an hour without any action. I noticed he was not plying deeply against the bottom, however. With some splitshot added, my imitation minnow went a little deeper. That made the difference.

The Bear Lake record cutthroat is 18 1/2 lbs. Utah fishery biologists have expressed the belief this lake could rival Nevada's Pyramid or Walker Lakes for oversized cutts, or Idaho's Blackfoot Reservoir for sheer number of 3-4 pounders. Bear Lake has not yet quite reached that status . . . or for that matter, its own potential. It does offer excellent trouting in spring and fall. Fisheries biologists have sufficient faith in it to maintain a hefty cutthroat stocking schedule. These cutts, it should be added, pick up a unique coloration, with caramel-hued sides and a bluish snout. Hence the local phrase, "blue-nose cutthroats." For some reason, Bear Lake rainbows are normal in coloration, and remain rather small in size.

In mid-January, cisco anglers gather with dipnets to extricate a rare fish of about 7-9 inches long from Cisco Beach on the east side. It's a time for beach fires, often built with old tires, and for blankets. The cisco offers top table fare, especially when smoked. Anglers also catch a Bear Lake whitefish, which like the cisco, is found only in this water. In some years the catching is done through the ice; but in most winters, this deep and wind-swept fishing hole does not freeze.

Bear Lake is reached from Utah 89 between Logan, and Idaho. Best access from the Salt Lake City-Provo area is via Evanston, Wyo, north into Utah then west at the junction eight miles north of Randolph on Utah 30. There are many motels in communities along the west side of the lake, and recreation vehicle parks there and at Bear Lake State Park. Much private property seals off the south and west sides. Access and pulloff camping is best on the eastern shoreline.

It is expected that Bear Lake will be stocked with Chinook salmon. The lake has plenty of forage fish for salmon. They key will likely be spawning room, as the lake is fed by only two small inlet streams. Time will tell on this one, but keep an eye out for Chinook fishing in the future.

ECHO RESERVOIR — Once considered marginal for trout because of its relatively "warm" elevation north of Coalville in Summit County, this lake began a few decades ago to produce shingle-sized rainbows. The scenery is a little barren. Shoreline fishing can be slow. But trollers have often "killed" the rainbows with triple-teasers and other flashing lures, as well as bait.

Personally, I like the Weber River inlet best and have taken many nice rainbows by walking the mud flats. Best summer fishing has often been in the first few stream riffles above flat water. Many of the fish find the lake too warm in July and August, but they know where to find a cooling effect. It isn't particularly comfortable walking shade-less mud flats in mid-summer, but the fishing can make an angler forget the heat. Best fishing in the lake itself is usually in spring and fall.

The lake has produced 5-lb. rainbows on occasion, and rarely, a big cutthroat. The area above the outlet spillway, in the southwestern corner, is also good when current is created by high water spilling to the lower Weber. Trout can congregate in this outlet flow.

Echo has little camping. About the only place along the shoreline with trees or shelter is a small resort on the east side. The reservoir is also subject to heavy late-season drawdown, with soft mud making wading difficult on the east side. Most bank fishing is done at the inlet, or steep west side banks, below I-80. About the only pulloff is at a rest stop.

To reach the boat ramp on Echo, you will need to exit at Coalville or from I-80 at the mouth of Echo Canyon. The ramp and a small general store are located, on the middle north shoreline via a dirt road. Since most of the banks are on public land, access from shore is not a problem.

ROCKPORT (WANSHIP) RESERVOIR — This water, within an hour of Salt Lake Valley, on U.S. 189, attracts much fishing pressure. Some anglers sit with bait rods for hours on end here hoping for a repeat of the 7-lb. brown they once read about in the newspaper. Most simply opt for a "nice" rainbow. I've had my best luck, although it can grow a little crowded on weekends, at the Weber River inlet. Respectable rainbows are taken in this area, especially in dim light of dawn and dusk. With ample casting room, many fly-rodders ply it after dark. If the feed and timing are just right and the rainbows go on a feeding binge, 2-4 pounders can seemingly strike from almost anywhere near the Weber River inlet.

Your best bets are with a flashing lure-like spinners, or if fly fishing, match the insect hatches. Several anglers have done well here with a greenish nymph, possibly simulating a fresh-water shrimp. I've had my best success on the inlet end with a double renegade, including one evening taking several rainbows from 16 inches to over four pounds.

There are few camping places on the lake but a state park and pulloffs on the Weber River inlet end can handle some overnighters. Most of the lake is surrounded with public land. Camping areas on the south end require paying a state park fee, but day-use fishing is free.

DEER CREEK RESERVOIR — Once managed almost exclusively for trout, this easily accessible water along U.S. 189 at the top of Provo Canyon, eight miles west of Heber City, is rapidly transforming into a largemouth bass and walleye fishery. Therefore, it will be covered in the chapter on warm-water fisheries.

However, many oversized trout have been caught on this lake, including a 22 1/2-lb. brown beneath the Charleston Bridge at the Provo River inlet on the northeastern corner. Salt Lake City angler Gean Snow coaxed an 8-lb. brown from the surface of this lake, again near the Provo River inlet, on a dry fly. I've taken 16-18 inch rainbows in the Provo and Wallsburg Bay areas.

While the dominant fish species of the future seems to be the walleye, with some black bass and perch, trollers occasionally hook rainbow or brown trout. This is particularly true in the deeper waters from Provo River channel past the island to the dam. In the spring, bait anglers do very well on the north side of the island about mid-lake. Note: by late summer, the "island" may be only a peninsula. Be careful about driving on the wet shoreline, as vehicles become trapped.

Being a culinary water supply for Salt Lake City and Provo, this lake will

A number three spinner simulating a sculpin is something a big brown trout can't seem to resist.

probably never be chemically treated, a major reason for its future lying with warm-water fishing.

EAST CANYON RESERVOIR — Located on Utah 65 only 18 miles from Salt Lake City via the turnoff at Mountain Dell off I-80 at the top of Parleys Canyon, this lake on the receives heavy fishing pressure. Nevertheless, it can yield numerous rainbows and a few cutthroats. The problem is that much private property prevents access, although there is a public launching ramp for boaters. Access is also limited on upstream East Canyon Creek. A resort has bought up much of the land around this scenic lake and there are few camping possibilities.

The lake suffered a severe winter kill in 1988-89, but was restocked with 9-12 inch "catchable" rainbows, and will be stocked again for 1990. Biologically, it has the capability to grow fair-sized trout. I've enticed rainbows to 18 inches on bait from the east side.

East Canyon is also reached via Utah 65 from Henefer and Utah 66 from Morgan. Coming and going, the region is rich in wildlife, including mule deer.

JORDANELLE (under construction) — This future reservoir, six miles north of Heber City, Wasatch County, alongside U.S. 40 is expected to become a viable trout fishery in the early 1990s. Jordanelle should provide more consistent trout fishing than Deer Creek. It could be very good in the first few years of filling, the usual period when newly-inundated vegetation and minerals enrich water, engulf terrestrial life forms, and promote rapid trout growth. When the lake "settles in," it should also produce stable rainbow and brown trout fishing. Respectable brown trout have long been present in this section of the Provo River. Just how good the fishing will be for large trout depends upon unkowns such as water levels, and quality, number of fish stocked, and that sometimes difficult-to-pinpoint factor, abundance of feed.

Jordanelle is earmarked for some of the state's most spacious and luxurious campgrounds, longest ramps, etc. Most of the ground around the lake is publicly owned through the condemnation process.

MOUNTAIN AREAS WITH HIGH LAKES

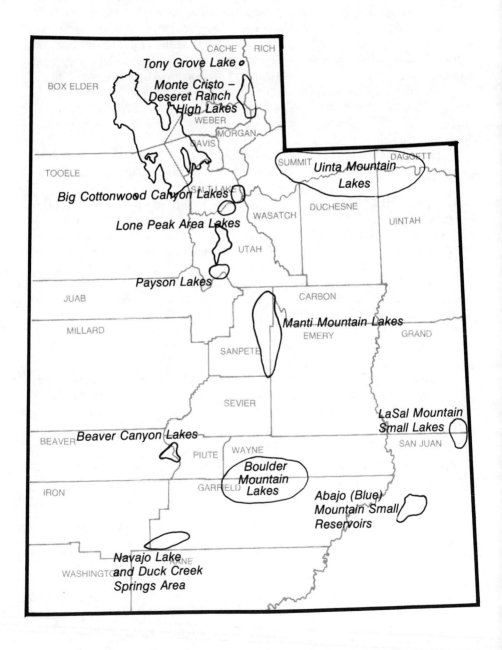

CHAPTER FIVE

High Country Trails

Anyone who has been in Utah very long falls in love with its high country. That includes the Uintas, Boulders (Aquarius Plateau to Escalante Mountain), Thousand Lake Mountain, Manti, Wasatch, Cedar, Beaver, Fishlake, Diamond, LaSal and other alpine highlands.

The alpine waters have a chapter of their own because esthetic qualities over 9000 feet in Utah are unique, and the challenge is different. Numerous waters are not accessible by vehicle. Higher altitude fish behave differently. They tend to feed more on the surface, gladdening the heart of fly fishermen. They have a different set of idiosyncrasies, including feeding times — usually in mid-day when lowland fishing is slowest. Seasons are shorter, with an emphasis on timing. Then, too, the highlands visitor does not want to wander far sans rain gear and mosquito repellent.

The Uintas Mountains, from Kamas to Flaming Gorge, from the Uintah Basin to Wyoming, are the continental United States' only major east-west mountains, towering to 13,528 feet at Kings Peak atop the Uinta River drainage. Some 10 streams flow in U-shaped canyons from these glacially-carved mountains. There are so many lakes that some are merely numbered. Access is via Utah 150 on the West, and many county and Forest Service roads . East of Utah 150 is the massive High Uinta Wilderness Area. Many of the unpaved roads shown on maps are four-wheel drive only.

Boulder Mountain rises dramatically to ll,400 feet elevation in Wayne and Garfield counties. A giant volcanic plateau, it is 22 miles across the top. The map shows it as a tableland ridge-connecting to the Aquarius Plateau and Escalante Mountain, then descending to Parker Mountain. Some 80 alpine fishing lakes are found here. The plateau is reached via Utah 12 from Torrey to Boulder and by a lacework of pioneer era dirt roads.

Thousand Lake Mountain (a misnomer, possibly the intended name for Boulder Mountain just across the Fremont River) rises to a little over ll,000 feet. Realistically, it has about 25 trout-filled lakes. Best access is from Utah 72 just south of Forsyth Reservoir in northwestern Wayne County. This elongated north-south mountain, on the Fishlake National Forest, rises sharply above the communities of Bicknell and Torrey. Side roads are mostly four-wheel drive.

Manti Mountain, referred to in many Sanpete and Emery County sporting goods shops as that "wonderful mountain," courses north-south for some 100 miles. The highest point is at South Tent Peak, ll,285 feet altitude. Skyline Drive runs the scenic length of the westernmost ridge, from U.S. 6 on the north to Twelve Mile Canyon above Mayfield on the south. Skyline is joined with many east-west side canyons originating out of valley communities like Ephraim and Manti on the west, and Orangeville, Huntington, Ferron on the east.

Cedar Mountain, east of Cedar City, includes Navajo Lake, Duck Creek

Springs, and Aspen-Mirror Lake, with access via Utah 14. Farther north, Fishlake Mountain and nearby Mytoge Mountain embrace Fish Lake, Johnson Reservoir, and small lakes north to Salina Canyon. Access to the east slopes is from Utah 72.

Beaver Mountain, between Beaver and Junction, has several dozen scattered lakes, some natural and others resulting from dammed creeks. Elevation is to 10,000 feet and above. Best known of the Beaver lakes is Puffer, up Beaver Canyon, north from Utah 153. This region also boasts Mt. Belknap (k is silent) and Delano Peak, pushing up beyond 12,000 feet. Setting is in conifer-aspen scenery with campgrounds. The road is paved on the west side, but turns to dirt and myriad switchbacks at the summit toward Junction.

The Wasatch Mountains, famous for skiing, also hold many trout-filled lakes, particularly in the glacial basins of Big and Little Cottonwood Canyons, near the ski resorts. With trailheads less than an hour from Salt Lake City, many are not exactly undiscovered or seldom-visited. The Wasatch rise to nearly 11,800 feet at Mt. Nebo above Nephi. Access is via many paved roads.

Other mountain ranges, including the Henry and Deep Creek Mountains, have no trout lakes. Other small alpine lakes include Manning Meadow Reservoir and a few ponds on Monroe Mountain. Manning is to open for cutthroat trout fishing in 1991, according to state biologists.

THE UINTAS — As far back as I can remember, I was cajoling someone who was "old enough to drive" to take me into the Uintas. Early favorites were the lakes east of Kamas, those north of Duchesne and Roosevelt, and the North Slope reached via the high plains of Wyoming. Before age 30, I had spent more than 300 Uinta nights camping above 9000 feet, and many more days fishing. In my opinion, the esthetic quality and wilderness values of this range, including high "baldies," emerald meadows and air-clear water, equal the alpine scenery and quality of experience anywhere.

First, a little history. Some of the lakes like Alexander and Buckeye, Trident and Haystack, which were so productive of good fish, have become far too accessible and popular now for any hearty recommendations. Alexander, about five miles up the Spring Canyon road off Utah 150 (plus a quarter mile hike to the east) was once my all-time favorite, yielding a number of 3-4 lb. brook trout. Alexander is a lake where one step into shallow water means sinking thigh-deep in bottom plankton. Marsh-soft lakes like this one often hold large trout in the Uintas, especially at the relatively lower elevations like Alexander's 9300 feet elevation. The lower the lake, of course, the longer the trout-growing season. With the ice departing in June, or even mid-July, then returning in late September, highlands trout have but three months of growing season. In the cold water, they they may only advance in length one inch per month, while valley lakes fish might add two inches per month in size.

However, whenever I hear people say the high lakes are not biologically capable of growing big trout, say, deep-bellied brook trout to 17-19 inches long, I know first-hand it is not true. On one of Alexander's "high lakes" openers (July 1 in those days) I witnessed dozens of 14-inch plus brook trout taken, along with a few rainbows to 20 inches. Many of these lunkers fell prey to a nightcrawler in

Alexander's deepest sector, a pocket in the southeast corner. I also watched a friend, Deral Barton, wrestle a 3-lb. brown trout from the lily pad area on the south side of this oval-shaped lake. The downfall of Alexander was in being "discovered" by hundreds of construction workers building the Duchesne Tunnel years ago. Fishing pressure was extremely heavy for some two years. Average size of trout fell considerably. After that, trash fish turned up in the lake. The construction workers are gone and the lake is still recovering. Slowly.

The feed conditions haven't changed. The lake is still rich in plankton and insect-laden moss beds and yet harbors a few monsters, albeit much more sophisticated than before. Alexander dispels the notion that all high lakes are "feed-poor."

But such tales of oversized trout are not merely to reminisce about the past. The angling challenge is to discover other "Alexander Lakes" not so well known. Other "feed-rich" lakes with less fishing pressure are out there , but it requires effort to find them.

How did a brown trout get into Alexander when it is Utah practice never to stock browns in flat water? Well, as the hatcherymen explain it, sometimes when you buy fish eggs, a "stray" species gets mixed in. I know of a 21-1/2-inch brown caught from one of the Cuberant lakes in the upper Weber River basin. I also know of a 7-lb. rainbow lifted from a roadside lake in the Blacks Fork area, where only brook trout are supposed to be. Exceptions do occur.

Where, then, are the **Uintas' best trout fishing lakes?**

Let's talk about some "old favorites" in which fishing quality has held up. One is Pinto Lake in the upper Rock Creek drainage, on a marked trail some 13 miles southeast of Mirror Lake. It's a favorite of boy scout and en masse expeditions. But any time I have fished Pinto, with its many bays and coves, angling is fairly fast for 10-13 inch cutthroats. This is basically true of other lakes in the upper Rock Creek region, including Pine Island, Lost, and Grandaddy. Add Lym Lake which once produced a 4-1/2 lb. cutt on an orange flatfish, but most of its chunky cutthroats fall prey to a rock roller bait or imitation. This little larval form of the caddis fly can often be found in the inlet creek. Lym is a 3-mile hike from Mill Creek after driving as far as you can go on an old logging road on the North Slope, Bear River drainage.

Other lakes along Utah 150, include Teapot, Pass, Moosehorn, Butterfly, et al. They have relied mostly on put-and-take rainbows and lately, orange-hued albino rainbows. A lake off the main highway, like Buckeye, above Alexander, or the many within a few miles of Trial, like North Twin, offer better possibilities than those alongside pavement. Even a water slightly out of sight, such as Lock above Haystack, or Maba, off the road from Marshall-Hoover-Shepherd in the upper Duchesne River drainage, are more likely to produce. Some lakes, like Marshall, despite its relatively easy access with four-wheel drive have such a rich supply of fresh-water shrimp that they can still cough up a 15-inch cutt or brookie. An unsubstantiated rumor was circulated about a 7-lb.cutt being taken from smoke-colored Shepherd. If so, it is not likely to be repeated due to today's much-improved road access. One of the best roadside lakes just off Utah 150, is also one of the most popular. Mirror is a great place to take the kids rafting or canoeing early in the season because brook trout and albino rainbows are bunched near the outlet end. A few whoppers have occasionally been caught from this lake.

Lake Types - While I have emphasized marsh-type food conditions here, it must be said that some mudflat drawdown lakes also produce good fish, including Whitney on the West Fork of Bear, Sand in the Weber drainage, and Five Points in the Yellowstone. Other lakes in rocky ledges with little vegetation, like Superior, appear bereft of life, especially if you part their surface at the wrong time of day. Many of these "barren looking" lakes offer fast fly fishing. If you see no surface action, especially early in the summer, try sinking a nymph, like a wingless caddis or mosier stone fly imitation down deep. Use a sinking fly line, or a water-filled bubble with monofilament and spin rig.

But my favorite is the undulating and relatively shallow marshy "pasture" lake, where you might imagine a baby dinosaur rearing its head; one with many coves and points, where you can reach insect-slurping trout with a fly rod. These lakes often offer lily pads, always a tough snag. Yet, fly fishing can be unforgettable.Such a one is swamp-lined Ouray, across Rocky Sea Pass into upper Rock Creek highlands, along with Lightning and Helen lakes, all about 12-14 miles back pack or horse ride east of Mirror Lake. In such places, you find yourself wishing time and schedules would just go away so you could fish forever.

To summarize, the Uintas have three types of lakes:

1. **Marshy**, with lily pads and moss, and wet or perhaps, floating shorelines. Bottom is often too soft to wade. Shallow bays provide a "pasture" effect with sunlight growing heavy moss beds. The moss invites many under-water insects, beetles, plus snails and bottom food. This means good trout, but with so much to eat, they are usually hungry for only short feeding periods. Brook trout usually inhabit this type of lake. Be sure to fish deep.

2. **Mud flat types** are usually due to major drawdown behind a dam. Many natural lakes in the Uintas have a small concrete dam for additional water storage. Although not much in esthetics, these lakes often grow nice trout. Best fishing is in the late summer-early fall, when fish are congregated in lower water with less feed. Both brook and cutthroat trout thrive in these lakes if at least 12 feet deep in winter to carry sufficient supply of dissolved oxygen.

3. **The rock-ribbed type** has sizeable fish less often than the other two. The primary factor is whether fresh-water shrimp are present. Some rock-bed lakes above timberline do have rapidly-growing fish because of the shrimp or "scuds." Trout are usually cutthroats sensitive to insect activity. Since you can't judge a book by its cover, these lakes are worth trying.

A major factor for growth of large trout is ample feed coupled with lack of angling pressure. Overstocking can bring stunted fish if none are removed by anglers. The ideal situation is a lake with much food but few fish, meaning more feed for each. If fish are lunker-size, there are fewer of them. A given water can support 200 trout of one pound each, or a third that many weighing three pounds each.

Many of the trout and grayling you'll catch in the Uintas will average about 9-12 inches long. But on some lakes like Duck via the Crystal Lake trail, plus others on the upper Provo River, you can frequently catch them that size fast and furious with the right fly pattern. My recommendation is a size 8-12 artificial in yellow, black, gray or black hues. These are the natural colors of the world at 9000 to 12,000 feet. Of them all, I have found the yellowish and double-jointed Siberian wood-ant, a sparsely-hackled nymph with a shiny body, to be the top trout-attractor in alpine waters. I suspect it appears as some sort of immature upper echelon caddis. It works less often in lowlands. Another favorite is the caddis-in-shell, which appears to be a rock roller larvae attempting emergence from its many-pebbled case. But the conventional stone and may fly imitations, gray hackles and mosquito, black gnat and ginger quills, will often get the job done. Renegade, Adams, all of the conventionals also work well if the size is approximately number 8-16.

While a spinning rig and water-filled casting bubble will reach to the middle of many of these small Uinta lakes, there are many one-two acre ponds where a fly rod will reach feeding fish. In my opinion, the lighter outfit offers much more refinement and fun. I usually carry both a "splash" pole with spin reel and an ultra-light Browning fly rod so that I'm prepared for feeders wherever they are. Some anglers, especially backpackers, may prefer a "double duty" combination outfit which breaks down into five or six pieces for easy transport. These are fine as "combos" but with the extra ferrules, are not the lightest when it comes to casting a fly all day.

But back to geography. Some regions, like the beautiful Naturalist Basin south of Mt. Agassiz, do not seem to produce large fish. Others, like lakes in the upper Yellowstone north of Duchesne, all seem to grow trout in the 2-3 lb. range. Even lakes in the barren rock slides above timberline may produce good fish, especially those with fresh-water shrimp as a trout forage food. The largest lakes do not necessarily raise the best trout. On one expedition into the upper Yellow-

Slab-sided brook trout like these are routine in many high country waters.

stone, I could entice nothing over 11 inches in the sprawling Spider Lake, nor Gem or Bluebell. Kindest waters were Drift and Doll Lakes, scarcely showing on the maps. My best trout from that drainage, brookies to nearly three pounds, came from nondescript ponds little more than large beaver dams. Of course, the larger Five Points, Superior, and particularly Tungsten and North Star up a remote trail in the treeless tundra, have a reputation for large trout. But several small "swamps" have also surprised anglers with net-filling brook trout, including one named Upper Lily Pad on the South Slope's Heller Basin-Dry Gulch area. Dead Horse Lake has that colorful name on upper Blacks Fork, but some of the largest cutthroats in this drainage are found within the mundane label of G-76, a dull name (which doesn't even follow the normal Uinta nomenclature rule) in a dull tundra setting. I couldn't wait to get my family to Hell Hole Lake on the Bear River drainage, where we found only 9-inch cutthroats. But the cutts at Kermsuh Lake (huh?) were considerably larger. Likewise, McPheters. I didn't have much complaint , however, about small trout in nearby Upper Stillwater Fork of the Bear, because this magnificent peak-and-meadow country reminds one of the best in British Columbia. If you want a memorable camping trip by from the road, try Christmas Meadows on the Stillwater.Watch for the sign on the North Slope off Utah 150 some 10 miles south of the Wyoming border. There are many lakes along the North Slope road over Mt. Elizabeth east of 150, although fishing pressure is not light.

   Timing is extremely important. I like to fish a few days after ice-out (not the very day ice goes, since water is still too cool for cold-blooded creatures to feel hunger) because the trout become ravenously hungry after their winter-long food drought. You can determine when this will be for a given back-in lake by comparing to one by the road. For instance, when the ice is gone from Moosehorn, just below Bald Mountain Pass at about 10,500 feet, I know it will likely be gone from other lakes at about that altitude. Better wait another week, however, if the lake is in north slope shade. I fished Pyramid one July 10th when the ice hadn't yet melted from a shaded cove.

   Be aware, too, that many early summer trails are filled with snowmelt water. For some, you may need hip boots *en route* to the lake. In autumn, cold nights kill insects and fish go one a luau binge for them through about late September. Sometime around middle October when temperatures plummet even in daylight, fish metabolism will slow again. The fish will then be dormant at alpine altitudes until the following spring, about mid-June in the lowest Uinta lakes. The earliest I have ever seen ice defrost on Moosehorn was in the dry year of 1977, when lakes at ll,000 feet opened by June 8. Trout were hitting about anything from June 12 to about June 18.

   Large lakes may require several days to find the fish. Interestingly, the best trout may be within a medium cast from banks, in neither shallowest or deepest water. About 5-10 foot depths are often best. I like to fish just off the deep water, usually the opposite side you enter from, the latter being against the mountain. Don't overlook the 2-5 foot depths either, because penetrating sunlight grows moss there holding food which trout seek. Fly fishing is often best near shore if there is cover like lily pads and overhanging grass. Key places are inlets, where food normally enters a lake, and at outlets where current also carries food to fish. The nice thing about outlets is that they are usually filled with floating logs and debris which form cover, shadows, and a natural base of operations for fish concerned with both security and a quick lunch.

I have found Uinta fishing to be best in middle of the day, from 9 a.m. to 1 p.m. when sun is brightest, temperatures highest. This in turn causes wind currents, cold air mixing with warm, stirring insect life and blowing food about the lake. Consequently, after hiking through the night with flashlight to reach dozens of Uinta lakes at dawn, I have come to a comforting conclusion. You don't need to be there at first light of day. I have put away my flashlight.

The fishing will often cease at about 1-1:30 p.m. in most lakes, since fish are satiated after a morning's food-gathering activities. In many lakes, you can set your watch by it. One day at Fire Lake a friend began giving his catch away because he didn't want to stop fishing. I told him he wouldn't catch any more after 1: 30 p.m. I still wonder if I placed a curse on him. Even that evening, when small trout ringed the lake, the big ones didn't strike again until just before dark. This is a typical day in the Uintas. Hike or camp or cook in the afternoon. A full moon with few clouds may allow fish to feed all night, then seem to have lockjaw the following morning. But at some time of day, Uinta trout will usually go on a feeding spree, even if just for a short time.

The **top lunker-producers** often have a combination of fresh-water shrimp and remote location. Such is true on the upper Whiterocks in Teds and Workman lakes which have consistently grown football-shaped brook trout. Ditto for the Whiterocks' Queant and Chepeta, the latter having yielded numerous 4 lb. brookies over the years. The West Fork of Whiterocks, along with upper Ashley Creek drainage, and the Uinta's east end hold respectable trout in lakes with names like One Fish and Mystery and Red Belly. Decent roads, when dry, take anglers into jump-off points for wildland backpacking at Paradise Park and Pole Creek Reservoirs. The maps show a road from Pole Creek up to Chepeta Lake on the Whiterocks; but it is extremely rough. Most anglers hike into the region. Paradise is located north of Whiterocks, Pole Creek off the Red Cloud Loop Road, with signs marking the way from U.S. 44 north of Vernal.

For oversized cutthroats, the Red Castle Lake region on the North Slope's Smiths Fork drainage has grown some of the biggest: three-pounders in the upper lake, some nearly as big in the larger "main" Red Castle and nearby waters. The extreme beauty of this drainage has drawn many an angler, so it takes more work now for the best fish. These are large lakes, with a raft (horse-packed in) a big help. Motors are not allowed on most Uinta lakes.

A drainage with colorful cutts is the Burnt Fork country west of Spirit Lake. The latter has a lodge, one of the few in the Uintas since other resort accommodations were discontinued at Mirror and Trial Lakes. Spirit Lake is a supply point for forays into nearby high country north and west, including the three forks of Sheep Creek, and Burnt Fork. Several lakes nearby, including Tamarak, have produced arm-long rainbows. Fish Lake, in the Burnt Fork area, produces nice brook trout on caddis fly patterns. One evening on Fish, five miles from Spirit Lake, a fly rod with caddis imitation spurred brook trout action as fast as I've seen in the high country.

On one backpack over Burnt Fork and into the upper Uinta River from Island Lake, over an 11,200-foot high pass which nestles Divide Lake, I found a number of fat cutts and two-pound brookies in Rainbow and Verlie Lakes. Rainbow Lake has produced rainbow trout to six pounds and brooks to four. My best on this trip was a 2-1/2-lb. brook. On another trip, I found a lake which did live up fully to its advance billing. This one was Picture Lake in the Lake Fork drainage, where I hooked three cutts in the 18-20 inch range within half an hour. Crater Lake in that same drainage, a unique glacial water where one step off the bank can put you in some 100 feet of water, yielded dozens of cutts in three hours. The latter lake seemed "dead" until an early afternoon shower. Then I caught a cutt on a spinner, opened it up, found red ants. Tying on a simulating royal coachman, I had tight lines for two hours. Other Lake Fork waters with respectable trout were Gates, Lambert, Clements and the little super-clear Aspen, a jewel for eager 13-inchers on any fly with a light leader.

I have found adjustments or "gimmicks" to be necessary in many high lakes. For instance, on one trek into the upper Henrys Fork, I found spawning cutthroats in Cliff Lake which had their minds on something besides food. But in a slightly lower lake, the cutts were hungered by warming waters, yet not ready for the eggs and milt routine, and cooperated nicely. In another, Blanchard, I missed the inlet on the first search, catching little elsewhere around the lake. When finally locating inlet current behind some low-growing brush, I found the feeding trout. Through the morning, not one refused a delicately cast Siberian wood-ant. On Buckeye, I couldn't catch a fish until carefully lowering a bait into a deep pothole cavern near an inlet.

One of my most exciting quests over the years has been for the **Arctic grayling.** My best, up to 18 inches long, have been in lakes of the the upper North Fork of the Provo, including Buckeye and Blue Lake. One evening I caught several grayling in the stream above Buckeye which would run at least a pound or more, never thinking to have them entered in the state angling records. Utah's record grayling at just a little over one pound hails from Whiskey Island Lake, a short hike from a dirt logging road off Utah 150. Daggett lake on the east end once produced good grayling but has less nowadays. One of the largest populations of self-propagating grayling are in Fish, Round, and Sand lakes in the Weber River drainage. Check for populations from year to year which are not too numerous, for grayling can reproduce so rapidly as to stunt out, leaving little feed for growth.

The Weber drainage is less than 1 1/2 hours from Salt Lake City, but this steep terrain is the least explored in the western Uintas. You can get into the Weber's three forks via the cut in Notch Mountain above Trial Lake, from the high ledges past Little Hidden, and the trail past Dean and Notch Lakes off Bald Mountain Pass. A fourth trail takes you past Big Elk and Erickson lakes to Smith-Morehouse Creek and Reservoir in the Weber drainage on the road to Holiday Park. There are many roadless lakes here with trout which have never felt an angler's hook.

Incidentally, hiking in from the main Weber River trailhead at Holiday Park looks easy enough on paper, but the bottom trail connection is on private property and not marked. The route is also extremely steep up Dry Fork, not recommended for anyone in less than excellent physical condition. The Cuberant lakes, in the Weber drainage, provide fast fishing for brook and cutthroat trout. The smaller ones seem to offer better angling than the big Cuberant No. 4. Incidentally, no one I've talked to knows how these lakes received their unique names. Ditto for Ibantik north of Trial. Most Uinta names come from early pioneers, like Lambert, or mountaineering scientists like Gilbert and Agassiz, or apparently, after some map-maker's girl friend. Names I like best tie with the geography, like Cliff or Meadow or Notch.

An unusual twist on the Cuberant lakes basin is that it has been the object of an official "investigation" by the UDWR official concerning reports about "a large and strange animal" which makes "considerable noises" at night. One angler I know dismisses it is an attempt to keep anglers from discovering the excellent fishing in that country, like the old saw about big trout, "yet watch out for the rattlesnakes." But another veteran angler verifies the same as occurring to him on a 1989 solitary backpack. The reader can make up his own mind, whether the Uintas are harboring some mystery animal in wild surroundings, like the okapi discovered in darkest Africa in 1947 . . . or an indication of someone attempting to safeguard good fishing. In any event, you heard it here first!

Joan and Gem Lakes, high in the Duchesne, are the only lakes being considered for golden trout, since they have not flourished in the upper Uinta River's Atwood area. Gem has produced slab-sided brookies in the past. There is only one lake in these mountains where splake are stocked, East Shingle Creek on North Fork of the Provo. No Uinta lakes are stocked with lake trout.

One strange thing about Uinta nomenclature: lakes named "Hidden" usually are difficult to find, giving up respectable fish, while lakes named "Lost" are trailside with a less prolific harvest. I like Hidden on the North Slope of the Provo, having caught many plump brookies there, although I couldn't find the lake once when forgetting to bring a map. Little Hidden on the Middle Fork of the Weber is also one ravine away from finding easily, with two-pounders not unusual. The best offering for oversized brookies in these lakes has been a size three silver Mepps spinner, the same lure I've found so highly valuable on lower waters. If the moss is thick, I use a spinner behind a bubble to keep the lure from fouling.

Baiters also have considerable success by rigging half a night crawler about a rod's length behind a casting bubble. The value of the bubble is that it will sink the bait slowly, with fish often taking the offering on the way down. A gentle retrieve, effected by raising and lowering the rod tip, making the crawler appear to be washing ashore, is also highly effective. The great angling mystery of high country is that there are no worms or nightcrawlers where the air and soil are thin, yet fish immediately recognize these baits that they've never seen before as food to be taken advantage of. On one lake I found a not-supposed-to-be-there grasshopper (the elevation is too high for them, say the biologists) and found the fish attacked it eagerly. Two trout fell to the 'hopper on two casts.

Somewhere among the 100-mile long, approximately 40-mile north-to-south Uintas, including both the northside Wasatch National Forest and southside Ashley, are approximately 1500 lakes. Most of them hold trout, the precise ones enumerated in the Uinta Mountain Lake booklets published by the UDWR. The first printing of these publications explains how to reach the various waters, their elevations, camping possibilities, availability of horse feed and expected size of fish. The reprints did a better job of explaining lake locations, along with improved maps. They said less about lunker potential, apparently because it placed too much fishing pressure on some lakes, while others were ignored. For example, Anchor Lake on the Weber was publicized as "having stunted fish," so anglers shunned it. Thus, trout multiplied even more. Then with more mouths for less food, the residents became smaller than ever. Lakes publicized as having large fish were rushed by anglers, at least those near roads. Poorer fishing usually resulted within a year or two.

Some lakes just never have had sufficient food to grow respectable trout, one being Clyde Lake on the upper Provo. In lakes with food problems, the UDWR has learned to plant fewer fish. If the lake was on a three-year aerial stocking cycle , it is changed to five. When a shallow lake unexpectedly winterkills, of course, angler input to the UDWR is helpful to resume the regular stocking cycle. Anglers should report lakes they believe to be winter-killed.

Most Uinta lakes can be located by following up creeks or sometimes, dry creek beds to the first level terrain below ridges and cliffs. Most lakes are glacially-carved basins below snowmelt runoff. Most Uinta lakes also have outlet streams, even only if via early summer overflow.

Streams coursing from the Uinta range include, west to east, and north to south, Provo, Weber, Bear, Blacks, Smiths, Henrys, Beaver, Burnt, Sheep, Carter, Brush, Ashley, Whiterocks, Uinta, Dry Gulch, Swift, Yellowstone, Lake, Rock, Duchesne. Lower stretches are covered in other chapters, but it should be said these upper rivulets and brooks offer excellent fly fishing for pansized trout above 9000 feet, especially in remote terrain. I once saw a 20-inch cutt in a tiny tributary of the Yellowstone, up from Hell's Canyon and over the Swasey Lakes trail. Most Uinta trails follow these streams from road's end for a time, then abandon steep canyons to wend over ridges. Major trailheads at road's end also provide horse unloading ramps; some popular trailheads have bulletin boards and maps of the drainage. Good trails grace most lake basins.

The book *High Uinta Trails* by Mel Davis has trail descriptions on reaching the many Uinta lakes. A forest service map of the Uintas shows many lakes well away from roads. For contour maps, the U.S. Geological Survey, 125 S. State, St., Salt Lake City has index maps to show you names for all maps in stock. These maps are a bargain for any Uinta Mountain lake-hunter.

Moon Lake, north of Duchesne, a huge reservoir on the Lake Fork River, has kokanee salmon with stocked rainbows. While it once produced a 16 1/2 -lb. brown trout and a 9 1/2-lb. cutthroat, the highly fluctuating lake at road's end is not a consistent lunker producer. Known as a picturesque water with pansized rainbows, it is most valuable as a trailhead resort stop for those heading into the upper Lake Fork waters. The lake seems deep and cold enough to harbor lake trout, but so far as I can find, it has never been tried.

It should also be mentioned that some pretty good fishing can be found on the **lower Uinta foothills reservoirs**, not covered elsewhere, reached by four-wheel drive to trailhead sites. This includes Splash Dam on the North Fork of the

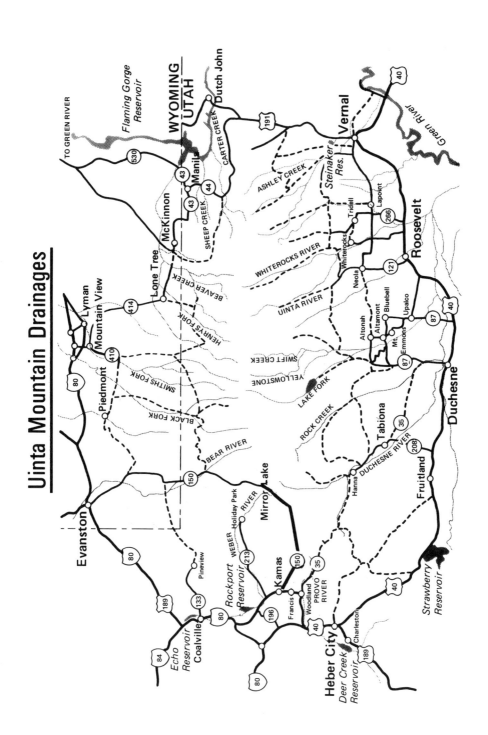

Uinta Mountain Drainages

Duchesne above Defa's Ranch, a similar "collection" lake at road's end on the Yellowstone, U-Bar Ranch ponds on the Uinta, etc. China Meadows area offers beautiful stream and lake fishing near road's end on Smiths Fork, etc. Good gravel roads at the top of Sheep Creek Canyon in Daggett County take anglers to fast brook trout fishing at Browne Lake and to cutthroats at Sheep Creek Lake. The east Uintas receive less angling pressure than the west.

Fortunately, there are many remote regions rarely visited, with few footprints or litter, and with oversized muley bucks, elk, bobcats, and moose.

Following is a list of horse-packers serving the Uintas: **West slope**, Piute Creek Outfitters, Kamas, 84036. **South slope**: Duchesne River area, Defa's Ranch, via Hanna, 84031; Moon Lake, Lake Fork area, Mt. Emmons, no zip listed; Whiterocks area, Whiterocks, 84085; Uinta River area, U-Bar Ranch, via Roosevelt, 84066. **North slope**: Spirit Lake Lodge, contact at 40 Stauffer Lane, Murray, 84107.

Note: other services should be available in the near future on Rock Creek drainage, Rock Creek Ranch, via Duchesne, 84021. Services are subject to change without further notification. Check with UDWR, 1596 W. North Temple, SLC, 84106 for additional information.

Mountain climbing and fishing often work well in combination. A good trek is Kings Peak via the Henrys Fork drainage. You can camp at Henrys Fork Lake 17 miles up-trail from the road, then have about four more miles to the peak. Bring the USGS maps labeled "Mt. Powell "and "Kings Peak" and study them closely. You don't want any "thousand foot surprises"! Climbing Kings is not a piton and rope type of thing, but being in good shape helps.

Uinta Lakes with special species are:

Grayling: Leconte, GR 1632, Norway Flats, GR 104, Cirque, WR-33, Y-20, Gandy, Picture (or Picturesque), Ewe, Big Dog, Farney, Hoover, China, Summit, Whisky Island, Trial, Washington, Fish, Round, Sand, Allen, Daggett. Also: Weir, Marjorie, and Blue have a few remaining grayling from previous stocking and natural reproduction.

Albino rainbow, stocked at a "catchable" 8-12 inches, are likely in the following roadside lakes: Butterfly, Mirror, Moosehorn, Pass, Lyman, Marsh, Trial. Mill Hollow Reservoir also has albinos. It is located on the Uinta National Forest (just south of the Uinta Mountains proper) on U.S. 35 east of Woodland and then southward on a marked gravel road.

The only Uinta lake listed by the UDWR as having splake species is East Shingle Creek Lake. This is reached via the Norway Flats road off Utah 150. At Norway Flats, hike several miles to the northwest. The map shows it as on the west side of the ridge from Big Elk Lake.

BOULDER MOUNTAIN, AQUARIUS PLATEAU — Some of the West's best trout lakes are located in these mountains. Not only is fishing pressure much less than in the northern Utah waters so close to the Wasatch Front, but trout grow much faster. Southern Utah fisheries biologist Dale Hepworth says the mineral-rich (basalt bed) location of Boulder lakes, plus the presence of moss beds with fresh-water shrimp and other aquatic foods, promotes rapid growth. The brook trout, in particular, take on a slab shape in such lakes as Pleasant and Raft on the Boulder Top and Horseshoe, Donkey, Blind, Fish Creek below the rim.

On one trip onto Boulder in late August, 1989, I also looked at several cutthroats in the 18-inch category cruising the surface of lakes below the southwest rim. I had reached this part of the Boulder over miles of rock-strewn roads. Except for access on the west side off Parker Mountain, and the road up Pine Creek to Cook's Lake, most roads require four-wheel drive vehicles.

I saw nice trout rising in Raft Lake, and hooked fat brookies on a spinner in lush little Pleasant Lake, despite arriving in late afternoon. Local conservation officer Leon Bogedahl, Torrey, says the Boulder trout seem to feed best from about noon to 3 p.m., some two hours later in the day than in most Uinta Mountain waters. Perhaps a more southerly latitude and warmer temperatures have something to do with it.

From one point on the north plateau rim, I looked at Green Lake directly below me, Donkey off to the far left. To its right (east) were Middle and Lower Lakes, Solitaire, Round and Left Hand Lakes. From a point several hundred yards to the right, I could see below me Blind, Pear and the depression where Fish Creek Lake-Beaver Dam Pond should be, according to the Dixie National Forest map. It was on these north slope lakes where Milt Taft, Bicknell, caught his state record 7 1/2-lb. brook trout. He also took a number of *Salvelinus fontinalis* in the 5-7 lb. bracket from those waters. No other alpine lakes in Utah have yielded brookies of this size. If one does, it will likely be another Boulder lake that does it. The Whiterocks River drainage of the Uintas has yielded a brookie or two to nearly five pounds, but not as many as the Boulder.

Incidentally, angling strategy may have to include casting over many bankside moss beds. There are many in these lake which can make casting difficult from shore. One technique is to bring a small raft. Another is to fish deeper water. I would get a leadhead jig or spinner between those moss beds to entice the best fish. Taft used a small spoon-like lure. Bait on bottom would work away from the moss beds. With flys, try larger wet flies and bucktails for best fish. But in deep lakes, you'll usually have to fish deep.

You have to be careful about reading the maps when it comes to lakes on the Boulder. Some like Elbow look good on paper, but are so shallow that in a dry year they are nearly gone. Some winterkill despite that sizeable blue coloring on the map. In fact, Hepworth lists Cooks, Miller's, Chuck's, and others as subject to periodic kill. Many like Chuck's can also produce excellent brooks when not killing for three-five years in a row. Also, some of the Boulder Top lakes like Raft, although growing trout to 18 inches in good water years, do not offer best camping possibilities. They are located in an open meadow with no cover from storms, nor much shade from sun. Unfortunately, the Boulder Top, all 22 miles across its longest diameter, is not blessed today with the same esthetics as found beneath the rim. The top is riddled with eroded swales containing little grass, heavy on the dust. Why this should be so is covered in a later chapter on Utah's Fishing Future.

My favorite lakes are the natural waters, like those just beneath the north rim, with shorelines mirroring conifers, waters clear and scenery superb. Two roads connecting from U.S. 12 just north of Grover, and the cutoff road to Teasdale, wind upward to such lakes as Donkey and Blind; roads struggle in the last few miles, and while one finally wheezes to those in the vicinity of Donkey, the Blind-Pear-Fish Creek trio require about a 3-4 mile hike or horse pack. It is not likely these roads will be improved, since emphasis is on quality experience. For the same apparent reason, a series of booklets describing precise location and access, plus big fish potential etc. of these Boulder lakes did not undergo a second printing as did the Uinta Mountain series. Little has been printed on the Boulder lakes and how to reach them. You can obtain a map by writing the Dixie National Forest headquarters in Cedar City.

Bown's Reservoir on the southeastern slope is one of the few roaded large lakes in this mountain country. A mecca for rainbow trout fishermen who want quick access, it can be seen and easily reached off U.S. 12. Several campgrounds are found along this sector of 12, including Bown. There are none on gravel-dirt roads elsewhere on the mountain. Incidentally, Bown's is often referred to as "Lower Bown's." But the "Lower" has been dropped since "Upper Bown's" shows on modern maps as Oak Creek Reservoir.

Unlike the Uintas, the streams which course from the Boulders are short-lived. Descent is rapid and the surrounding dry lowlands gobble the water up quickly. Some excellent fly fishing for brook trout is found in Pine Creek on the east side of the mountain for a few roadless miles. This one flows into the Escalante River drainage. Another Pine Creek, a tributary of the Fremont River on the west side, has silted in at the bottom of Boulder. Dixie Forest officials have fenced in some acreage on Pine Creek on west side meadows, with some fishing for small trout. This can be reached from the road which departs Utah 24 east of Bicknell, then leads to the south side of the Boulder. A rugged trek extolled only by the hardy is one along the roadless stream through Box Canyon-Death Hollow in the Escalante River drainage directly north of the town of Escalante. The upper Escalante River provides some trout pools to the toe of Boulder Mountain, but quickly turns to warm and troutless flow in the Escalante Desert.

Grayling are found on the Boulder in Cook Lake. Plans are to stock more grayling in the future. Splake have been planted in Blind Lake. An oppossum shrimp, the same trout food available in Fish Lake in Sevier County, has been stocked in Blind Lake to assist rapid splake growth.

The Escalante escarpment boasts little flatwater, most notable being Pine Lake, a put-and-take rainbow fishery, with a few brook trout, at 8,000 feet. Take the well-graveled Utah 22 route north from Bryce Canyon National park, and turn toward Escalante from a point just south of Widstoe Junction. It is five miles from Utah 22 to Pine Lake's campground.

THOUSAND LAKE MOUNTAIN — Someone misnamed this one years ago and the map-makers never corrected the error. The mountain has about 25 lakes with trout, many reached only via four-wheel drive. Several are lunker lakes, making the mountain worth an angler's time. Deep, Meeks, and Round Lakes are three favorites with anglers and campers.

Like the Boulder, this giant mesa's waters seem to have the proper environment for rapid trout growth, a major reason being presence of fresh-water shrimp. Local conservation officer Leon Bogedahl says, "I check out a 4-lb. brook or cutthroat caught here every once in a while. I'd say most of the deeper waters on Thousand Lake, like those on Boulder, are capable of producing above-average trout." As with other high country, lakes which are too shallow can winterkill if temperatures remain severe for long periods. You can't always believe names as labeled by maps. So-called Big Lake is one of the marginal fisheries. One lake, Floating Island, has been "stunted out" with brook trout populations and was to be restocked by 1991-92 with rainbow trout and/or the Bonneville strain of cutthroat trout.

Much of the mountain receives little fishing pressure, at least in relation to waters near the Wasatch Front. Many of the lakes, again like the Boulder lakes, are just beneath a cliff-like lava rim. There are several campgrounds, including Elkhorn, as marked on U.S. 72 pavement near the turnoff to Forsyth Reservoir. Much of this mountain is roaded, although roads deteriorate the farther south you go. To protect quality, fisheries biologists would also like to shut down roads leading directly to the more popular lakes. For maps, contact the Fishlake National Forest office in Richfield, Sevier County.

The same offerings which work on other alpine waters prevail, including small dry and wet flies, bait, spinners. And like most highlands, expect plenty of rain and mosquitoes. Read over the sections on Boulder for best angling techniques. One problem, as with Boulder lakes, is getting over shoreline moss beds. A life raft can be easily transported to several roadside lakes.

The only lake listed by the UDWR as having grayling on this plateau is Grass Lake.

WASATCH RANGE — From north to south, you'll like the fat brook trout and albino rainbows from Tony Grove Lake, east of Logan, seven miles by paved road from U.S.89 in Logan Canyon. Tony Grove is a deep and beautiful natural mountain lake with scenic camping nearby. A scuba diver once told me he had seen brook trout in this water "as long as his leg." But most of those caught have been a healthy 12-14 inches.

Farther south are many deep, clear lakes in and around the scenic and precipitous Big and Little Cottonwood Canyons, an hour from Salt Lake City. Let's examine those in Big Cottonwood first: Blanche, Lillian and Florence are found on Mill B Fork, a three-mile climb off the highway to Brighton. The Mill B sign is located on a side road several miles up-canyon, just below a series of highway switchbacks. These small but deep lakes are located in glacially-carved granite, and at times, feature hungry, pansized brook trout. Large fish are not likely. Most anglers get well down into the black depths with bait.

From the Brighton area, an angler can be at the west meadow's Silver Lake in 10 minutes. At stake are hatchery rainbows, with a few natural brook trout. Above is Twin Lake, a deep reservoir with more brook trout. On the trail north of Brighton some two miles are Mary, Martha, and in the cirque above, Catherine Lake. The latter is a good one for fly casting to ll-inch brookies. Martha, a shallow water, frequently winterkills and is seldom stocked. Mary is a deep glacial-ravine lake in which anglers once dredged up 10-15 lb. lake trout, although today's catch is mostly brookies. Angling pressure is greater on these alpine lakes than on Uinta waters. Catching a big laker in Mary is still possible. The habitat remains unchanged in a splendid cliff-guarded setting. None of these Big Cottonwood lakes are accessible via horseback, for horses are forbidden on a major metropolitan city watershed.

Little Cottonwood Canyon offers more alpine fishing lakes, with brook and cutthroat a little less sophisticated due to extremely steep trails and longer distances. Lakes include Upper and Lower Red Pine and White Pine, and, with a few nice trout taken on the same flies which work well in other high country. Another lake in the ledges, difficult to locate, is Hardy. All are stocked every several years. Anglers hiking into Upper Red Pine say the trout are respectable in size, but highly temperamental. The idea here is to go as much for the alpine scenery as the fishing. The trail signs to these lakes can be seen on the highway which leads to Alta and Snowbird.

Farther south, in American Fork Canyon, are Tibble Fork Reservoir and Silver Lake, reached via good road on the North Fork route. The view is magnificent looking north to Mt. Timpanogos. There are some small hike-in lakes above Silver Lake. These waters all feature pansized rainbows and brookies, although an occasional 5-10 lb. brown is hauled out of Tibble Fork's deeper moss bed pockets. Such a fish usually feeds nocturnally and shows little during daylight hours. Bait or lures imitating minnows entice the best fish, with smaller trout falling to flies. Tibble Fork and the stream below is as air-clear as water gets, and camping is popular throughout this entire canyon, especially in fall when the oak and aspens change color. The all-paved road connects on the east end with movie actor Robert Redford's Sundance resort and U.S. 189 in Provo Canyon. The route is often crowded with sight-seers and hikers. At the mouth of American Fork Canyon is Timpanogos Cave National Monument.

Other high lakes are found on what is called Payson Mountain or the north slope of Mt. Nebo, highest in the Wasatch. These lakes, however, are put-and-take trouting, with many scout troops and nearby residents taking advantage of them via a good road. The only lake on the Wasatch being stocked with grayling at this time, according to UDWR fisheries biologist Glenn Davis, is Red Creek Reservoir on Payson Mountain.

MANTI MOUNTAIN — This elongated series of ridges and spur canyons, named after a geographical area in local Mormon literature, has more trout fishing than first meets the eye. I had spent many days exploring the Manti, but as recently as August, 1989, discovered many new trout waters. Electric Lake is a relatively new trout reservoir on the upper Huntington River and draws considerable attention. The deep, south end, accessed by Utah 31, is a favorite of many trollers and baiters. I like the upper inlet end best because 12-15 inch cutthroats prowl the surface there for insects. The north end is reached via Utah 264 up Eccles Canyon from the Scofield region, or a turnoff from 31 to 264 at the top of Fairview Canyon. There is no road between, so you choose the end you want, or launch a boat at a ramp on the upper end to get between points.

But more typical of Manti lakes is Gooseberry, a few gravel miles off U 264. The lake is a popular one in a treeless green meadow, a scenic area where elk or deer might also be spotted morning and evening. Fishing is temperamental for pansized rainbows and cutthroats. The upper end mud flats offer fly fishing possibilities in early summer but are soft and shallow later in August with fish moving into deeper water. The outlet Gooseberry Creek joins Fish Creek for some 12 cutthroat-laden miles to Scofield Reservoir, much of that distance roadless. You can be dropped off at Gooseberry and be picked up on the gravel road at the bottom. The same is possible in several roadless Manti canyons, including Left Fork of Huntington River for seven roadless miles below Miller Flat Reservoir. The lake itself has a good trout population in substantial water years. But heavy drawdown in drought years means loss of fish. Check the surface to see if the trout are there; when they are, fly fishing can be fast but mud shoreline sometimes makes wading difficult.

Along Utah 31 are many lakes with catchable rainbows such as Cleveland and Huntington. Near U264 not far from the upper end of Electric Lake are several fine fly fishing lakes, including Boulger and Bench (also known as CCC Pond and Beaver Dam Lake). Both lakes fatten rainbows and cutthroats on fresh-water shrimp. A simulated pattern can bring fast action. On one warm summer day I detected no slurping fish on Bench, but two hours later, there they were, rising in such unison it appeared as boiling water. The takers were 13-inch rainbows hitting right on the surface. In the meantime, nearby baiters looked on in frustration. I did not see any one fishing with bait catch a fish during the time I was there. It was clearly an insect-gorging frenzy. The fish did not look to the bottom. Some of the best Manti fly fishing is found in these smaller lakes.

A mile by gravel road above Bench are the Fairview Lakes, one lake at high water, two in late summer. They offer rainbows to three pounds, some of the fastest growing trout on the Manti. Fishing can be fast in the deep channel between the two lakes, but otherwise the shoreline is muddy and shallow. The lake is best plied from boat. Try a trolled spinner or minnow imitation. There is one complication with these lakes, however. They are surrounded by private property and no public camping is allowed. But since Fairview is stocked by the state, public access cannot be legally denied to the lake or its shoreline.

Many trout lakes are visible from Skyline Drive which hugs the entire Manti backbone for some 100 miles. Anglers will find the likes of Logger and Snow Lakes, while side canyons offer more hidden waters like Deep. All offer fat rainbow trout, with some of the largest found in Deep, a natural lake nestled in an almost unnoticed basin. Snow Lake on the treeless Manti top doesn't offer much for camping. But it can excite the fly angler who looks at those rising rainbows. Logger, a shallow, wind-churned and murky fishing hole, is a favorite of baiters who wait out respectable rainbows right alongside the dirt road access.

Reached by four-wheel drive near the top of Six and Twelve-mile Canyons are many lakes which also offer excellent fly fishing for cutthroats in air-clear ponds and lakes. For variety there are lakes like Emerald, possibly the best on the mountain for chunky brook trout. Ferron Reservoir across the divide from the top of Twelve Mile is a favorite of many fly anglers. Ditto for Willow, on down the

Ferron Canyon road. I have seen the lake surface alive with feeding rainbows on a summer evening in these east slope Manti lakes. If you explore around the many side canyons you can come up with good fishing almost anywhere. There are also many small roadside streams high on the mountain, and a few controlled flows in ditches and canals, which nevertheless hold trout. Fairview (Cottonwood) Creek emerges from a tunnel near the summit, with fast fishing for rainbows often found at the permanently-shadowed tunnel mouth.

Fast fishing can also be found in foothill lakes. An example is Yearns Reservoir, barely out of the town of Manti. Rainbows there like the Siberian wood-ant on a summer evening. Fly fishing action is best in high water years, since drought-year fish are concentrated and skittish. With the sun off the water, however, they begin feeding with the first long shadows.

Other Manti lakes include Island, oxygenated by a UDWR-placed windmill which prevents winter or summerkill. Recreational use on the Manti is high; so is livestock operation, with sheep apt to be almost anywhere. Campgrounds are found in the side canyons, but scarce on top.

Angler-explorers cannot trust all the roads they see on Manti maps. Heavy flooding in the middle 1980s washed out some county roads which have not been rebuilt. This is especially true on Six and Twelve-Mile roads, and many on the upper east slope above Joe's Valley Reservoir. The latter roads can be slippery and dangerous when wet. Best maps can be obtained from the headquarters Manti-LaSal National Forest office in Price and communities with district offices.

Manti Mountain is a main cog in the Great Western Trail which runs from Mexico to Canada. This route for hikers and/or horsemen winds over public lands through Utah in several mountain ranges. It follows Skyline Drive from Salina Canyon on the south to Tie Fork on the north. There it joins Spanish Fork Canyon and the Wasatch Range. The trail route will gain more attention in the future as it is improved and publicized.

FISHLAKE MOUNTAIN — The only other major fishery on this high plateau besides Fish Lake is Johnson Reservoir. Johnson offers excellent rainbows which fatten quickly, and enjoy bait, lure, or fly. I have my best success on the lake near its outlet with a spinner or black leadhead jig. Fishing is often good right off the east side road. Late in the summer Johnson may draw down in low-water years to churn mud with the first wind and offer a murky challenge. It then sends a muddy flow into the Fremont River. The lake is fed by a creek from Fish Lake on the south and Seven-mile Creek on the northwest. At some 8,500 feet it offers a cool summer climate and ample forest service campgrounds on week days. On weekends, they may be filled late in the day.

The Fishlake region has some small lakes north of Johnson served by four-wheel drive roads, including Rex Reservoir on public land. It is a stocked rainbow fishery best reached from Salina Canyon. Check the Fishlake National Forest maps for small streams in the area.

LASAL MOUNTAINS — Most of the lakes here are located near the foothills. They are primarily stocked rainbow fisheries and include Don's, Hidden,

Fisherman has a lake to himself. A typical Uinta scene at 10,000 feet.

and Oowah. Baiting and lures work well, but fly fishing offers variety in a scenic setting. Check with the southeastern region for additional information on both LaSal and the Abajo Mountains in San Juan County. Maps are available from the Manti-LaSal National Forest in Moab, Blanding or Price.

CEDAR MOUNTAIN — Cedar is home of Navajo Lake, a turquoise jewel at 10,000 feet, just off U.S. 14 east of Cedar City. It has never gained a reputation for large fish. It is a beautiful place to catch 10-12 inch brook and rainbow trout .So is nearby Duck Creek Springs, a natural moss-laced spring with a dam deepening the water table on the east side. Fly fishermen love this one, wading almost anywhere to coax 11-13 inch rainbows. A 12-lb. rainbow was once landed here just to prove the lake's food-producing capabilities, but today there are more anglers with smaller fish. Fish subsist on fresh-water shrimp and caddis hatches. Just east on U.S. 14 eastward is Duck Creek Village, with a consortium of services, including hotels and restaurants, and people beating the summer heat. They also mean more pressure on Duck Creek. Another lake east of Duck Creek Springs is Aspen-Mirror, which puts out some good rainbow and brook trout fishing for a delicately-presented fly pattern. Aspen -Mirror has grown large rainbows, but a 10-12 incher is more likely today. It is a short hike from road's end. (for Kolob Reservoir, see Iron County.)

BEAVER (TUSHAR) MOUNTAINS — has the well-known fishery at Puffer Lake on the left fork road in Beaver Canyon. Rainbows here have attained some size in the past. Now, fishing pressure mandates a daily fare of more small rainbows than a few large ones. Along and immediately accessible to U.S. 153 are many small lakes like LeBaron and Kents, amid a conifer setting. LeBaron is the only lake in this region managed for grayling. Fly fishing is a good way to get them. A spinner works on larger fish. Sitting them out with bait is a popular way to coax a bite from trout on the deepest ends of the reservoir lakes. A few large browns have been caught from these waters, one on an unlikely tidbit of liverwurst that a lunching angler decided to try as an experiment. Fly anglers can also find caddis hatches and willing brook trout in the upper lakes and connecting streams. Scenery is superb throughout pine and peak-studded Beaver Mountain. Mule deer and wildlife are abundant. The north Beaver terrain is listed officially on Fishlake forest maps as the "Tushar Range." Check with forest officials in Beaver for maps.

DIAMOND MOUNTAIN — Some drawdown irrigation reservoirs on Diamond Mountain north of Vernal include Calder, Matt Warner, Crouse reservoirs, etc. These lakes are reached on the road to Diamond Mountain as marked off U.S. 44, with the turnoff 20 miles north of Vernal. The mountain, named after prospectors who "salted" the area with fake (even cut) diamonds to gain financial backing, offers widespread access on dirt roads. A road on the north end crosses the Green River into Browns Park. The entire region has place names recalling notorious local outlaws like Matt Warner and Charley Crouse, Butch Cassidy's close friends from a century ago. Although the region is well roaded, there are few services available.

CHAPTER SIX

Small Waters — Big Trout

Utah is blessed with many small trout streams and lakes. Some hold good trout. This fact may be known by only a few local anglers, who are likely to become rather tight-lipped when asked about it. In fact, some secretive types may check their back trail to see if they are being followed . . . but we can tell you here about some of these productive waters.

As a further clue, watch for fisheries which are stabilized and have a year-around or spring-fed flow. A constant supply of water usually means larger fish than a fluctuating snowmelt-dependent fishery. This is important in a state with widely varying fisheries habitat.

Each county water, not covered earlier under large streams and lakes-reservoirs, is listed alphabetically, with streams preceding lakes.

BEAVER — The **upper Beaver River** is almost entirely diverted for irrigation purposes at the canyon mouth, but above that provides put-and-take rainbow fishing, with small browns. Canyon scenery is beautiful up to 12,000-foot high plus peaks in the Tushar Mountain watershed. But alas, snowmelt flow, anchor ice with tough winters and lack of abundant feed make for few big fish on the upper Beaver. Some large spawners may make their way up into the stream from Minersville Reservoir in late spring and early summer.

The best chance of catching a good brown trout is apt to be in **springs and marshes just west of Beaver** which connect with the Beaver River. The year-around flow there has grown browns to seven pounds. They are fewer now, but the fresh-water shrimp still grow trout quickly. Wading and casting is hampered some by the moss and algae.

BOX ELDER — **Box Elder Creek** (Brigham City Creek) east of Brigham City, flows from Mantua Reservoir, near the town of Mantua. The creek has a few small natural cutthroats and stocked rainbows. A small, deep and hidden reservoir on the stream alongside U.S. 89 harbors some good browns. **Box Elder Creek inlet** on the southeast corner of Mantua has an occasional large spawning cutt in June.

In the Raft River Mountains, southwest of Strevell (Idaho), **Clear Creek** grows small cutthroats and rainbows . It is the only Utah drainage which flows to the Snake River and Pacific Ocean. To reach this beautiful little canyon you start in from Idaho, then wind up slightly over the border into Utah. To reach Strevell, drive west of Snowville on Utah 30 and Utah 42.

Locomotive Springs, located in flat sage country about 35 miles south of Snowville, can grow whopper rainbows. Spring-fed ponds and outlets flow into

Great Salt Lake. Rainbows up to two and three pounds are taken in the winter months on bait, flies, or plugs. Thick moss snags heavy lures. Fishing is not recommended here in the warm months due to mosquito problems. Rainbows to 8 and 10 lbs. have been taken. Take the county road south of Snowville toward Kelton and the "Locomotive Springs Waterfowl Management Area." The esthetics aren't much, but everything suddenly looks like the Garden of Eden when you hook into a giant rainbow.

Mantua Reservoir is primarily a warm water fishery but grows some good trout. The county also has two drawdown irrigation reservoirs in the northwestern sector, **Lynn** and **Etna Reservoirs**, near the communities of those names. They produce respectable rainbows in good water years.

CACHE COUNTY — No other county in Utah has any more lunker potential than this one, although some excellent brown trout fishing from the past has been reduced by man-made stream alterations. **Rock Creek**, which can grow decent browns, joins Blacksmith Fork from the north about two miles below Hardware Ranch, the state's only elk-feeding refuge. Look for brush-lined beaver dams away from Utah 101.

Temple Fork of Logan River is a major source of the Logan's cold, clean water , but with a rapid flow, and rocky stream bed, it's mostly small trout. Keep an eye out for rattlesnakes. The author once killed a rattler near the confluence of Temple Fork with the main Logan River.

Little Bear River: This stream sometimes nearly dries up below Hyrum Dam near the town of Hyrum, but a few nice browns often wash to the spillway hole directly below the dam. The stream can grow respectable browns above and below Hyrum.

Paradise Creek, and others in southern Cache, have pansized browns, with an occasional spawner from Logan-Blacksmith. The **sloughs at extreme upper end of Cutler Reservoir**, via U.S. 30 west of Logan, have sizeable Logan River coldwater fishery brown trout. Away from the Logan inlet, it's a largemouth bass fishery.

The Logan River along U.S. 89 east of Logan has three numbered impoundments. **First Dam** at the canyon mouth produced that behemoth 37 3/4-lb. brown trout mentioned in Chapter Three. Nowadays it yields more rainbows than browns, but despite easy access and heavy fishing pressure, the moss-lined lake depths still grow slab-sided trout. In hot summer weather, go deep. The **Second Dam**, nearly obscured from U.S. 89, and hemmed in by cotttonwoods along the bank, has been a favorite of lure casters, despite its smaller size and lack of back casting room for fly fishing. Best brown so far was 12 lbs. **Third Dam**, several miles up-canyon, has a 23-pounder to its credit. The giant brown hit a dry fly on top and was featured in a story in Outdoor Life several decades ago. The open, shallow inlet end has fly fishing possibilities Since I was a youngster fishing this reservoir for two-three pound browns, much of it has silted in; but the chances of catching a good brown exist. Best offering is a rock roller, or imitation.

First and Second dam on Blacksmith Fork — Smaller lakes than Logan impoundments, with less angling pressure, they have good browns and some excellent fly fishing in late summer drawdown. When low, fish are skittish. Use rock rollers and imitations. Some oversized browns move from lake to the deep upstream channel.

Hyrum Dam — is a favorite of boat trollers, with 12-14 inch rainbows the usual reward. Some problems with trash fish and temperamental trout in late summer heat. Located several miles west of the small community of Hyrum.

Porcupine Reservoir — A deep, very cold lake, located in the mountains southeast of Hyrum via Utah 165, it offers rainbows, a few browns, splake, and kokanee salmon. Like Flaming Gorge's Sheep Creek, the kokanee can make for a colorful kaleidoscope of finning crimson, but September fishing is closed. If trouble finding it, follow Little Bear River up from town of Avon.

Newton Reservoir near Newton is a marginal trout fishery, with some rainbows of size in good water years. **Gitten Springs** west of Smithfield has a few respectable rainbows. **Ballard Springs marshes**, near Providence, feed the Blacksmith Fork, with an occasional large brown trout. **Wellsville Reservoir** has good rainbows in high water years.

CARBON — The county has one excellent brown trout stream in the **Price River,** sometimes called **Lower Fish Creek**, below Scofield Reservoir. It's nine miles of roadless canyon, but easy walking along railroad tracks. Browns to three pounds are taken primarily on bait and lures. A few smaller rainbows. Good fly fishing, wet, nymph patterns, especially in mossy sector just below Scofield. Some top fishing for cutthroats in beaver dams on **Upper Fish Creek** above the reservoir, better away from road which accesses west side of Scofield. Many anglers fail to notice the tiny brooklet a few minutes north of Upper Fish Creek. Known locally as **Pondtown Creek**, it has nice cutts in the beaver dams.

DAGGETT — Few people to compete with you here, but fair fishing in the creeks entering Flaming Gorge Reservoir. This is especially true during the early summer when rainbows may be spawning. **Sheep Creek** has also has pan-sized trout and camping facilities on east end of Uinta Mountains. Fishing is not open in fall when kokanee are running. The creek below Browne Lake and other Uinta waters offers small cutthroat fishing.

DAVIS — Limited trout stream fishing in small and steep Wasatch Front from Bountiful to Layton. **Mueller Canyon Creek** up from Bountiful is probably the most vehicle-accessible and popular, with substantial local angling pressure. **Farmington and Centerville Creeks** have small cutts and stocked rainbows. Designated camping facilities in the canyons.

DUCHESNE — Located where it catches snowmelt from south slope of the Uinta Mountains, Duchesne (Doo-Shane) County is blessed with many trout streams. The Strawberry River below Starvation Dam carries respectable browns, with an occasional 2-6 pounder taken right inside the Duchesne City limits to the Duchesne River. Friends and I have taken some 18-20 inch browns on Mepps spinners and other minnow imitations. Best fishing is in the spring-early summer,

before low water. Big browns hold tight to cover. Rainbow trout are stocked below
the dam on two channels, the east side with the main current. A dirt road winds
from the plateau on the east side of the dam down to this stream where shaded
camping is available.

Below Strawberry-Soldier Creek Reservoir, some 20 miles west of Duchesne, the above stream is known as the **Wild Strawberry River**. Set aside as the
state's first fly fishing only water, after a request in 1965 by the Utah Chapter of
Trout Unlimited, this clean-flowing stream wends through a quiet and charismatic
canyon of cliffs and solitude for eight roadless miles directly below Soldier Creek
Dam. You can also drive to road's end from the east side, via the Strawberry
Pinnacles (natural rock towers) road south from U.S. 40, connecting four miles
east of Fruitland. Excellent fly fishing for browns and cutthroats to 20 inches,
occasionally right alongside the road. The mosier pattern, a simulated stone fly
nymph which resembles a heavy-bodied captain, is uniquely successful to this
stream. Most of the Wild Strawberry Canyon from the Pinnacles upstream was
preserved for sportsmen via timely purchase by the Nature Conservancy organization. Camping is is not allowed in this canyon, but you can stay overnight in
Timber Canyon which joins the Wild Strawberry about seven miles upstream from
the Pinnacles.

Red Creek and **Lower Currant Creek** mingle flow a few miles upstream
from the Pinnacles, then join the Wild Strawberry downstream from Camelot
Resort. From there down, an occasional lunker is possible in the deeper holes.
Branches and brush mean many snags, so bring ample hooks and lures. To reach
the lower Strawberry, remain on the east road at the junction near the Pinnacles.

North and lower West Forks of Duchesne River — See Wasatch County.

Red Creek Reservoir — not much for esthetics, with a major mud flat
drawdown lake, but capable of growing fat rainbows and cutthroats. In drought
years, the fish will be concentrated near the dam's deeper water. Access is north
of Fruitland for some 15 miles on a good gravel road.

Big Sandwash Reservoir — Rainbows to 14-18 inches long are often
caught here, with possibility of a larger brown. Location is between Duchesne and
Roosevelt off U.S. 40. Drive 12 miles north from Bridgeland. The lake is a popular
one with trollers. Some good trout are also caught by lure casters off shoreline
points and edges of coves.

A series of marshes draining to the Lake Fork River, south of Moon Lake,
known as the **Frog Ponds**, offer some fast fly fishing for small brook and rainbow
trout. Head north from Mountain Home. The ponds can be seen on the east side
of the road, which is rather "wash-boardy" across the Ute Indian Reservation.

EMERY — The **Huntington River** is a small but productive brown trout
stream coursing down the east side of Manti Mountain. Some sectors are marked
fly fishing only. Access is via U.S. 31, out of Fairview, Sanpete County, or
Huntington, Emery County. The **Left Hand Fork of the Huntington** (marked
on the highway) also provides excellent angling for medium-sized browns. The
latter sometimes muddies quickly in a rainstorm, although I've caught browns on

dry flies even with murky water. The main Huntington just below Electric Lake is extremely clear, with 10-16 inch wary browns visible in the deep holes. Keep a low profile. Some put-and-take rainbow fishing near Utah 31 all the way to the Utah Power and Light plant below mouth of canyon. Camping in designated areas or other pulloffs along stream in the canyon.

Another fine stream not far away is **Straight Canyon Creek** below Joe's Valley Reservoir. Access is west of Orangeville on Utah 29. The road continues beyond Joe's Valley on dirt access to the reservoir's feeder creeks, including **Seeley**, with fishing for small cutthroats. Creek below dam has small browns willing to rise in the clear water for stone fly imitations like a double renegade. **Ferron Creek**, south of Orangeville and east of Ferron, has scattered browns below and above Millsite Reservoir before canals divert stream.

Joe's Valley Reservoir, located on the southeastern toe of Manti Mountain, is an azure blue water encompassing a large valley. Not generally known for whopper trout, some good ones are nevertheless occasionally taken. A just under 13-lb. brown was subdued in the summer of 1989, on a minnow-imitation lure cast from the bank. Cutthroats to five pounds have been caught. The lake also has some 3-5 lb. splake, the fast-growing lake and brook trout hybrid. Rainbows, regular and albino are also found here. Trolling is usually productive. Some fly fishing in late summer at the western side inlets. A paved road around the north end takes boaters to a ramp on the west side. Ample camping spots, and some services at one east side location.

Millsite Reservoir is some 10 miles west of Ferron. Shoreline access and ramp are located just east of the region's only golf course. This is a favorite of many locals who wait out rainbows and cutts with bait. Some evening fly fishing.

GARFIELD — This county contains some of the state's best stream fishing. Much of it is little known and little-fished due to isolated location and only rural populations. Air-clear **Mammoth Creek** southwest of Hatch, has the feed to grow respectable browns. Try the roadless canyon sector above the fish hatchery southwest of Hatch. A good county road extends some 10 miles west of the hatchery to a long, open and scenic meadow with good fly fishing. At one time, it was even compared to Idaho's Silver Creek for open riffles graced with large trout. There is some private property in upper meadow. Erosion and loss of cover, plus fishing pressure, have removed some of the undercut banks, along with large fish habitat. In meadow, avoid bright days with heavy line-leader shadows, as fish are wary. Below the meadow, Mammoth Creek spills into a lava canyon with good fishing away from the beaten path. Large flies simulating the adult hellgramite (stone fly) and the caddis fly (adult rockroller or trichoptera) are best. Note: stopping in at the Hatch Fish Hatchery is worth an angler's time not only to discuss fishing on Mammoth Creek, but to witness the 12-15 lb. splake kept on display there. This hatchery is the main source of splake for stocking throughout Utah.

Asay Creek, which joins Mammoth to form the **upper Sevier River** some 1 1/2 miles below U.S. 89, is not quite the brown trout stream as is Mammoth. Asay shelters a few medium-sized browns, but is mostly put-and-take rainbow fishing. An interesting morning might include fishing down Asay Creek to the Sevier confluence, then down the larger stream for the possibility of a nice brown or large whitefish. The main Sevier is drained by canals in some sectors, but where there is water, you might also find trout of size downstream to Circleville.

Another little-known trout stream in Garfield is **upper East Fork of the Sevier** a dozen good gravel road miles north of Bryce Canyon National Park, or south of the community of Antimony. A roadless sector of lava canyon fed by spring water has good browns. An angler can walk into the canyon from the road south of Antimony. Side streams hold respectable cutthroat trout during spawning seasons. The East Fork directly below Tropic Reservoir runs only intermittently, as water is diverted. The stream above Tropic offers fly fishing for feisty trout in small beaver dams. Ample camping is available in gentle meadow terrain.

Panguitch Creek above the town of that name is a mostly secret resource known only to local anglers. The stream rarely flows through town, save in spring runoff. At times in summer there is no visible flow from Panguitch Lake on the Dixie National Forest. However, accretion springs gather to provide some pretty fair fishing for 10-13 inch rainbows-cutthroats. You can locate the fishing by simply driving to Panguitch Lake, then walking into the canyon below.

Eastern Garfield County below the Boulder has few trout streams save **Calf Creek** and the upper **Escalante River** on their way to Lake Powell. However, the entire region is an interesting and beautiful place to hike for a week, and Calf Creek Falls (on a trail as marked off U.S. 12) is the highest waterfall in Utah.

Tropic Reservoir west of Bryce Canyon, via a marked county road off U.S. 12, has the rich moss beds needed to grow nice trout in good water years. Lures and bait are best in early summer, with flies working as water warms.

Bowns Reservoir — was covered with Boulder Mountain. The lake was named after the father of Casey Bown mentioned in the Dedication Page. The Bowns fished and hunted this wild country decades ago, and built the lake as an irrigation and angling lake.

Wide Hollow Reservoir — This potential rainbow trout fishery, only two minutes off U.S. 12 west of Escalante, was chemically treated in 1989 to kill bluegills. It should have 9-12 inch rainbows by late 1990 if water supply allows.

GRAND COUNTY — The site of Arches and Canyonlands National Park, this county has little trout fishing, except the high lakes in the LaSal Mountains. **Castle Valley Creek** draining this area yields small rainbows.

IRON — Some stream fishing for cutthroats and self-propagating wild rainbows in the **Right Hand Fork of Coal Creek**, east of Cedar City along U.S. 14. Only other streams may have trout wash in from upstream reservoirs.

Paragonah Reservoir, located up-canyon from the town of Paragonah, has an excellent, self-sustaining rainbow trout population, 12-17 inches. Excellent fly fishing late in summer.

Yankee Meadow Reservoir, in the canyon above Parowan, has spring-fed cold water, with brook trout and rainbows. Fish are not known for size, but esthetics and fast fly fishing are there. Hatches vary. At times in mid-summer it is choked with algae blooms and difficult to fish.

Hooking a good rainbow on the East Fork of Sevier River.

Newcastle Reservoir is located in the extreme southwestern corner of the county, near the town of the same name, 30 miles west of Cedar City. Good fishing for rainbows to three pounds. Trolling is popular with triple-teasers, minnow imitations. Crayfish are abundant and bait fishermen using crayfish tails or parts also score well from bank.

JUAB — Good angling possible for small brown trout in **Salt Creek** Canyon east of Nephi in brushy sectors.The small flood-control dam on this stream can offer occasional good trout fishing, but fishing is usually better by "trouble-shooting" back in the hard-to-reach sectors. Some streams in Deep Creek Mountains near Nevada border, like **Trout Creek**, have been discovered to contain a pure strain of natural cutthroats present when pioneers entered state. The same is true on the Pilot Mountains north of the Deep Creeks where "pure" cutts have been discovered. Check with the current angling proclamation, or a county conservation officer on open seasons year to year. Access is via dirt roads for some 70 miles north of Delta or 90 miles west of Vernon. These roads are usually four-wheel drive, or pickup. Another route is from U.S. 93A south of Wendover into Nevada and back into Utah on gravel-dirt roads. Much of this desert country is near the historic old Pony Express Trail.

Burraston Ponds — These spring-fed ponds, now under UDWR control, are a great place to take the kids. They offer 10-14 inch rainbow trout alongside dirt roads and plenty of camping room. Get off I-15 and look for the sign two miles south of Mona. The air-clear water provides excellent fly fishing. A constant water temperature often offers very good winter-spring fly fishing before it is available in the snowmelt-fed fishing holes. Outlet streams from the ponds are infested with chubs and offer a trout only when one swims through the outlet dams.

KANE — Little stream fishing. **Duck Creek** flowing from Duck Creek Springs southeast of Cedar City alongside U.S. 14, offers intermittent fly fishing. Water flow is not consistent, and then it disappears . . . some say to be reborn at a lower elevation in Mammoth Creek.

The **East or Main Fork of the Virgin** above Glendale can be fast for small brown trout, with limited access due to marshy terrain and private property. The Virgin holds browns in brushy pockets all the way to Orderville and slightly below. This is one for an angler who doesn't mind tight places in a narrow ravine fishery.

MILLARD — While this county has no large trout fisheries, it has a few excellent small ones, like **Chalk Creek** above Fillmore and **Corn Creek** above Kanosh. Chalk Creek has some natural browns, but is mostly a put-and-take rainbow fishery. The stream fluctuates widely with spring runoff and early fall low water. Corn Creek, sustained by spring flows from the north hand fork, is a more consistent fishing hole, with respectable brown and rainbow trout in brushy areas away from road. If the creek is flooding, try the spring-fed north fork. Stream rehabilitation here by the UDWR and forest service via log check dams after severe flooding in 1983-84 have slowed current velocity and halted canyon gouging.

The **Sevier River** below Yuba Dam is primarily a walleye fishery, but I have lifted some 13-18 inch rainbows from the colder riffles. The stream is best fished spring and fall, as hot weather and mosquitoes can be a problem. The large waterfall dumping from Yuba to the cavernous spillway hole below yields an occasional nice brown. Another sector of the Sevier, along U.S. 132 above Leamington, produces a few scattered browns in the cutbanks and deeper riffles.

MORGAN — There are three major trout streams, all tributaries to the Weber River. **Stoddard Slough** is a moss-choked, canal-like creek, but it has a steady, spring-fed flow and a few scattered oversized browns. The largest I know of is a 12-pounder, caught in 1988; but pressure and access have combined to make such trout wary and difficult to fool. Fish between the moss lanes. Browns seem to subsist on fresh water shrimp and sculpins, so imitations thereof frequently work. From the old fish hatchery to the Weber, this stream flows through some private property, but good fishing may be found from road right-of-way.

East Canyon Creek, above and below the reservoir of that name, has a potential good cutt or two, although pressure is heavy on weekends. Much private property, so the angler will have to gain permission or face limited fishing.

Lost Creek is (no pun intended) pretty well lost as a fishery because local landowners removed bankside trees, with anchorless banks caving in, and erosion silting the stream. Fish wherever there is brush. Best up high near dam. Some good cutts may flow through **Lost Creek Reservoir**. It has good fishing for medium-sized rainbows and cutthroats. Fly fishing can be good in late summer, with float tubes or boats. Mud flats make wading difficult. The entire fishery is reached via gravel road north of Croydon, from I-80.

PIUTE — Some brown trout fishing in the **Sevier River** near Marysvale and the same stream below Piute Reservoir. Rainbows are stocked. Roads below Piute Reservoir are slippery when wet. **Otter Creek**, running into the reservoir of that name, contains good browns near Greenwich and along Utah 62 in the long meadows where current flows beneath overhanging banks or brush. The stream is laced with suckers and chubs in deeper pools, but trout lurk where flow brings cooler water and ample dissolved oxygen. In fact, the trash fish problem became so bad in the fall of 1989 that the stream, and Otter Creek Reservoir itself were chemically treated, then restocked. This means that the 18-20 inch trout this creek once produced cannot be expected again until about 1992. They grow quickly in this feed-laden water, however. Above Greenwich, the flow is small, with under-sized brook trout. Just above Otter Creek Reservoir, the creek runs straight and shallow, with a poor fishing due to a poor hole-to-riffle ratio. Another potential fishery is the canal which carries water from the East Fork-Sevier, via a small diversion dam near Antimony, to Otter Creek Reservoir. It was also chemically treated, but could be a fishery with restocking and time.

Directly below Otter Creek Reservoir, the creek has a few wary lunkers down to the East Fork-Sevier covered in "The Best Streams."

RICH — Some stream fishing is found in Bear Lake feeder creeks, including

Swan Creek just south of Idaho border. The latter may have spawning cutthroats at times, with "normal" fishing likely to be hatchery rainbows. **Woodruff Creek** draining into the town of that name has some hatchery rainbows, with larger trout possible washing down from Woodruff Reservoir.The **Bear River** below Woodruff Narrows Dam, just across the Wyoming border, has a few good cutthroats making their way down from the dam into Utah farmlands.

  Woodruff Reservoir — has small brook and cutthroats. It is located west of Woodruff, via dirt roads off Utah 39. Some fly fishing. Small boat launching site. No camping refinements.

  Birch Creek Reservoir — is a large lake, off U.S. 39 west of Woodruff, scenic and a popular camping spot. Alas, it seems to have very poor feed and grows mostly small trout. It is closed in some years. Perhaps in the future, the lake's biological problems will be corrected.

  SALT LAKE — Many small trout streams are located east of Salt Lake City in scenic canyon settings; but with three-quarters of a million people located nearby, the fishing is relegated mostly to put-and-take. **Parleys Creek** has offered good cutthroat fishing right into the city limits in times past. Now, like nearby **Mill Creek and Big Cottonwood Creeks**, it's mostly stocked rainbows. It has been possible to catch 12-14 inch cutts and an occasional brook trout out of **Little Cottonwood Creek** from canyon mouth to Alta-Snowbird ski resorts, but that would be rare today. **Red Butte Reservoir**, long closed to the general public, has produced browns to 14 lbs. **City Creek**, the same one which sustained early Mormon pioneers when arriving in 1847, has small cutts and brown trout. Call the Salt Lake City Parks Dept. regarding vehicle access. **Emigration Creek**, the route into Salt Lake Valley as far back as the Donner-Reed party in 1846, has a few small cutts and planted rainbows. Residential takeover of this canyon has removed and destroyed some of this stream, as has I-80 in Parleys Canyon.

  The best fishing for skillet-sized trout in these streams is often in Big Cottonwood Creek from the switchback curves, about five miles up-canyon on the road to Solitude Ski Resort, through the Spruces Campground to Silver Lake. Ditto on Little Cottonwood a few miles above the canyon mouth, and in pockets east of that nearly to Alta. With heavy snowmelt coming down the Cottonwood streams, best fishing is in late summer-early fall. Fish are scattered, and may require risking a snag.

  Mill Creek in the lower valley near Main Street has produced brown trout to 10 1/2 lbs. but that era is pretty well finished. The lower stream now produces a few decent browns in the deeper sectors near Main Street, but most of it is sealed away behind private property. Still, a good brown is occasionally taken, usually beneath a bridge or in deep, permanent shadows. In Parleys Creek, some of my best fish over the years has been behind or beneath poison ivy, railroad ties, bridge abutments.Salt Lake City may be one of the few large cities in the Lower 48 where trout fishing is possible almost within the shadows of skyscrapers. When heavy flooding had to be diverted in the early '80s down State Street, a youngster hauled out a 13-inch rainbow in front of commercial shops between downtown buildings.

  Spring Run, below the confluence with Big Cottonwood Creek at 9th East near 48th South, still yields a few small and wary brown trout. Spring Run once produced browns and rainbows to seven pounds when electro-shocked by biology classes from the University of Utah. The big fish seemed to disappear when the VanWinkle Expressway was constructed and cutbanks removed in the name of flood control. Focus on any cover or brush. Fish are not in open water.

The **Jordan River** connecting Utah Lake southward to Great Salt Lake, has been tabbed as a potentially excellent brown trout stream over the years, but industrial pollution and channel dredging have harmed it considerably. A friend once caught a 23-inch brown as far downstream as the 33rd South area, although the best fishing is now from 64th South upstream. Rainbow stocking is heavy near the bridges at 90th South and up to the Point-of-the Mountain. I've witnessed 3-lb.browns electro-shocked in brushy riffles above 90th South.This is a good place to take the family for a spring outing. Fishing is slower in warm weather.

Mountain Dell and upper Parleys creeks, with tributary **Lambs Canyon Creek**, east of Salt Lake City, all offer opportunity for small cutthroat fishing. Focus on brushy holes with a short line.The reward could be wild cutts of resplendent hue and color. Some rainbow trout "sweetening" is also likely to take place near major holidays. These are good places for kids to "get lost" for an afternoon. Note: Mountain Dell Reservoir in Parleys Canyon is closed to fishing to protect a culinary water supply.

Some trouting is also possible with periodic stocking in such places as **Bell Canyon Reservoir** in the foothills of Lone Peak, southeast of Salt Lake City, but the lake is privately owned. Check with the UDWR, or local water companies.

Great Salt Lake, with no outlet and one-fourth (28 percent) salt content, does not sustain fish life, except for large carp in the fresh water inlet bays.

SAN JUAN — Like Grand County, it has few trout streams. **Mill Creek** provides wild brown trout fishing, with rumors of a few large rainbows in times past. If so, they are not there now. Location is in the LaSal Mountain foothills. **Indian Creek** also provides some small trout in the general area. This is a large county, but most fishing is for warm water species. **Monticello Lake** near the LaSal Mountain foothills has rainbow and brook trout, plus a campground. **Recapture Reservoir**, in a wide ravine several miles north of Blanding, also offers pansized rainbow trout fishing, as do Blanding number Three and Four reservoirs. Ditto, **Lloyds and Foy's** reservoirs near Monticello. Foy's was built by the state specifically as a trout fishery.

SANPETE — This county has fishing for every taste. The little **San Pitch River** which springs up near Milburn, has wild brown trout fishing in the beaver dams and cutbanks. It is not for the lazy, however, as fishing might require bucking brush, wading across mud pockets and casting to tight places. The stream may dry up below U.S. 89 just north of Fairview, but it picks up additional marsh-fed water for some 10 miles of trouting down to the Mt. Pleasant area. Near Ephraim, the flow seems to turn too torpid for trout, but fair to good brown trout are taken in between. April-May and autumn seem best, with heavy irrigation diversion sending fish into hiding. Try to catch it just before or after spring runoff as high and murky water off the Manti makes trout difficult to locate. I caught a 16-1/2 inch brown in this stream in July, 1989, in the spring-fed sector above U.S. 89 by eye-droppering a spinner down between oakbrush roots.The historical record from the Sanpitch is a 7-lb. brown.

Pansized trout can be taken from several roadside brooks containing freshwater shrimp alongside U.S. 89. Keep an eye out for any running water in Sanpete County.

Small reservoirs near Fountain Green and Moroni provide rainbows in good water years to 13 inches, with some fly fishing available. Check locally for access on county roads.

Nine-Mile Reservoir — Measure it nine miles south of Manti. This large and shallow lake grows rainbows to 3-5 lbs. It is moss-laden with many insect hatches and excellent fly fishing morning and evening, especially in early summer. A boat or float tube helps fly anglers work moss beds.The spring-fed inlet near U.S. 89 usually holds some wary rainbows. Deepest end near the dam attracts baiters. Lure-tossing can be productive in deeper pockets. Easily accessible, it is often pressured on weekends.

Palisade Reservoir — This beach-lined lake a few miles up Six-Mile Canyon from U.S. 89 has stocked rainbow trout with slow-to-middling angling. It is more popular as a swimming and water skiing lake, and may prove better as a warm-water fishery in future.

SEVIER — Eastern Sevier County has some fine small creek fishing. One short but favorite trout stream is **U-M Creek** which tumbles from Forsyth Reservoir through a steep lava canyon for some four miles down to Mill Meadow Reservoir. The roadless canyon is not for the faint of heart, since hiking is steep. Nice rainbows move down from Forsyth and take up residence in the swift waterfall holes. There may also be some carryover fish through the winter, although the stream rarely flows in the winter. Neverthless, most of the 12-15 inch rainbows I've taken here were in healthy condition even in low water. There is little room for fly fishing. Spinners and minnow imitations worked deep are best. The lower end near Mill Meadow has camping space. Ditto on the upper end below Forsyth, but only with four-wheel drive; note the sign leading to Forsyth Reservoir, then drive to dam around and below.

Seven-Mile Creek feeding Johnson Reservoir has cutts in the brushy sectors, and in the meadows, below cutbanks. Trout run 10 to 17 inches. This is ruggedly scenic terrain, with fine camping opportunities on the Fishlake National Forest.

The **outlet to Koosharem Reservoir (Upper Otter Creek)** along U.S. 24 was chemically treated in 1989. It normally offers small brook trout and some rainbows. However, as you near the community of Koosharem, the stream cuts fewer pools, with smaller fish. **Lost Creek** east of Salina has natural populations of small brown trout not far from I-70.

Clear Creek, in the southwestern sector near Joseph, may course down in direct view of I-70 but it is provides a clean, cold habitat for very nice rainbows and a few browns up to three pounds. Get a line beneath rocks and banks to connect with a 10-13 inch rainbow. I fished it in middle of the day in July, 1989, finding trout cooperative and feisty on a small spinner. The biggest problem can be getting off the freeway, but watch for turnoffs near the confluence with Sevier River, Fremont Indian State Park and access roads to Cove Fort. The stream departs the freeway up-canyon with more good fishing. The freeway here has actually helped anglers by providing public access and stabilizing stream banks.

Forsyth Reservoir on the Sevier-Garfield County boundary along U.S. 72 has fat and fast-growing rainbows with very good fishing in late summer's drawdown. These trout will often take the right fly, so check with hatch of the day. Many boaters take rainbows to 16 inches on bait and lures. Camping is not luxurious, but plenty of space is available on the east side meadow. Access roads are slippery when wet. This lake is a favorite of local anglers because fish are usually cooperative. The lake is deep near the dam; fish there if water is low and warm in summer.

SUMMIT — Ah, here's one you'll appreciate! Offering Swiss-type mountain scenery, it offers so many trout waters you could fish one a day for the entire year. Streams coursing down the Uinta North Slope number in the dozens, include five forks of the **upper Bear River, Black's Fork, Smiths Fork, Henrys Fork and three forks of Beaver Creek**. Access from the Wasatch Front is via Utah 150 north of Mirror Lake. These are mostly small cutthroat fisheries on the Wasatch National Forest. Lodgepole pine, Englemann spruce and verdant meadows mean considerable wildlife and camping opportunities. The several forks of the Bear offer scenic hiking and camping, but poor feed and tough winters do not allow rapid trout growth. Lower Blacks Fork shows up in early angling literature as a good trout stream. Mormon pioneer Wilford Woodruff, an Englishman who tied his own trout flies, says his artificial patterns used on Blacks Fork in 1846 "outfished local bait fishermen three to one." The stream is yet a fine fly stream, and is reached via the road over Mt. Elizabeth east of Utah 150. The **main Bear, Hayden Fork and the Stillwater Fork** offer more exciting esthetics and camping than big trout. Fishing gets better if you hike upstream from roads. **East Fork-Bear** has 10-11 inch cutts hitting almost anything resembling rock rollers or stone fly larvae. A small grey hackle yellow or immature caddis pattern will gather attention. The **West Fork** offers slightly larger cutts. There is access at north end of Whitney Reservoir off Utah 150. The Bear grows larger near the Wyoming border, but size of trout does not keep pace. Another tributary of the Bear is **Mill Creek**, reached east of the Boy Scout Camp. The pansized cutts in grass-lined Mill Creek hug the bank, so get deep and close to structure. This is beautiful country with the Uinta skyline nearby. Bring warm clothing. Henrys provides the best fishing for 10-13 inch cutts, frequently in sight of the careful fly caster. Henrys is reached over the Mt. Elizabeth road, east of Utah 150.

Burnt Fork and several forks of Sheep Creek flow from the east end of the Uintas in this county. Access is from the road's end at Spirit Lake Lodge, south of Utah 43. Watch for trail signs. Burnt Fork is a favorite of mine because it hosts a brilliant cutthroat which at first seemed to be a hybrid golden trout. It is not likely, since no goldens have been planted in this part of the Uintas. Note: Burnt Fork is diverted for irrigation before reaching Utah 43.

From the Uintas flow several streams westward, including **Chalk Creek, Beaver Creek, Wolf Creek**. Chalk Creek above Coalville is a small cutt fishery, with an occasional 16-incher. The upper end holds much private land, with an eroded watershed which muddies Chalk Creek with the first sign of precipitation. A friend, Dee Smith of Salt Lake City, does well here with spinners, or dead minnows, half a dozen miles up-canyon, beneath tree roots. Best fishing is often after spring runoff in late June or early July.

Beaver Creek is actually two fishing waters: the stream above Kamas with small cutthroats in the brush, and the spring-fed flow below town with the chance of a big brown. Trout were once coaxed out of lower Beaver to 10 lbs. and more recently, six. The best fish hug shadowed cutbanks. Most open and pathside holes have been worked, so focus on the "far casts" and small riffles not easily fished. To reach the upper Beaver, take Utah 150 toward Mirror Lake. To find the lower Beaver, with larger fish potential, drive about five miles west of Kamas, then take the road which winds northward along the low range of hills. This road will eventually take you to the Weber River near Peoa. A small brooklet coursing through Peoa holds a few wary brown trout all the way to the Weber. Some of the land here is posted. Lower Beaver has little camping room, but upper Beaver on the Wasatch forestland has numerous campgrounds.

Wolf Creek, a tributary of the Provo east of Woodland, is a stream with some small cutts and brook trout in the brush-lined riffles, and an occasional large whitefish. The stream is reached via Hailstone Junction and Woodland.

The Provo has several other small tributaries, including the **North Fork** east of Kamas. Away from Utah 150, it has small cutts and brook trout usually willing to hit a small fly pattern.

Western Summit County has several small creeks like **Silver (sometimes called Kimball)** which flow into East Canyon Creek. Silver has proven it can grow large browns. My largest was a butterball fat 4 1/4 pounder, 100 yards from I-80. However, a chlorine spill from a treatment plant near Park City in 1988 killed many fish. The stream should recover with stocked trout by 1991. New housing subdivisions are crowding much of this creek from Snyderville downstream. Nevertheless, the feed is there and if the water remains unchanneled and unpolluted, respectable fish are possible. Another small creek tumbles through the farmyards near Wanship to reach the Weber, carrying a few overlooked brown trout. A friend also caught and returned a 4-lb. brownie recently from an unnamed brook which enters the Weber not far from Wanship.

Many of these streams and roadside lakes on the western Uintas are stocked with albino rainbows from the Kamas Fish Hatchery several miles east of Kamas. They make a spectacular scene, thousands of them together in bright orange color, perhaps worth a stop enroute along Utah 150. Emphasis in this entire region is on fishing, with bait for sale along almost any road on weekends and people talking trout during any waking hours.

Several lakes not included in the Uinta chapter include **Stateline Reservoir** near the Wyoming border on Smiths Fork, and nearby **Meeks Cabin Reservoir**, shared with Wyoming. Both offer cutthroats, some browns, stocked rainbows. Since Meeks Cabin dam lies in Wyoming, check from year to year on license requirements. The road here borders many small lakes within passenger car access. **Marsh, Bridger** and a few others yield nice brookies if fished from canoe or life raft to get where average shoreline anglers can't. No motors are allowed on many of these small Uinta lakes.

On the west Uintas, **Smith-Morehouse Reservoir** east of Oakley, has an unusual name and scenery to match, and is worth a camping night or two. Trout are traditionally small, however, because the lake is drained in fall of tough water years. A small pond near the reservoir oft-times has chunky cutthroats. The stream below, **Smith-Morehouse Creek**, has a few natural cutts and stocked rainbows, both in the canyon sector and upon leveling out in the valley before spilling to the Weber River.

TOOELE — Several small cutthroat streams, including **Clover, South Willow** in the Stansbury Mountain area west of Tooele. Trucked-in rainbows "sweeten" deeper water. Campgrounds are available in several canyons here, including South Willow. **Vernon Creek**, filling the reservoir of that name from the south, is a small spring with pan-sized browns, and the possibility of a good spawner in the fall.

Vernon Reservoir — This one is a "sleeper," mostly unknown on the Wasatch Front. Yet, it grows hefty brown trout, with bait and lures good from shore, and in late summer, fly fishing. The lake, on a county dirt road about 10 minutes south of Vernon, is a favorite of local residents using bait, spinners and streamers. Moss beds bring a challenge at times. Most of the real estate is Bureau of Land Management domain.

Settlement Canyon Reservoir — This irrigation reservoir in the Oquirrh Mountains above Tooele has good fishing for small-medium rainbows, with the possibility of a nice brown. Usually heavily stocked for holidays. Trolling or fishing off points will usually work.

UINTAH — With no lack of trout waters here, this is one of my most frequently-visited counties. **Jones Hole Creek** on Diamond Mountain, northeast of Vernal, has steady water flow and fresh-water shrimp which grow 2-3 lb. rainbows and browns. It gurgles for nearly five miles to the Green River as a clear, moss-billowing trout stream with very careful stalking likely to pay dividends. Few waters in Utah can match it for sheer production of trout poundage per cubic square foot. An interesting side visit is the federal Jones Hole Fish Hatchery. Ample camping in the area, with Dinosaur National Monument nearby. The trip from Vernal, via Utah 149, then north as marked, requires several hours, but is worth the effort.

Brush and Ashley Creeks on the southeast Uintas are on a par with the other South Slope streams, although smaller fisheries. Brush Creek has medium-sized cutts. Ashley has lost some of its excellent brown trout fishery to the flood control channelizing of the stream, but is mounting a comeback if no further channeling is done. The streams are served by county roads north of Vernal. **Little Brush Creek** and small trout are also accessible from U.S. 191.

Local irrigation diversions, including the Maeser Canal system, may also hold trout. Such waters are stocked in the late spring alongside paved roads.

Also see the chapter on Fee Fishing-Hunting for information on the Ute Indians' massive array of fishing opportunities in eastern Utah.

Steinaker (Stanaker) Reservoir — This one five minutes north of Vernal, alongside U.S. 191, is in a rehabilitative stage after being illegally stocked with largemouth bass and bluegill. In October, 1989, the UDWR chemically treated the lake and for 1990, planned rainbow trout in the deeper, colder sectors with largemouths in the shallow coves."Before we would restock rainbows, however," said UDWR fisheries biologist Glenn Davis, "we received a promise from area bass clubs that they would do all in their power to prevent any more illegal stocking. Most destructive is the bluegill population which reproduce rapidly, eat trout eggs, and stunt out so they are little good to anyone. We must keep the bluegill out, or we will not stock any trout or bass in the future." The lake could again produce 2-3 lb. trout in 1992.

Red Fleet Reservoir — Located up U.S. 191 from Steinaker, Red Fleet was also illegally stocked with bass. Chemical treatment was set for 1990, followed by trout restocking. "It is to be managed as a trout fishery," said Davis. "If there is illegal warm water species introduced, we will cease to stock trout." History shows that the lake, in a scenic setting, is capable of growing slab-sided rainbows. Other draw-down irrigation lakes not far from Vernal, with good trout fishing in high water years, include **Bullock and Cottonwood**. Access is via U.S. 40 a few miles north of Gusher. Bullock usually provides faster fishing for rainbows than Cottonwood. **Brough Reservoir** has nice rainbows in deep water. It is located east of Roosevelt, 4 1/2 miles south on Utah 88. The lake is 1/2 mile west of the road. None of these lakes have services nearby.

UTAH — Much fishing water here in spite of being the state's second most populated county. There are many tributaries to the Provo River, including **South or Vivian Fork** tributary in Provo Canyon below Deer Creek Dam. Electroshocking surveys indicate browns here reach 14-16 inches. Another fine but little trout stream is **Hobble Creek** above Springville. This one, long a favorite, has dwindled in productivity from the time 17-inch browns were caught in the brushy sectors. It is now mostly 11-inch browns with a few small cutts in the brush. A catch-basin dam near the mouth of the canyon is stocked with rainbows, plus a few browns. The left hand fork has little flow, few trout.

Diamond Fork — Just over the divide from the headwaters of Hobble Creek, upper Diamond Fork flows southwesterly as a small stream with cutts to match. Log dam rehabilitation has helped the fishery. Fishing is better after Diamond Fork picks up water flow from Strawberry Reservoir via a tunnel into Sixth Water Creek and becomes a 10-foot wide river. Some chunky brown trout inhabit its deeply-scoured holes.The confluence is 8.3 miles above the Uinta National Forest Service sign on a county road which is well marked off U.S.6, only about 20 minutes south of Provo. Diamond Fork has trout all the way to the Spanish Fork River. My best in October, 1989, was a 17-incher taken on a sculpin imitation, although I've seen browns to four pounds in years past. There are several pulloffs along the stream, and a forest service campground. **Sixth Water Creek** is reached by vehicle only at the bottom end and at top where the Strawberry Tunnel emerges. In between are seven roadless miles of tumbling riffles and wild brown trout, plus good cutts and rainbows moving in from the Strawberry tunnel as an added bonus. An angler can be dropped at the top of Sixth Water and picked up at the bottom. Only four-wheel drive or truck should be used here, due to steep clay roads which are very slippery when wet. Both Sixth Water Creek and Diamond Fork are usually difficult to fish in early summer's high water, but offer excellent angling in late summer-early fall after flows subside.

A number of other nearby tributaries, including **First to Fifth Water creeks**, also hold small cutts. A 5-lb. brown trout was once electro-shocked by conservation officers on Fifth Water. A thing helping this lacework of small creeks is that they are not near roads, and habitat is basically unaltered over the years. A map of the country east of Diamond Fork would be helpful.

Spanish Fork River — along U.S 6 has various stages of biological health in its journey to Utah Lake. In the far upper end, beaver dams provide some small cutt fishing. By the time it reaches Tucker and environs, it has usually turned to mud, yet the water is still cold enough to hold a few good brown trout. The Spanish Fork River also yields a few good trout below the confluence of **Thistle Creek**, itself a fine little trout stream for cutts to 15 inches and rainbows to 13. A quirk of this stream is that anglers catch trout beneath submerged houses, residences inundated and partially washed away in the small town of Thistle during the 1980's by a mudslide. I have watched from U.S. 89 as 12-13 inch rainbows were caught by an angler drifting a worm into one home's underwater kitchen. The only other place where trout are consistently taken on the Spanish Fork River is just below the infusion of cold flow from Diamond Fork. Thistle Creek itself is fed with **Benny and Nebo Creeks** off Mt. Nebo. Both are the home of hand-long cutthroat trout, interesting perhaps for the youngsters to stalk.

American Fork Creek — This is a small fishery, but one worth wading for its esthetics alone. No more clear water can likely be found anywhere in the world, as it cascades and eddies from Tibble Fork Reservoir in American Fork Canyon's North or Left Hand Fork. Fish are small browns with a few brook trout, and stocked rainbows. At the canyon mouth, the stream vanishes into a canal system. See Chapter Five for two lakes above Tibble Fork. Ample camping is available. **Payson Creek** at south end of Utah Valley also holds a few cutts and hatchery rainbows around holidays. Drive south of Payson on the Mt. Nebo loop road.

Deer Creek — This tributary of the Provo River just below the dam of that name "sneaks in" below U.S. 189 without being seen by most eyes. The air-clear creek is fed by Cascade Springs, where a visitor can view 10-inch long brown and brook trout from wooden walkways. No fishing is allowed there, but it does indicate what you can catch in Deer Creek below Cascade where fishing is allowed. From the bottom end, off U.S. 189, a four-wheel drive will put you in touch with 13-15 inch browns. Cascade Springs itself can be reached via U.S. 189, exiting to Sundance-Aspen Grove, then to the summit and follow the signs some seven miles east, all on paved road.

Spring Creek, which feeds the State Fish Hatchery just north of Springville,

Whiterocks River in Uintah County offers fall fly fishing magic.

holds clear and constant water flow, with some decent browns and stocked rainbows. Access is best on the road west of Springville to I-80. One sector flows in a pipe. Small trout are found on both ends.

Utah Lake — There are some inlets with an occasional trout. **Salem Pond** near Spanish Fork-Salem has grown a few sizeable rainbows in the past, but it is small, with limited fishing and used little save by local youngsters.

WASATCH — Like Summit, this county has much to offer an angler. **Spring Creek** feeding the fish hatchery near Midway has a few respectable "winter holdover" rainbows of size above and below the hatchery. The pools directly below the hatchery are biologically capable of growing very large trout. In years past, 10-pounders have been taken. Fishing pressure and private property mean fewer large trout accessible to the public nowadays. Upper Spring Creek is located from pavement between Midway and Heber City, east of the Provo River. The meadow stream here is stocked heavily in late spring. Spring Creek below the hatchery is reached via the Heber Creeper railroad racks north of Charleston.This entire region has small springs and creeks feeding Spring Creek or the Provo River, with the possibility of trout. A few are found on the northwest corner of Deer Creek. One flowing to Spring Creek is the meadow-meandering **Snake Creek**, with small browns and rainbows — unless nearby golf courses and developments eat up all of the water.

Inlet streams to Strawberry Reservoir, including Strawberry River, hold a few natural cutts, but not as many as years ago when willows and cover provided trout habitat. Streams here were sprayed and killed to deliver water more rapidly to downstream users. With the lands transferred in 1989 from the Strawberry Water-users Assn. to the Uinta National Forest, federal fisheries biologists say the streams will be rehabilitated to once again become trout fisheries. However, greatest value is to provide spawning beds for large rainbows and cutthroats. Of course, chemical treatment of the feeder streams along with Strawberry in 1990 mean no lunker catching for several years. Traditionally, the streams are open to fishing July l each year, with some spawners remaining until after that time.

Daniels Canyon Creek — Located on U.S. 40 above Heber City, this stream has little fishing at top and bottom, but some fair trouting in the middle deeper holes. A friend had to run downstream quickly one day with a 2-lb. brown on light line. Most of the fish are small cutts and stocked rainbows. Fishing pressure is heavy on weekends, but some trout "dig in" below bridges and brush. **Center Creek**, east of Heber City, has small cutts and stocked rainbows.

Wallsburg Creek enters Deer Creek Reservoir on its southeast corner, with some spawning fish moving up in season. Large rainbows show up occasionally in the spring. Although the reservoir is not known for harboring lake trout, a few large lakers have been caught in this stream, apparently moving up and liking the cold water temperatures. It also holds a few good browns, albeit much of it through Round Valley is shut behind private property.

Wasatch County shares **Wolf Creek**, a tributary of the Provo, east of Woodland, with Summit County. Look for small cutthroats with a few brookies and whitefish. Another shared stream is upper **West Fork of the Duchesne**, good for excellent scenery and 10-inch cutts. **Currant Creek**, shared with Duchesne County, is a fine little cutthroat, brown and rainbow fishery when not muddied by storms. Browns to nine pounds have been taken just north of U.S. 40. The most likely catch is a 10-15 inch cutthroat. The dirt road north of U.S. 40 leads 18 miles to **Currant Creek Reservoir**, with more good-excellent cutthroat fishing. Use a small spinner, or stone fly nymph. The entire canyon is a good get-away for camping, fishing and scenery.

WASHINGTON — Utah's Dixie has few trout streams in quantity, but a few in quality. One is the **Santa Clara River** northwest of St. George. Look for wild browns with some size from confluence with Moody Wash up to Pine Valley where you might locate a few brook trout. Two excellent stretches for sizable browns are in deep lava gorges upstream from Moody Wash to the town of Veyo; the other gorge is from Central to Pine Valley. Regional fisheries biologists say summer temperatures seem to put down the fish, so spring and fall are best. Rattlesnakes are known to abide here, so keep a vigil! In the summer, dress for heat.

One more stream is the **Virgin River**, with a hike-in to the **North Fork** which tumbles through Zion National Park, and offers excellent fishing for nice rainbows in the Zion Narrows on north end of the park. This is a back-pack expedition which should be attempted with extreme caution and preparation, since spring runoff and rainstorm flooding can trap an angler between steep canyon walls. If coming in from top, access is on Cedar Mountain in Iron County via U.S. 14. An angler can also take a one-day trek up-canyon to find trout. In the park, the stream is mostly put-and-take rainbow angling, with considerable pressure daily. Below the park, the stream warms and gives way to trash fish.

Kolob Reservoir — A high mountain lake, at nearly 10,000 feet elevation, this water is a fine one, featuring brook, cutthroat and rainbow fishing. The cutts have been known to attain six pounds, rainbows to three. Natural reproduction in high water years means excellent crop of fishing always coming up. In a low water year, like 1977, there is no guaranteed (purchased by water-user consent) conservation pool to sustain fish. Water level is usually high enough, however, to avoid such problems. Fishing on boats is best early in year, with late season bankside fly fishing. This is a beautiful fishery just north of Zions National Park, with access via the town of Virgin near the park's west entrance. The name "Kolob" is from Mormon literature meaning "nigh to Heaven."

Baker Reservoir — This lake on the Santa Clara River between Central and Veyo has whopper browns, with 5-8 lb. specimens taken almost every year. The temperatures are just right to promote rapid growth. Go deep in mid-summer. Troll a minnow imitation or bait. The lake is worth expending time and patience for a giant Salmo trutta. Other Santa Clara impoundments below Baker are warm water fisheries.

Upper and Lower Enterprise Reservoirs — Located in the northwestern corner some 10 miles west from the town of Enterprise, this pair of lakes on the Dixie National Forest, offers excellent rainbow trout fishing, especially the upper lake. Fisheries biologist Dale Hepworth says the upper lake has produced trout to five pounds in gill net surveys. In drought years, water quality suffers in the lower lake from lack of dissolved oxygen. The upper lake is about 400 acres, with the lower only a fifth that size. They offer a jump on the season with Dixie-like warm weather as early as March.

WAYNE — The Fremont River and Pine Creek have been mentioned with the Top Streams. Spring Creek up the Fremont River drainage from Loa, offers fair-good fishing for those willing to work the pockets. In this county, you never know when a canal or ditch, especially off the feed-rich, spring-fed Fremont, might produce respectable trout. I've caught rainbows to 19 inches as recently as 1989 from the Fremont below Mill Meadow, although the stream's intermittent flow indicates the fish must have moved down from the reservoir. Accretion flows through the county keep the Fremont alive even after it appears to be diverted and wholly dead. Forget the Fremont in and below Capitol Reef National Park due to high water temperatures.

Mill Meadow Reservoir — This readily accessible lake is located just barely south of the Sevier County line, up the Fremont River from the town of Bicknell, on the route to Johnson Reservoir. It is capable of growing football-sized rainbows. It is also a favorite of serious fly casters because of energetic trout, and treeless meadow terrain offering ample back-casting room. Many trout are also taken on bait and lures, boats, or bank. The fastest way to catch a whopper 4-6 pounder, however, is probably trolling a flatfish or Rapala around the moss beds. A shallow lake, it is often wind-whipped, but can pay dividends for those who stick it out. If you don't like it here, Forsyth and Johnson Reservoir are not far away.

WEBER — Tributaries of the **South Fork, like Causey Creek** below **Causy Reservoir**, offer pan-sized cutthroats. The reservoir itself is deep and best probed with lures. Some bays offer late season fly fishing. This one is in heavy moose country, so you might keep an eye out. To reach Causey, head east of Ogden, past Pineview Reservoir on the road toward Monte Cristo on Utah 39. Watch for the signs.

Pineview Reservoir — Primarily a warm-water fishery, Pineview nevertheless yields an occasional lunker rainbow. Best bets seem to be when trout are in shallow water, spring and fall. Spawners sometimes congregate on the east end to run up the South Fork of the Ogden River. Work the shallow bays there in April with lures.

Author's daughter, Cindy, with his 5-lb. largemouth bass from Lake Powell.

CHAPTER SEVEN

Best Warm Water Fisheries

Interest in Utah's warm water fishing is growing rapidly. A chapter on warm water fishing wasn't needed years ago, but it certainly could not be left out now. New warm water lakes have come into being, and some previously "empty" ones are now stocked to keep apace of new angling demands. Some of this demand has come from visitors and newcomers to the Beehive State who brought old angling habits along.

Utah's best warm water fisheries are listed alphabetically below. Also check species list to determine dispersion. Note: Utah has no warm water fish hatcheries at present, but brings many of the species in from outside the state.

Largemouth black bass are found in the following flat waters: Powell, Deer Creek, Mantua, Pineview, Utah Lake, Gunnison Bend, Rush, Steinaker, Pelican, Gunlock, Quail Creek, Cutler, Scipio, Blue, Mona, Delta-Millard Agricultural Dam (DMAD), Kanab ponds, Hyrum, Cottonwood, Newton, Huntington North.

Smallmouth bass: Flaming Gorge, Powell, Starvation, Brough, Cottonwood, Bullock, Newcastle, Rockport.

Striped bass: Powell.

Walleye: Utah Lake, Willard Bay, Powell, Deer Creek, Starvation, Yuba, DMAD, Gunnison (near Delta). Note: during late spring spawning periods, all inlets may also have walleyes.

Crappie (black): Pineview, Willard Bay, Powell, Gunlock, Quail Creek.

Channel catfish and bullhead: Utah Lake, Willard Bay, Powell, upper Flaming Gorge, Gunlock, Quail Creek, Redmond Lake, Yuba and upper Sevier River, Green and Colorado Rivers, Bear River below Cutler. Jordan River for several miles below Utah Lake.

White bass: Utah Lake, Powell, Willard Bay.

Northern pike: Powell, Redmond Lake, Yuba.

Bluegill: Pelican, Powell, Pineview.

Yellow perch: Deer Creek, Yuba.

Tiger Muskellunge, hybrid: Pineview.

Bonneville cisco: Bear Lake.

Green sunfish: Powell.

Chinook salmon: A future possibility in Bear Lake and larger Utah waters.

Note: crayfish are found in many Utah waters with smallmouth black bass. "Crawdads" are licensed under Utah law and are taken with worms or bait as are the fish species.

BLUE LAKE — This lake near the Nevada border has respectable largemouth bass and a few rainbow trout the angler can see in clear water. Despite its remote location, it is a favorite with SCUBA divers. The fish are extremely wary in the spring-fed clear water. To locate, take U.S. Alt. 93 about 20 miles south of Wendover through Nevada, past the U.S. military reservation, then east on unpaved road to Salt Springs area. Watch for signs.

BULLOCK RESERVOIR — This small lake is north of Gusher in Uintah County on U.S. 40; then turn north about four miles. It holds adult smallmouth bass transplanted from Flaming Gorge Reservoir. The fish were 1-2 lbs. in early 1990, and are growing rapidly in shallow coves. Trout inhabit deeper water. Crayfish abound in this lake, a favorite smallmouth food, so try any simulation.

BROUGH RESERVOIR — This lake is south of U.S.40 in Uintah County. Follow Utah 88 for 4 1/2 miles to within a quarter-mile of lake. It was heavily stocked with adult smallmouths running about 1-2 lbs. in the fall of 1989. Best lures, say local anglers, is a dark-hued jig.

COTTONWOOD RESERVOIR — See instructions to Bullock, since both lakes are near one another. This one also received adult smallmouths from Flaming Gorge. Cottonwood has one more plus, a heavy stocking of largemouth bass fry in 1989. These fish could reach one pound or more by fall of 1990. Some older largemouths are also occasionally caught in this lake.

CUTLER RESERVOIR — This large Cache County lake on the Bear River west of Logan has never really reached its potential as a warm water fishery. But it does yield largemouths in spring and fall. Bucketmouths are deep in the summer. The Logan River inlet has brown trout, with the fishery giving way to black bass and channel catfish down-lake. The best bass fishing is in the coves and structured or undulating shoreline. The size of this water, with few surrounding roads, makes it more conducive to boat fishing.

The **Bear River** directly below the Cutler dam for several miles in Box Elder County (access is north of Brigham City off Utah 69) has some of the state's largest channel cats.

DEER CREEK RESERVOIR — Located on the Provo River seven miles west of Heber City, this lake was once managed for trout. But, it is better suited to species like bass and walleyes. It has always carried a substantial perch population, one of the few in Utah. Residents of the area say that well before Deer Creek Dam was put in place in the early 1900's, springs and ponds in the region held bass. The largemouths now show in spring and fall for shoreline plug and spinner casters. However, the big news in the spring of 1987 and '88 was the mushrooming walleye run up the Provo River near Charleston. Several specimens were caught in the 12-13 lb. range, including what was once the state record at over 13 lbs. The latter was caught trolling in mid-summer and was not associated with the run in April- early May. As usual, the best medicine for walleyes has been minnow imitations, yellow jigs, etc. There are boating ramps at Wallsburg Bay, an area often good for respectable largemouths, and also near the island on the middle east side. An angler can walk down the west side railroad tracks for little-bothered shoreline casting, but a boat is a distinct advantage on this large lake.

DMAD — The Delta-Millard Agricultural Dam in Millard County was once a viable warm water fishery, but lost much of its resource in the heavy flooding years of 1984-85. Washed out dams were replaced, but much of the fishery must yet be restocked, probably with black bass and walleyes to be obtained out of state. This was also basically true of **Gunnison Bend Reservoir** near Delta. The water temperatures and feed are still there, however, with the possibility of fish taking on size by 1993.

FLAMING GORGE RESERVOIR — This versatile fishery has the state's best smallmouth fishing, along with the world-famous lake trout. The two species are found in opposite places, of course, but that is the beauty of the Gorge. The smallmouths favor coves and points, including structures around the marinas, making it a family-favorite species. In late spring spawning time, May to early July, families can catch smallmouths easily from a rocky or undulating shoreline, in a social setting, then have a delicious fish fry.

Friends and I have caught dozens of the red-eyed and feisty fighters just around the cove from Cedar Springs Marina. Also, on a late spring day, check the cove just north (over the hill) from Lucerne Bay Marina. The fish have a marked preference for green or smoke-or "motor oil hued" jigs; but small Rapalas also work well. Larger Rapalas in size 7 or more may also work for a1-2 lb. fish with greater courage than jaw size. The smallmouths have been numerous enough for bass clubs to catch hundreds of respectable fish for restocking in other lakes, including Starvation. Note: the smallmouth has a jaw which does not extend beyond a straight line with eye, and it is more heavily colored with black and bronze than the Utah largemouth.

The upper end of Flaming Gorge, where silt settles in from Green River and Black's Fork, provides some of the Mountain West's best channel cat angling. This is reached best by boat from Lucerne Marina or points north. Waiting them out with shrimp, minnows, or nightcrawlers will work. You won't have much competition when going after channel cats. The lake may also become a viable largemouth black bass fishery in the future, although they are not stocked at this time. The lake has several boating parks away from roads and ample camping room.

GUNLOCK RESERVOIR — This Washington County lake on the Santa Clara River offers hefty largemouths, but they can be difficult to catch. For the angler who has patience and is willing to experiment, this may well be one of the best bass fisheries in the state. Spring and fall are good times, but in a Dixie locale, winter fishing is not as cold or unproductive as say at Mantua farther north. The lake also has good crappie fishing every several years when the population builds up. Populations seem to fluctuate like rabbit cycles, according to southern Utah fisheries biologist Dale Hepworth. He also suggests anglers try an under-fished channel cat hot spot at the inlet and current areas on the lake. To get there, drive northwest of St. George to the little junction of Shivwits, then turn north.

GUNNISON RESERVOIR — This mud-laden lake near Nine Mile Reservoir in Sanpete County is not one of my favorites, since it is replete with carp. But it also carries some good channel cats and a few black bass for those willing to wait them out. Bait fishing is best.

HYRUM DAM — A marginal trout fishery, largemouth bass fry were planted in 1989 in this Cache Valley lake near the town of Hyrum. They should show up by 1991.

HUNTINGTON NORTH — Some largemouth bass fishing, but it often competes with swimming and boating at a state park and beach north of Hunting-ton in Emery County.

KANAB PONDS — These three small ponds several miles north of Kanab in Kane County have medium-sized largemouths, respectable bluegill, and green sunfish. Two of the ponds can be seen from U.S. 89. They are not large enough for a crowd, but do offer some angling diversion. The west side cliff area seems to have deeper water and larger fish.

MANTUA RESERVOIR — This lake near the little community of Mantua in eastern Box Elder County is a growing bass fishery, although it had a setback in 1988 when flooded-out marshes on Great Salt Lake seemed to send all of the birds to Mantua. There, they wreaked havoc on a newly-stocked bass and bluegill populations, with only larger fish surviving. Several anglers scored on four-pound largemouths in 1989 by lowering jigs and spoons between the heavy moss beds. The moss beds make for difficult fishing from shoreline, save at the southeast inlet area. The inlet is a potential hot spot during spawning time in late spring, but can be hard-hit by bank waders. The chub population is also heavy in the inlet at that time of year. Mantua was once a viable trout fishery, and still has a few rainbows and cutthroats. But the lake will be managed for bass and bluegill, according to Utah fisheries biologist Glenn Davis. He said in 1989 that bass and bluegill seem to be reproducing, and if bird depredation decreases (now that the Great Salt Lake has stabilized), Mantua should become a healthier bass fishery. At this time, bluegill seem to have size, but are not found in numbers.

MONA RESERVOIR — This heavily-fluctuating artificial lake in Juab County just west of Mona, visible from I-15, has some decent largemouths... there just aren't enough of them for fast fishing. A shallow lake, it is subject to winter kill. Mud flats make for tough wading; the deeper, north outlet end seems to have the best fishing. The lake is ignored, because good trout fishing can be found nearby. The lake has potential, but isn't a major warm water angling hole.

NEWCASTLE RESERVOIR — This western Iron County lake has both rainbows and smallmouth bass of respectable size. Take Utah 56 west of Cedar City near town of Newcastle. Some of the best fishing for bass is often in shallow coves in late summer drawdown.

NEWTON RESERVOIR — This northern Cache County lake, near the town of the same name, has been stocked with largemouth bass which could reach about 1-1/2 lbs. by summer of 1990. It is also a trout fishery, so concentrate on the shallow areas if after bass. The lake has some yellow perch and a few large channel catfish.

PELICAN LAKE — This oval lake southwest of Vernal in Uintah County, near Randlett, has produced world-famous bluegill exceeding the size of a large man's hand. Periodic cold winters have killed the 'gills, however, so you'll have to check with the UDWR office in Vernal from spring to spring. The first time I fished it, children could cast any fly from shoreline for quick action. Another year there were no bluegills. The largemouth bass seem to withstand even the the coldest winters, and a size 7 black or brown Rapala worked along the tules will attract bass sooner or later. A favorite way is to launch off Utah 88 at the deep bay in the southeast corner, then canoe or paddle silently along the heavy growth of reeds, casting parallel to them. Float tubes also work fine, since much fishing is found within a few hundred yards from shore. Some anglers anchor in the weed and moss beds to eye-dropper minnow imitations. I've had my best success for 3-4 lb. bass by casting in late April-early May to the moss beds with a Rapala, being careful in wading not to spook fish in the air-clear water. Watch on U.S. 88 for signs to the launch area on the southwest corner. The other access is via the east side dike road. Mosquitoes can be a problem in summer.

PINEVIEW RESERVOIR — Pineview has the state's easiest-to-find crappie fishery. Simply wade out in the willows on the east end in late April and early May and you should get into the crappie with a yellow or chartreuse jig. Get close to the willows. I witnessed two anglers one spring day . . . one with 11 on the stringer, the other with nothing. The two were standing within five feet of each other. The one with frequent tight lines placed the jig very near the willows, then twisted and turned the offering to resemble a lively creature of some kind. The successful angler said he knows of no better crappie fishery in the West.

This scenic lake with the three arrowhead-like bays is located 12 miles east of Ogden along Utah 39. I've had considerable success on largemouths on the northside bays, but bassing is admittedly tougher now than before. I'm not sure why, but bassing and trouting both seem to have given way in this mountain-rimmed lake to other species. Not only have crappie flourished, but tiger muskellunge (musky x Northern pike) are also doing well after being introduced several years ago. Biologists are also considering wipers, or a white bass-striped bass hybrid. This lake receives considerable experimentation, because it is a marginal fishery for trout and bass. The carp population is substantial in shallow coves, and the species sometimes become a nuisance for bait casters, especially when spawning in the spring. There are several campgrounds around the lake.

POWELL — Lake Powell is so important to Utah as a fishery that an entire book could be written about it. The 1800 miles of crimson and orange cliff-mirrored shoreline has to be one of the most beautiful artificial lakes anywhere. The 2-6 lb. largemouths caught here take on added significance with the resplendent scenery. The fishery is now a greater attraction with the addition of fast-growing smallmouth bass. It is one of the few lakes where I've taken walleyes of size in midday, and on a bright one at that. However, Powell is clearly at its zenith as a striped bass fishery. There are also some problems the angler should understand before going after stripers.

Several Aprils ago when seeking striped bass, I was told that "You've got to fish for them after dark in the deep water from a boat with bait." That may be one way to do it, but my first several arm-long stripers were from taken at mid-day from bank with lures. I had bought an Arizona stamp to a Utah license, fishing in and out of the boundary line north of Page. Several 4-6 lb. striped bass hung onto almost any silverish minnow imitation thrown. These were brutish and powerful fish which struck at Garland bass jigs, spoons, anything that moved in the deep back bays. Many of these fish moved up from very deep water to feed.

My next time out on Powell, it was the conventional: lower a half anchovy down about 35 feet in deep water in the old Colorado River channel. The striper is one of the few fish I know of which cares nothing for structure (contrary to black bass) and suspends in the middle of deep water, near neither top nor bottom. The fish simply suspend themselves in water some 300 feet deep. Another time in mid-summer, friends and I proved false the adage that stripers always move and feed in schools. We caught a single fish at a time by moving around. Best time to find foraging stripers on the surface, I've discovered, is spring and fall. Early November, temperature-wise, is tops. You may even spot birds gathered around the shad and bait fish chased by stripers when they are near the surface, an almost certain strike if you can get your offering in among the melee.

The record striper at Powell in 1989 records is 40 lbs. even. Many of the monsters are taken near or along the Moki Wall out of Bullfrog Marina. The species has moved up to Hite, and out to the San Juan and Escalante Arms. You can catch both stripers and black bass here. But stripers are now just about everywhere. Yet the striper hey day began to subside about 1986 as the fish out-stripped its major food supply, the thread-fin shad. Walleyes which made their way into the lake without benefit of stocking also fed heavily on both threadfin and striper fry. Now, there is some striper reproduction, but fewer are making it to adulthood. The larger stripers do fairly well feasting on a never-ending supply of carp. But there is a food gap in the middling striped bass sizes.The average size of fish since 1986 has dropped from about 3-4 lbs. to 15-17 inches. The most likely possibility of returning to the old days with long lines at the fish-cleaning stations is for a new forage fish. Utah biologists favor a rainbow smelt, but they must sell this idea to other states in the Colorado River Compact, and this can take time. For now, the possibility of catching fair-to-middling stripers is there, but it will take moving around more than before.

At the same time that striper populations mushroomed, the fish-per-hour catch seemed to drop on largemouths. Biologists say creel surveys on largemouth have shown an upswing since a partial demise of the stripers. Theoretically, the bucketmouths occupy a different, shoreline habitat niche than the open-water stripers, so they should both be able to grow *at the same time* in number and size. Yet it appears that largemouth fishing picks up when striper fishing declines. The UDWR is doing research to find why.

The lake was once a rainbow trout fishery, but is now being managed almost exclusively as a bass fishing hole. Almost any back cove, point, or pocket between rocks, or end of bay moss beds or surface flotsam is likely to yield bass and bluegill. I like to fish with a Rebel green plug, simulating a small bass, for largemouths. By attaching a second small jig up the line, bluegill can also be attracted. Doubles on bass-bluegill are often the result.

Crappie are likely to be at the end of bays in tree top stickups and among heavy moss beds. The best spots are in remote bays farthest from easy access, requiring several days on the lake. Storms can come up suddenly, so don't be under-boated or motored. On several occasions, I have taken houseboats out of Hite or Bullfrog, letting the family swim, suntan on sandy beaches, etc. , while I have found excellent bassing by walking the nearby shoreline. If a submerged boulder is found, work a Rapala or Rebel plug near it. If fishing from a cliff or point, I like to lower a spinner. Beginner bassers often do best by using waterdogs, available at marinas, along with anchovies. Strangely,the larger dogs seem best for all sizes of bass. Simply hook the bait through both lips and cast where the shallow gold water meets the deeper green. My favorite time is middle May when bass are spawning. One May day I also found that bluegill between sand bars would not leave a black fly pattern alone. A few days later, I could find no 'gills.

Hite has muddy water from the nearby Colorado River, but bass don't seem to let the murky flows bother them. Some 10 miles down-lake, you can find cleaner water, less floating log debris, and excellent camping sites. Water is green-clean at Bullfrog and into Halls Bay. Ditto up-lake from Wahweep, just across the Arizona line. The sandy beaches up-lake from Wahweep offer super channel catfish possibilities, especially fishing at night. If you are launching north from Wahweep, your Utah license is good almost as soon as you're out of the wakeless speed area.

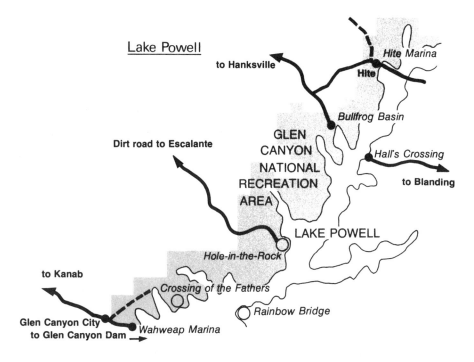

QUAIL CREEK RESERVOIR — This lake on the Virgin River, just up I-15 from St. George, broke its dam and flooded several years ago, yet much of the water and fishery remained. It has been a superior largemouth fishery. The lake should fill and be open most of the year in 1990. According to fisheries biologists, the lake has a unique inlet stream oxygenation system which allows fish to remain comfortable and healthy despite what would normally be heated summer drawdown. The cold and well-oxygenated water also allows a trout fishery in the deeper sectors. Crappie are doing well in Quail Creek, attaining size, although the UDWR is debating whether the ascent of crappie populations will be detrimental to other

Lake Powell, south of Hite Marina, is a wonderful place to cast for largemouth or smallmouth bass, crappie, and walleyes.

species. The lake has a large population of channel catfish averaging about 1-1/2 lbs. which anglers say are rather easy to catch. As for the bass fishery, it appears to be one of the best in state on middling to large sizes. An advantage over Powell is that Quail Creek's bass are easier to locate. A short boat ride will get you anywhere, and much of the structure along the shoreline can be reached from the bank. Anglers in the spring of 1989 reported many 3-4 lb. bass on the usual artificial worms, jigs, plugs, etc.. Camping space is not difficult to find in the area.

ROCKPORT RESERVOIR — This is a major trout lake, but has many smallmouths around point or peninsula structure. They will usually hit eagerly in mornings, or with sun off water.

RUSH LAKE — This is a relatively new reservoir on Utah 36 near Stockton, that appeared in 1985-86 after several heavy water years. It's not much on scenery nor camping opportunities. But it is stocked with largemouths which are thriving, and should reach several pounds by the spring of 1990-91. The shoreline is shallow, and is not easy to fish sans boat. You'll have to allow time to locate the bass; but spring spawning time would offer the best chance. Several other small "duck" ponds in this immediate region have pansized largemouths which are fairly easy to catch.

SCIPIO LAKE — This small, shallow lake on U.S. 50 southeast of Scipio in northern Sevier County has some nice but wary largemouths. Boats are best due to mud flats and moss beds. The water is murky, and is not easy to get close to structures without snagging. You may have to probe down with eyedropper lures to reach the best spots. Probably only veteran bassers with extra patience will score on this one.

STARVATION RESERVOIR — This sprawling reservoir a few miles west of Duchesne holds the state's best walleye fishing. While Deer Creek is an up-and-coming *Stizostedion vitreum* fishery, no water anywhere produces the number of large walleyes as does Starvation. One expert, Scott Cornia of Salt Lake City, has spent much of each fall's deer season hauling 10-13 lb walleyes out of this treeless reservoir. Cornia says he favors a medium-sized Rapala, trolling or casting along cliffs and ledges from dam to the bridge over U.S. 40 and continuing uplake. The fish are definitely most active in the spring spawning period, and in autumn. The wind-swept lake also has many coves and bays which could reward an energetic and hardy bank angler. The record "marble eyes" has fluctuated at this writing between Deer Creek and Starvation, with a little under 15 lbs. the latest record from the latter. However, fish are growing rapidly.

Starvation has a growing smallmouth bass fishery. Many 1-2 pounders caught by anglers from Flaming Gorge within the past several years were placed in tanks and transferred by UDWR biologists to this Duchesne County lake. Most are caught with dark-hued jigs. Smallmouth fishing is expected to be excellent by 1991. Late spring's spawning period, probably middle May, would likely fetch the best fishing for smallmouth bass.

The lake can be reached at the deep dam end via county roads off U.S. 40, plus a short hike. The upper end is visible and only a short hike from U.S. 40. There are several launching areas, with ample camping. Scenery is there if you like the cedar and sandhill landscape. Starvation may in time become a home to other warm water species such as largemouth bass and possibly crappie. Mammoth brown trout also show up occasionally on the end of a lure, so rig heavy. Water is usually slightly murky so a clear line is not a must.

STEINAKER (OR STANAKER) RESERVOIR — This lake five minutes north of Vernal on the highway toward Flaming Gorge was chemically treated in the fall of 1989. But while the trout fishery started all over, such was not the case with largemouth bass. Fishing clubs caught out many respectable bass which were held in tanks for replanting. Typically, the north end coves hold most of the bass. These are rather sophisticated fish which don't hit any offering in sight, although crayfish imitations have done well in the past. Nearby **Red Fleet** has illegally-stocked bass but it will likely be treated and managed in the future for trout

UPPER AND LOWER SANDCOVE — These small reservoirs on the Santa Clara River chain offer some lunker largemouth possibilities. With warm weather and year-round fish growth, the basser would do well to include these lakes on his must list. They are power-generating facilities operated by Utah Power and Light Co., so are subject to heavy drawdown and possible fish kills in drought years. The last severe year was 1977. To reach these lakes, between Gunlock and Veyo, take Utah 18 north of St. George and turn south at Veyo. Farther down the Santa Clara, just west of St. George, little **Ivins Reservoir** can also produce good bass in good water years. Bass less than 15 inches must be returned in some years.

UTAH LAKE — This huge Utah County water, a cutthroat trout fishery in pioneer times, has lost its coldwater fish due to agricultural and industrial pollution. If it can be cleaned up — a goal of a newly-contemplated Utah Lake Authority — it could be more of a bass and walleye fishery. Right now, it turns up a few largemouths near the stream inlets such as Provo River, and white bass during spring spawning periods. It has been hot as a walleye fishery, but fell off after flood control dredging of inlets in the middle 1980's. Still, at Lincoln Beach on the southwest corner, the Provo River inlet, Bubble-up inlet just south of Geneva Steel, etc. the lake still produces some good late spring walleye fishing. Best bets seem to be at dawn, dusk and after dark with a chartreuse or yellow jig-type offering. I've personally taken marble-eyes to 7 lb. on this arrangement and watched larger ones taken on a size 7 or 9 Rapala. One expert, Craig Williamson of Provo, suggests fishing the gravel spawning beds south of Utah Lake State Park. Another walleye specialist, Todd Yates of Salt Lake City, recommends early morning hours when the water is not "worked over by the competition." Choosing the best times can become a vital factor in getting best casting spots on the Provo River dike at height of the walleye run, and some good fish are taken, although not as many as in times past. Aside from spawning periods, the fastest walleye fishing appears to be around the island in the southern sector. Best method there is to anchor and cast jig or plug where deep meets shallow.

The lake has very good channel catfishing. Gean Snow of Salt Lake City suggests tossing out shrimp (available at a meat market) or nightcrawler in the lake's southeast bays, usually in water about 3-6 feet deep. Some anglers take along step ladders as a "temporary fishing camp" while wading about. Channel cats grow big in the lake, with the state record 32 lb., 5 oz. pounder hailing from Utah Lake.

It was taken at night on bait. Some experts like the "stink baits" such as chicken livers.

WILLARD BAY — This fresh water lake on the Weber River, north of Ogden, is sometimes thought to be salt water due to its proximity to Great Salt Lake. However, it contains warm water species in abundance, including black crappie (try the north side dike), walleye (try the west side dike), and channel catfish (almost anywhere). It is a favorite of many warm water anglers due to its accessibility, and fairly good consistency in turning out good fish in the spring. The walleye is a target here, with best fishing in May along the dike structure. Cast parallel to the dike and walk softly to avoid spooking fish. Access to the west dike is from a point well south of the lake, near the large Smith-Edwards store easily visible on U.S. 89. The lake has several camping spots on the northeast end. The lake is also large and basically square, with little undulating shoreline or structure to choose from. The fish are just there in open water for the most part, requiring considerable casting. Inlets are very good in spring spawning seasons, but these areas are sometimes closed to fishing.

YUBA LAKE (ON SOME MAPS CALLED SEVIER BRIDGE RESERVOIR) — This lake has been a popular perch and walleye fishery, then suffered from winter kill in drastic water drawdown in the early 1980's. The perch didn't come back, but the walleye have. I caught a 5-lb. walleye from shore with a black lead head jig in late April, 1987. Fish have put on considerable weight since then. Some of the best fishing is in the Painted Rock launching area, as marked, off Utah 28 southeast of Levan, Juab County. An angler can also reach the dam area off a marked exit on I-15, some 15 miles southwest of Levan. While fish can be caught from bank, a boat is a definite advantage. Several large Northern pike have also been caught by trollers on this lake's upper end. Since walleyes hang fairly close to shallow structure, plugging to specific willow and/or moss bed hangouts is often the best approach. Frequent snags in bottom moss is likely in Yuba, but it is near the vegetation that many of the best walleyes are taken. Bring plenty of tackle. A camper will find plenty of room to pull off at Yuba. Several dirt roads wander along the south shoreline. State park launching and mooring facilities are found near the dam on the west end. Located in a remote area, Yuba has few other services.

Note: Other minor and locally important warm water fisheries being managed for largemouth bass include: Holmes Creek Reservoir south of Ogden, ponds in the Layton area of Davis County, and small ponds west of Salt Lake City. As bass anglers well know, even small "farm ponds" like these can grow nice bucketmouths. Sevier Lake and Clear Lake marshes south of Delta in Millard County once had viable fisheries, but low water table in the past few years indicates little chance of rapid comeback.

CHAPTER EIGHT

Utah's Fishing Future

Utah's fishing resources are endangered. Stream fisheries cannot long withstand such impacts as channelization, dredging, roadway encroachments, inundation by dam construction, erosion, poor watershed management, and outright dewatering. Lake and reservoir fisheries are also harmed by extreme drawdown, and pollution. Loss of habitat is a far greater threat to fishing than hordes of anglers ever will be. Even stocked fish can't survive if there is no habitat.

Some severe impacts on stream fisheries include: the Utah Highway Dept. leveling the banks of Spring Run in south Salt Lake County in the name of "flood control;" the channel alterations to the Provo River from widening U.S. 189 in Provo Canyon; the same to Cache County's Logan and Blacksmith Fork Rivers; dewatering of streams amid competition for water; industrial and agricultural pollution of waters like Utah Lake and the Jordan River. The Central Utah Project envisions a large scale sacrifice of Uinta Mountain trout streams to farm and industry. All this while recent studies indicate tourism, with quality fishing, hunting and outdoor recreation, has emerged as Utah's number one money-maker, far out-stripping agriculture or mining, the "traditional" sources of income. Tourism adds up to $2.2 billion revenue per year income in Utah, according to a 1990 U.S. Fish and Wildlife Services survey. Fish and wildlife accounted for $533 million of it; by comparison, skiing brings in $426 million, livestock industry, $260 million, and oil-gas industry, $260 million. This is one reason to protect Utah's natural resources.

In 1965 I attended sessions with the Central Utah Water Conservancy District at which officials stated outright they would not plug any environmental considerations into their engineering equations. Those same officials and legislators, hearing complaints from groups in the 1980s then stated: "Well, environmental groups should have lodged their complaints earlier; now you come along and block construction of the CUP. That's irresponsible."

No, I was there in 1965 as the first president of the Utah Chapter of Trout Unlimited, when it requested minimum flow guarantees on Rock Creek, Wild Strawberry River, West Fork Duchesne, Provo River, and even for Utah Lake where the first CUP plans engineered for water levels below fish survival. Water conservancy district officials said they absolutely would not comply with such unreasonable requests. Later, an "Environmental Awareness" forced the district into semi-compliance. These CUP planners are still reluctant to protect the natural resources which have proven ever more valuable monetarily and esthetically.

The CUP planners are still not certain how much angling-scenic-outdoor recreational habitat must be destroyed in the project's attempt to move water. The U.S. Bureau of Reclamation simply marched down the upper Provo River in the 1960s with tractors, gouging the productive trout stream into a sterile canal. Now, the public relations program of the CUP claims they are "enhancing" Utah's fisheries with reservoir construction. In this they have been consistent, for that's what the CUWCD said in the 1970s — while plans called for dewatering half a dozen trout streams. One of them was the Wild Strawberry below Soldier Creek Dam which was to have a special, highly-publicized "oxygenated" outlet, while not providing enough water for fish to survive anyway! Many trout died before bare minimum flows could be agreed on.

In a 1989 newsletter, Utah Rep. Wayne Owens said of the CUP: "It began as an imaginative concept to capture unused runoff from the south slope of the Uinta Mountains, but various pressures have pushed the project to the brink of fiscal and environmental irresponsibility . . . the streams and rivers of the Colorado River basin must not be depleted to the point of harming the fisheries or the environment." He said the project would have dewatered 186 miles of eastern Utah trout streams if something had not been done. Ever since elected, the ecologically responsible Owens has been promoting legislation which would provide protections.

The water conservancy district seemed to have a change of heart in the late 1970s and decided to allow higher minimum flows than the original 6,500 acre feet required to meet downstream water rights on South Slope Uinta streams. Will those commitments made in a meeting with then Gov. Matheson be honored? I was present at that meeting and it was considered binding. But I also watched as water users attempted to wriggle out of commitments in the Provo River pact for minimum flows in 1988 after a poor water year. I also saw a PR campaign by the CUWCD in the summer of 1989 which claimed the district had *always tried to improve fisheries throughout the CUP planning . . .* " If so, why was every government agency, state and federal, and every private conservation club, plus every professional biologist's group, opposed to the CUWD fisheries plan?

All sportsmen are encouraged to write their representatives and senators, and tell them how they feel about protection of natural resources. Explain that the problem is, once gone, these God-given resources cannot always be returned — not for any amount of money.

Interestingly, that was a lesson the USBR learned when officials attempted to un-do their "flood control" carnage of the upper Provo fishery. The bulldozers had removed insect-laden mosses upon which trout subsisted, along with all the cutbanks and shelter. All that remained was a sterile canal. "The damage was irreversible and it was finally decided no amount of money could bring it back," one state fisheries biologist told me. The upper Provo, after some 30 years, has begun to recover somewhat, but it may be a long time yet. Where anglers once caught 2-3 lb. browns consistently, only expensive hatchery rainbows, pale and flaccid, and considered vastly inferior to wild brown trout, can now survive. Research at Utah State University shows that only one-eighth as many trout are found in a stream after even mild channelization. The latter also greatly diminishes esthetics, driving sportsmen away. As a practical matter, wherever you might seek fish in streams, skip the devegetated or channeled stream. They will have few trout.

A stream protection law which the author helped draw up in 1970 attempted to prevent damage to naturally flowing streams. It called for input by biologists in the Dept. of Natural Resources if any individual or entity wished to alter the beds or banks of a stream. The exceptions, insisted upon by the consumptive water-users before House Bill 79 could pass, was to allow changes only for "flood control and prevention of soil erosion." This has proven an unfortunate loophole. Since that time, I must admit failure in my efforts for a viable "Stream Protection Law."

The State Engineer, who must pass on all Utah water law interpretations, provides a very broad one on what constitutes "flood control" and "soil erosion." Thus, water-users can still do what they please on Utah steams. Furthermore, the State Engineer has not provided for a "recreational use" of water to be considered a "beneficial use," This negates even purchasing water to be left in streams for public recreational uses.

The Utah rule is: "The water must be *diverted* from the stream to be considered a beneficial use." That's the way it is in much of the West. But Montana, with its many trout streams, managed to change this antiquated law. Utah will do so only if sportsmen and citizenry vigorously seek such a change for the public benefit. If so, the Stream Protection Law could be given some teeth. All that would be needed is the elimination of six words: "Except for soil erosion and flood control." The important thing is that wildlife and recreational uses do not consume the stream water. It is still delivered to consumptive users downstream. Both types of users, if cooperating, could utilize the water for their different purposes.

Why should such valuable natural resources as the Weber near Oakley or the Provo below Murdock Dam and west of Heber City be wholly diverted, precipitating a loss which is irreversible? All it takes is five minutes to destroy a fishery requiring years to mature. Several hundred thousand license-buyers have a valid right to complain. And should.

Rep. Wayne Owens stepped in during the spring of 1989 to invoke Provo River water release agreements, thus preventing loss of this fishery via too-low winter flows. He was contacted by concerned sportsmen, proof that the "little guy" can make a difference. It should be added that the Provo River is not "safe" yet. There are those who would like to divert all of the flow to Salt Lake County, but Provo City claims prior water rights. Fishermen should root for keeping more water in the stream farther downstream. All of Utah County would benefit with a Provo River, for how can you have a Provo River Parkway without a Provo River? This region could have an excellent brown trout fishery right through the community of Provo if water remains in the stream. The same is true of the Jordan River in Salt Lake County, for the stream is a viable brown trout water until multiple drains pour pollution into the river from approximately 64th South to Great Salt Lake.

In other waters with cutthroat and brook trout, it takes only a modicum of agricultural wastes to destroy the fishery. Do you care? You need to say so . . . to county commissioners, local and national legislators, and other decision-makers. Many waters now rely too heavily on stocked rainbow trout. Hatchery fish cost in the dozens of dollars per pound, plus the cost of repairs to Utah's old and dilapidated fish hatcheries. With less pollution, and more protected habitat, many streams could boast self-propagating cutthroat and brown trout fisheries — all at almost no expense to the state or sportsman. Of special value are the two

Cottonwood Creeks southeast of Salt Lake City. Skiing development in those canyons is being watched to make certain it does not endanger fishery or culinary water supply. It seems that if the Winter Olympics ever do come to Utah, the Cottonwood Canyons should still be protected from further development or people pressures.

Some streams have been victims to development, including Parleys Creek east of Salt Lake City. Parleys once produced myriad pansized cutthroat and brook trout in the upper reaches until I-80 replaced it with wall-to-wall concrete. Emigration Creek succumbed to real estate development. Progress? Maybe. But these streams are resources which become more valuable as tourism becomes our number one industry and outdoor recreation our number one pastime.Citizens need to recognize their worth before they are gone forever.

The Green River, with the mushrooming angling pressures being placed on it, needs careful attention to flows. Highly-fluctuating water releases which have trapped and drowned unsuspecting anglers must be stabilized. Perhaps it will require more lawsuits to convince the Bureau of Reclamation. Besides, water levels differing as much as three-four feet a day does nothing at all for the fishery. A study is needed to determine what brings in more money, power users, or fishing dollars. I suspect the latter.

The Weber River east of Ogden after being turned into a sterile channel by flood control and highway construction. This is typical of several Utah streams as they near cities.

Other problems can be resolved by looking for more of the right species to stock in Utah's barren waters, where trout and perhaps bass are not quite right. Hopefully, Utah fisheries personnel will continue to look for the right fish to stock in places like the lower Sevier River. There are a few walleyes in the Sevier below Yuba Dam, but surely something more could be put in there to compete with the carp.

The sportsman's best hope is for legislation responsibly protecting fishing, hunting, and outdoor recreation in the early 1990s. Rep. Owens has said, "Spending for fish and wildlife values in Utah has been chronically under-funded over the last few decades, while demand for use has increased dramatically... " Focus must be placed on watershed acquisition and protection. For example, the Boulder Mountain watershed above Pine Creek and the Fremont River in Wayne County. Floods in the early 1980s inundated and silted-in Pine Creek and the Fremont. Why should this suddenly happen now, in this day and age? The Fremont River, once such a productive brown trout fishery that it grew browns to five and six pounds on a regular basis *without expensive hatchery stocking* began filling in with heavy silt, then spread out. Bicknell Bottoms was lost both as a fishery and as grazing ground for cattle.

What caused this? Some said "just a chance flood" in the heavy snow years of 1983-84. But Pine Creek had not silted in for eons of time, then did so every year for nearly a decade. What was happening upstream on Boulder Mountain? I put that question to the Dixie National Forest office in Cedar City, the U.S. federal agency held responsible to see that such things don't happen. The Dixie office admitted it was "a regrettable incident of erosion" and said steps are being taken to rectify the situation. "We are also concerned with the current condition of Boulder Mountain. We have long been aware of this area's uniqueness and conflicts..between various resource values. Recently, we have attended to two problems on the Boulder Mountain which have an impact on watershed condition: roads and livestock grazing."

One resident of Wayne County said he had traveled the world over to find the best brown trout stream on which to spend his retirement years. He decided on the Fremont. But there are now only a few pockets of brown trout fishery remaining on this once productive stream.

What can the Dixie forest do to bring back the Fremont? The UDWR has been asked to determine the cost of removing silt from the Fremont, spread a meadow wide and several inches deep. But the UDWR determined it would be throwing money away to clean out a channel which would just silt in again. The Dixie must spell out precisely how to prevent future silting. The *upstream* problem must be resolved. This is as clear a need for watershed acquisition as exists in the West. How to go about it? By removal of grazing animals from a delicate watershed? Less road building? More revegetating, with restrictions on use? Well, the Dixie forest people are supposed to be the experts. In the meantime, it would help if sportsmen wrote to their legislators and decision-makers, as well as the Dixie National Forest supervisor.

Will the great Utah brown trout fisheries of the past ever return? Possibly, but only if the lessons of the past have been learned.

The Fremont River in Wayne County has become silted in by erosion on Boulder Mountain. Author scans a one-time great trout fishery that needs help.

Have they? There are a few indications. The Utah Dept. of Transportation has begun to cooperate with fishermen and fisheries biologists in the widening of the Provo Canyon Road, but only after many public meetings with a large outcry. Movie actor and environmentalist Robert Redford got into this one several times to point out that the agreed-on safeguards of stream and canyon were not being followed. It does at times appear, after being hit on the head several times, that UDOT decided, "Hey, there really are people out there who *are serious* about protecting the Provo River and the canyon esthetics." UDOT engineers seemed quite proud of the "fish condos" they had built for bankside fish cover, although they were merely rebuilding where the highway was altering the channel for the *second* time. But as some concerned Brigham Young University biologists have said, "It is better than a decade ago. It bears further watchdogging."

Years ago, I heard the same thing about "watchdogging" from Utah State University biologists. It's a good thing someone was keeping vigil. Sure enough, the local county commission sent bulldozers into the Logan River, destroying biota-laden streambeds, straightening out cutbanks and cover, lifting it all from a trout stream (along with the trout themselves) onto ugly, meaningless dikes along the river. All this merely shifted flooding problems from Fifth West to Sixth West and on downstream. The same thing has happened extensively on the Weber River.

There is no engineering study to prove deepening of a riffle stops water from surging downstream. And the elimination of logs or debris under which trout live does not really stop water from its inevitable downstream destiny. In fact, research by a Salt Lake City engineering firm, Urban Technology, indicated decades ago that a stream's bed, if once dislodged, is more apt to wash out and become deposited downstream, solving nothing . . . and destroying any indigenous stream fishery.

There is one positive note: the Ogden River at the mouth of Ogden Canyon, which had been channeled and denuded in the name of flood control decades before, has been rehabilitated for fishermen with bank stabilization and new vegetation and trout should flourish again. It will take time for nature to heal, but man is helping instead of harming this time around.

The emphasis here has been on protecting stream fisheries, because flat water in Utah is not nearly as endangered as are streams. New reservoirs are created annually. However, flat water fisheries are also losing in some instances where water is drawn down to the point where fish die. The only absolute way to prevent it is to purchase what is known as "conservation pool rights." These rights have to be bought up for anglers just as a farmer buys rights to water his crops. But they are expensive. The UDWR does not have such rights in all Utah reservoirs. Too often money is not allocated because the angling public has been considered a "last user." But this should change with the today's emphasis on tourism and outdoor recreation.

Another problem in lake fisheries is pollution. In Utah Lake it is agricultural pollution. Phosphates and nitrates have turned what was a trout fishery in the early 1900s to the present channel cat and white bass fishing hole, and even that is now endangered. But for some reason nothing has been done. On occasion, planners talk of dredging out the lake, but this should be done only with the careful input of UDWR biologists. Any dredging near stream inlets in the spring would almost certainly destroy spawning fish and their eggs.

Cold-water fisheries can be affected by acid rain and other pollutants. Radioactivity has even been discovered in Utah's high mountain lakes, according to University of Utah radiologist Dr. Robert Pendleton. All waters must be monitored to make certain the fish and the fishing environment are not irreversibly destroyed. Sewage treatment is now in the talking stage around Bear Lake. The challenge is to get an agreement with Idaho. What affects one side affects the other. Another problem is watershed management. For example, denuding of the watershed around Strawberry Reservoir allowed heavy siltation to take place. Hopefully, U.S. and Utah governmental agencies will have the courage to protect these resources in the face of anyone who wants "special privileges" which diminish public uses.

But time will tell how well we protect our outdoor heritage.

There are other problems, political ones. For example, after UDWR director William Geer spoke up for sportsmen's interests on the Provo River and disagreed with anti-wildlife interests, the reward he received for it all was to be dismissed in December, 1988 by Gov. Bangerter. He was the second director to be fired within several years, a thing which has to send a message to all fish and wildlife leaders. Do not campaign too vigorously for natural resources. The Dept. of Natural Resources actually carried out the governor's order, making sportsmen wonder how much state officials really cared about protection of natural resources. It should be repeated that these were political dismissals — there was never any hint of biological wrong-doing. Sportsmen should be crusading for a logical system, for the sake of continuity if nothing else, where wildlife resources directors are appointed or terminated on a merit system by a committee, perhaps the present Utah Wildlife Board. It would mean the director could be fired for malfeasance in office ... but not at the mere whim of a politician who may or may not know anything about the state's fish and wildlife. Furthermore, a wildlife resources director receives all but a miniscule part of his budget from sportsmen's license purchases. Why should he then have to comply with the same requirements as those directors who spend taxpayer dollars? Shouldn't the UDWR director answer in some way to the sportsmen or their representative?

Lastly, a serious fisherman in Utah, or anywhere, should be looking out for the public's interests (and his own) by joining a sportsmen's club. Most decisions in Utah are not determined merely on an *issue* basis so much as *how many people want it that way?* Numbers talk. You can be effective as an individual, yet probably far more so by being a representative of a sizeable organization. Politicians may never have taken a biology class, but their future depends on listening carefully to groups like the League of Woman Voters (who challenged the Central Utah Project) or the Utah Wildlife Federation and its affiliated clubs, the Federation of Fly Fishers, the Stone Fly Society of the Wasatch, Utah Chapter Trout Unlimited etc.

First, of course, you must be informed, take the matter to your group, decide on a course of action, testify at hearings, and contact the decision-makers. Sportsmen can make a difference.

There is one more thing: the state can never keep up with several hundred thousand meat fishermen. The more waters set aside with conservative limits and more emphasis on fly or lure-only angling, the more resource that will remain for ourselves and our posterity.

All anglers should consider releasing a fish unharmed. I recall when friends asked me why I returned several four-pound trout in one day. "Did you know that in a cold stream it could take up to six or seven years for a fish to attain that size?" No, they didn't. In alpine waters, it could be longer than that. As Trout Unlimited puts it, " A trout is too valuable to catch only once." Oh, and one more thing: obviously anglers will have access to more waters if they act responsibly. Some of that water is on private land. Entry is sometimes allowed for those who promise — and follow through — on closing gates, picking up litter, *etc.* And even if it is on public land, wouldn't you want it left clean for you? A beer or soda pop can in a clear, sparkling trout stream is an incredibly irresponsible act. Hopefully, none of us will be part of it. Instead, we can be part of the solution rather than the problem.

Note on the next page the many records which were set in 1989. For example, the walleye record was set four times in 1989, twice at Deer Creek Reservoir and twice at Starvation Reservoir. All of these fish topped 13 lbs. The striped bass mark at Lake Powell was nearly broken several times with fish just under 39 pounds, until beaten by a 40 lbs. even fish. Two long-standing cold water species marks were also busted in 1989, the Arctic grayling adding one-half ounce, and the mountain whitefish mark taking on an ounce to record size. Splake, introduced into Utah just a few years ago, are attaining size rapidly, with larger specimens expected soon.

Also note that some fishing waters possess several different names. UDWR official records show Northern pike and yellow perch records under "Sevier Bridge Reservoir" but are listed here under the water's more well-known name, Yuba Reservoir. The smallmouth bass caught on Midview Reservoir, Ute Reservation, is listed with both names of this lake, Midview and Borham. A few records like the cutthroat trout from Strawberry Reservoir may never change.

Note: See the list of rules for entering YOUR FISH into the Utah record books. Study the procedures carefully to qualify.

Curt Bilbey, Vernal angler, with the world's third largest lake trout, a 51-1/2 pounder from Flaming Gorge.

Current Record Fish for the State of Utah

As of Feb. 15, 1990

SPECIES	YEAR	WEIGHT	LENGTH	GIRTH	FISHERMAN	LOCATION
BASS, Largemouth	1974	10 lb 2 oz	24 1/4 in	20 in	Sam LaManna	Lake Powell
BASS, Smallmouth	1983	6 lb 12 oz	20 1/2 in	17 1/3 in	Roger L. Tallerico	Midview Res.
BASS, Striped	1989	40 lb	45 in	25 in	Bill Hook	Lake Powell
BASS, White	1970	4 lb 1 oz			John Welcker	Utah Lake
BLUEGILL	1983	2 lb 3 oz	10 5/8 in	14 1/4 in	Calvin Davis	Pelican Lake
BULLHEAD, Black	1984	2 lb 7 oz	17 in	10 1/4 in	Ray Johnson	Utah Lake
CARP	1960	30 lb 0 oz			Ralph Merrill	Great Salt Lake Marshes
CATFISH, Channel	1978	32 lb 5 oz	39 3/4 in	22 in	LeRoy E. Mortenson	Utah Lake
CHUB, Utah	1987	1 lb 11 oz	13 1/4 in	11 in	Ray Johnson	Starvation
CRAPPIE, Black	1982	2 lb 11 oz	15 3/4 in	13 1/4 in	Jerry H. Little	Lake Powell
GRAYLING, Arctic	1989	1 lb 1 oz	13 7/8 in	8 1/2 in	John S. Becker	Whiskey Island Lake, Uintas
PERCH, Sacramento	1987	2 lb 13 oz	15 3/4 in	14 1/4 in	Ronald J. Brinkman	Garrison Res.
PERCH, Yellow	1984	2 lb 11 oz	15 1/8 in	9 3/4 in	Ray Johnson	Yuba
PIKE, Northern	1986	22 lb 0 oz	44 1/4 in	17 1/2 in	Dean E. Johnson	Yuba
SALMON, Kokanee	1984	5 lb 5 oz	23 3/4 in	14 1/8 in	Ray Johnson	Flaming Gorge
SCULPIN, Mottled	1987	0 lb 1.12 oz	5 3/8 in	3 1/2 in	Jeremy G. Bone	Spring Creek (Springville)
SUCKER, Bluehead	1988	2 lb 6 oz	19 1/4 in	9 1/4 in	Rick T. Wardle	Weber River
SUCKER, Flannelmouth	1985	2 lb 7 oz	19 1/4 in	9 in	Ray Johnson	Flaming Gorge
SUCKER, Utah	1988	6 lb 6 oz	24 1/2 in	13 in	William Mehn	Weber River
SUCKER, White	1985	1 lb 13 oz	17 1/2 in	8 in	Ray Johnson	Flaming Gorge
SUNFISH, Green	1988	0 lb 12 oz	9 3/4 in	8 1/8 in	Catherine A. Ablard	Montez Creek Reservoir
TROUT, Albino	1987	1 lb 2 oz	14 1/2 in	4 1/4 in	Brian Archuleta	Joes Valley Reservoir
TROUT, Brook	1971	7 lb 8 oz			Milton Taft	Boulder Mountain
TROUT, Brown	1977	33 lb 10 oz	40 in	25 in	Robert Bringhurst	Flaming Gorge
TROUT, Cutthroat	1930	26 lb 12 oz	45 1/8 in		Mrs. E. Smith	Strawberry Reservoir
TROUT, Golden	1977	0 lb 13 1/2 oz	14 1/2 in		Breck Tuttle	Atwood Creek
TROUT, Lake	1988	51 lb 8 oz	45 1/8 in	31 3/4 in	Curt Bilbey	Flaming Gorge
TROUT, Rainbow	1979	26 lb 2 oz			Del Canty	Flaming Gorge
TROUT, Splake	1989	5 lb 6 oz	22 3/4 in	13 1/2 in	Reed Davis	Fish Lake
WALLEYE	1989	14 lb 10 oz	30 in	22 1/2 in	Kelly Thomson	Starvation Reservoir
WHITEFISH, Bonneville	1982	4 lb 4 oz	21 in	13 3/4 in	Deon Sparks	Bear Lake
WHITEFISH, Mountain	1989	4 lb 7 oz	21 3/4 in	13 in	Blair Newman	Lower Provo River

CHAPTER NINE
Fee Fishing and Hunting

Fee fishing and hunting has been popularized in the last few years by an increased number of sportsmen willing to pay for privatized fishing and hunting. This chapter covers fishing-hunting clubs and the Indian tribal lands and waters.

UTE RESERVATION — The Ute Tribe controls the one million acre Uintah-Ouray Reservation, including the Hill Creek-Willow Creek drainage south of tribal headquarters in Ft. Duchesne, Uintah County. The tribal rights also include the south slope of the Uinta Mountains below the Ashley National Forest line. This extends from about the 6,500 foot level to nearly the 8,000 elevation on these drainages: **Rock Creek, Lake Fork, Yellowstone Creek, Uinta and Whiterocks River.** As of 1990, the federal courts are trying to determine how much of eastern Utah the Utes control. Either way, the Utes own some of the best fishing waters. A tribal angling permit (by day or season) is required to fish and/or camp along these fisheries.

The permit is worth the fee because the resources are in a strategic location and because some sportsmen won't pay the extra fee . . . thus thinning out competition. So, the same fine trout stream which yields fat and resplendent trout to the fly angler on the national forest does the same on the Ute Reservation — with perhaps a third as many fishermen.

Take Yellowstone Creek, north of Duchesne. One day when I had been catching 10-inch cutthroats on this stream, I bought the tribal permit in Mountain Home and went a quarter mile onto the reservation. Fish were several inches larger and far less educated. This is generally true across the entire south slope of the Uintas. On Rock Creek, the Utes own the Lower Stillwater with its capacity for large brown trout. Some nice browns are also taken on the Uinta River opposite the Ute village of Whiterocks. The Utes also boast excellent fly fishing on the Frog Ponds south of Moon Lake along the Lake Fork drainage.

On **Towave** (Ta-wahvee) **Reservoir and Hill Creek** south of Ouray, I found some of my best trout fishing of the past several decades. Many of these trout were four-pound cutts introduced several years earlier as pansized fish by the Bureau of Indian Affairs. Many anglers found fast action here for not only hefty cutts but nice rainbows, and upstream from Towave, excellent brook trout fishing. Below Towave, sizeable cutts which likely spilled through the dam, showed up on the taking end of almost any offering. I recall hooking 20-inch cutts on brown or yellow bucktails imitating grasshoppers and silver streamers resembling minnows. More anglers have discovered Towave and are willing to drive the 51 rough miles on an oft-rutted and slippery-when-wet four-wheel drive route. The same biological food conditions which fattened these fish are still there: fresh-water shrimp, beetles etc.

A just-over 10 lbs. cutthroat was taken through the ice in the winter of 1988-89 by a Ute angler, according to tribal fish-wildlife officials.

Towave was stocked with brown trout which reached up to a size of 2-3 lbs. in the fall of 1989. Normally, brown trout will grow faster than other trout, but they are often more difficult to catch. I doubt any size browns will be as cooperative as those four-pound cutts which used to hit a silver flatfish or Rapala with every reasonable cast, especially in spring and fall. Trout put on weight as quickly in Towave as any water in Utah. Federal biologists said they were amazed at trout in Towave increasing about 2-3 inches per month, from April to September. By contrast, trout in the high Uinta lakes manage only a single inch per month in summer's peak growth.

Another 35 dirt miles or so up Hill Creek from Towave you can also try your luck in **Weaver Reservoir**, set in scenic aspen country. Weaver is more beautiful than the cedar-surrounded Towave. It also holds more pristine water than the often murky Towave. But trout grow a little slower in the colder Weaver, running around 10-15 inches on the average, cutthroat or rainbow, in the summer of 1988. The trip to Weaver can be worth the time and effort just to observe the wildlife, bald eagles, mule deer, wild turkeys, and possibly, elk.

Roads into upper **Hill** and **Willow Creek** can be confusing and badly rutted but are also upgraded from year to year. Basically, you can expect dry, gravel roads across the lower sandhill sector of the reservation immediately south of Ouray, but as higher elevation is attained, roads become more challenging. Check with the Ute Tribe Fish and Wildlife Dept. in Ft. Duchesne for access maps on specific waters to be fished. Also write for a angling proclamation, as opening dates are usually staggered with Towave opening in April, Weaver in May, streams above in June, and some waters open year round.

The Utes have many flat water fisheries, including **Midview, Twin Potts and Cedarview**. Cedarview has sported brook trout fishing in the past. Access to these lakes is fairly easy due to foothill locations on the Uinta south slope. Some, including Midview (also called Borham) sport warm water species such as slab-sided smallmouth bass and nice walleyes. Midview produced a state record nearly seven-pound smallmouth in 1983. Twin Potts, normally a popular rainbow and lake trout fishery, suffered from drawdown in 1988 and faces re-stocking.

Bottle Hollow Reservoir, viewable from U.S. 40 east of Roosevelt, is now being converted from a trout fishery to a warm water fishing hole, possibly for bass. Trout have not done well in the 69 degree water. If the Utes do get a viable fishery out of this one, access will be easy with camping nearby.

Licensing: Ute angling licenses can be obtained at Uinta Basin sporting goods stores and at some sporting goods stores on the Wasatch Front. A one-day angling license in 1990 cost $4, with $1 a day for additional fishing. The Utes require camping permits for any overnight stay on tribal property. Costs are listed in the angling proclamation. Boating permits are required on the larger lakes. All floating craft are banned on smaller waters like Towave and Weaver.

BIG GAME HUNTING by non-Indians is no longer allowed on the Ute Reservation , but if it is ever is again, I would rush for a license. Locating mature four-point bucks is fairly easy south of Towave. I have also witnessed many elk on the reservation, taking a five-point bull on my initial wapiti quest. Average bucks and bulls graced the view from many back roads in upper Hill Creek. Black bear and cougar are found in this outback, particularly along the Green River's Desolation Canyon, south of Flat Rock and Wild Cat mesas, West Willow Canyon and to the divide at 8,200 feet looking south from the top of the Book Cliffs ridgeline. One day after a skiff of snow, reservation guide Lee Hadden showed me dozens of large bruin tracks around previously killed cattle and deer carcasses. Bear claw marks show on many aspens in upper Hill Creek. Bobcats haunt the cliff country almost everywhere.

After building a trophy big game clientele via Nu Tu Veep Expeditions on upper Hill Creek, the Utes suddenly decided in the early 1970s to restrict this hunting to members of the tribe only. Ute officials said in 1990 they "have no intention of changing restrictions in the near future."

The Utes do allow **small game hunting**, including good pheasant hunting near Ft. Duchesne, waterfowl along the Green River, and excellent upland bird shoots for forest grouse and cottontails south of the Green River. In good years, chukar partridge hunting can be exciting in the terrain north of Towave. It is closed now, but "bird numbers are on the increase," the Utes say.

In the past, the Utes required state licenses be purchased prior to tribal fishing-hunting permits, but that requirement was waived several years ago.

This is Be Prepared terrain, where extra gasoline, water, food and sufficient time to appreciate the scenery are recommended. So are four-or at least high clearance two-wheel drive vehicles. This territory contains some of the wildest undeclared wilderness in the Lower 48. You can drive for nearly one hundred miles without seeing any civilization.

OTHER INDIAN FISHING-HUNTING: The Navajo Tribe controls southern San Juan County. Check with tribal headquarters in Window Rock, Ariz. The Goshute Indians have jurisdiction over big game hunting on west side of the Deep Creek Mountains near the Nevada border, so contact that office in Ibapah, Tooele County. The Shivwits Indians own a small portion of land in southwestern Washington County, with contact at any local BIA offices.

DESERET LIVESTOCK RANCH — encompasses a quarter of a million acres in Morgan and Rich Counties. Owners limit entry to a handful of hunters each year, basically for removal of surplus deer and elk competing with cattle. Some of the top trophies in the state hail from this undulating aspen-pine-oak terrain. For the past few years the top archery-taken elk have come from this ranch. Costs for a week's elk quest ranged upward of $7,000 in 1988. Check with Deseret Land and Livestock, Woodruff, 84086. For information on other large ranches which offer fee fishing and hunting, contact the Utah Farm Bureau, 5300 So. 3600 West, Murray, 84107.

PRIVATE SPORTSMAN'S CLUBS — One of the largest in Utah is the United Sportsmen, Sandy, with control of approximately one-half million acres for

Bragging-sized cutthroats like these are taken on Hill Creek and on many small streams on the Ute Indian Reservation.

deer and elk hunting on private ranch property. The club leases large acreages during the hunting seasons, pays landowners for any broken fences, insures against damages etc. Much of **Chalk Creek** above Coalville, private land which has long been closed to the general public, is now under jurisdiction of this club. Other properties are utilized in places like **Tabiona-Hanna, Scofield, Minnie Maud country.** For details, contact the U.S. at 9119 So. 150 West, Sandy, Utah, 84070, (801)-562-0054.

For information on bow shooting lanes, check with archery stores throughout the state. Many have lanes available just prior to the August archery deer season.

There are **other sportsman's clubs** in the state, particularly slanted to limited access deer and pheasant hunting. However, I am not familiar with many of them personally, and cannot vouch for their specific services. Many of these clubs focus on renting and insure landowners who have previously closed land to the public. Championing the idea of private fee fishing and hunting have been well known outdoor writers and anglers like Lee Wulff. Hunting writer Steven Johnson says that the clubs favor people "who have little spare time." Membership in a private sportsman's club is usually on an annual basis. Prices vary. Contact sporting goods dealers for further information.

So far as I know, Utah has none of the macho "controlled hunts" (like some I've seen in the mid-West) where a hunter simply peers into an enclosure and selects a "trophy." Furthermore, this sort of "guaranteed" approach does not appear challenging enough to include as "sport hunting."

GUIDE SERVICES — There are several fishing and hunting guide-outfitting services accessing the Uinta Mountains and one for the Boulder Mountain. Guides are not required to be licensed in Utah, therefore no list is filed with the state. Judging from clients' comments, there are other quality guide services available. I am familiar with the following horse-guide services to the **Uinta Mountains** for fishing in summer, hunting in fall: Whiterocks area, Joe Jessup, Whiterocks, 84085; Kamas, west end, Piute Creek Outfitters, Ranch Rt. 2, Kamas, 84036; Spirit Lake Lodge, call George Coonradt in Murray, 226-5562; Moon Lake area, call Gary Stringham, Mt. Emmons, 454-3153; Upper Duchesne drainage, including Grandaddy Lakes, Defa Ranch, Hanna, 84031. For **Boulder Mountain**, contact Don Sampson, Navajo Trails Ranch Camp, Box 88, Bicknell, 84715, telephone. 425-3469. (Sept. 15-June 15, Box 886, Los Altos, CA, 94022.)

Entire state, hunting only: Richard LaRocco, 175 N. Center St., Wellsville, 84339, telephone. 245-3252, home; 752-7774, office. LaRocco, a former Outdoor Life associate editor, has assisted many hunters to find trophy game in Utah. Private ranches are utilized. Hunting with LaRocco, I found him to specialize in locating trophy bucks via spotting scopes and many off-season hours afield. There are many **lion-bear guides in southern Utah**. One who specializes in lions is Val Robb, Paragonah, 84760. Several are located in St. George, Cedar City.

PRIVATE FISHING WATERS — Utah has many scattered private fishing waters or ponds. Interestingly, many like those in the Kamas area, feature fee angling a few miles from good-to-excellent public fishing holes. As one entrepreneur put it, "Sometimes the kids don't catch a fish, or perhaps Dad fails on a day when they aren't biting. We have the fish where anglers can find them." Such commercial enterprises usually keep water at optimum temperatures for constant fish hunger level, with little food available to speed up the catching process.

I do not condemn nor condone the concept of "easy" and artificialized fishing waters, but should point out that this is not to be confused with the skills required in subduing a *wild trout*. The catching may be fun either way, but outwitting a wild trout is by far the greater accomplishment.

Occasionally, Utah communities hold July 4th "Huck Finn Days" which encourage anglers to "scramble" for trout with pitchforks, hands or whatever is available. In my opinion, these may cheapen the idea of catching fish for sport and should not be confused with sport fishing.

Small farm ponds with stocked rainbows and fee fishing are scattered over the state. Check with sporting goods stores for information on these private waters.

COMMERCIAL SHOOTING PRESERVES — The state has many private pheasant shooting preserves. They must be registered with the state's Utah Div. Wildlife Resources, so check with them at 1596 W. No. Temple, Salt Lake City, Utah, 84116, or (801) 533-9333. With limited pheasant hunting in Utah, the preserves often provide best shooting opportunities. Prices vary, but shooting on a one-time basis is often possible.

DUCK CLUBS — The state has many duck clubs, especially in and around the south and east shores of Great Salt Lake. Waterfowl shooting was excellent prior to the 1983-84 flooding period. Some clubs altered services at that time, but with stabilized water levels, most have resumed memberships. Normally, some of the state's fastest waterfowl shooting, included Canada geese and swans, are found on these clubs. Contact sporting goods dealers and the UDWR. Memberships are usually on an annual basis, with prices varying widely.

Searching for a big muley rack in the Henry Mountains.

CHAPTER TEN

Utah's Big Game Picture

Big game hunting in Utah has extensive economic and social impacts. Mule deer in particular draw much attention throughout the state. For example, most school districts let classes out for several days around opening day of deer season, the third Saturday of October. Countless motels and restaurants talk about the autumn hunts "bringing in more revenue than any other time of year." Try any left turn from a highway, on the evening before the deer inaugural, toward Manti Mountain in Sanpete County or Pine Valley in Washington County . . . and it may take hours. The circus-like atmosphere resembles Christmas plus five college football games thrown in at once. With some 200,000 big game license-holders and perhaps three times as many family members in a convoy of vehicles headed for the hills, it is an annual ritual which must be seen to be believed.

Traditionally left home are myriad "deer widows" who have special department store sales in their honor — while the spouse is away. Some "ghost towns" in Sanpete and Emery and Millard or Iron Counties are re-peopled during the 11-day season only when hunters return to re-supply. That's the typical Utah venison quest scenario. With archery and early or late special permit hunts, some form of big game hunting occurs in Utah from August through November.

Utah went to a buck-only hunt in the early 1980s, but success is as high as in any other state in the West. Perhaps only Colorado yields as many deer per square mile of sage, cedar, oak, mountain mahogany, aspen and conifer as does Utah. The state has considerable "ideal" deer habitat, a fact not lost on the nation's major outdoor magazines. Outdoor Life in particular has had many stories set in this state about successfully meeting the outsized rack challenge.

Economically, it is difficult to measure the value of a big buck bounding into the sunset, or the sight of an October slope on fire with golden aspens, scarlet maple and oak. But studies show millions of dollars spent pursuing mule deer each fall in the Beehive State and that's after arriving hunters have already expended much on other preparations.

So, when hunters get excited about hunting in Utah, they have ample company. "Getting excited" includes tying on a deer tag for about 30 percent of those who go afield each season. Trophy bucks are taken by those who know what they're doing — usually those who wisely scout ahead year after year. As one veteran orange-vester put it, "A couple weeks' searching a year is too short a time to find the right buck." Most of the easy deer are now gone in vehicle-accessible sectors of the West and the smart ones know every ridge and arroyo far better than any hunter.

Utah has burgeoning **elk** herds. The state had only a dwindling carryover of pioneer-era wapiti in the early 1900s. But introductions from Yellowstone

National Park, as well as careful management and protection of range, have made elk so plentiful that open bull seasons are now the norm. Wapiti hunts can now also focus more on quality than ever before. A spike-only shoot in some regions encourages growth of mature bulls, something Utah needs more of. This has worked out in Montana, say local game biologists. It was experimentally begun in Utah a few years ago.

Moose, particularly in the northern sector of the state, are proliferating as never before. Moose hunt success is phenomenal. For the first time in decades, **Rocky Mountain sheep and mountain goats** are also expanding after introduction to places like the Wasatch Mountains' Lone Peak, Timpanogos, the Uinta high country, Tushar Range etc. Only a few can now be hunted, but opportunities may increase in the present reader's lifetime. The state has always had a fair number of **desert bighorn sheep** in the Cataract Canyon country of the Colorado River. **Antelope**, once abounding in Utah, fell away a half-century ago, but are returning in numbers from Three Corners to Parker Mountain and the West Desert.

One of the nation's few **wild bison** herds inhabit the rugged Henry Mountain terrain, so remote and unknown until recent times that it was the last major mountain range in America to be discovered, mapped and explored. An expanding private herd of buffalo lives on Antelope Island.

Black bears and mountain lions have been labeled as "game" in Utah, whereas a few decades ago they were considered predators to be shot on sight. Cougars are on the increase almost everywhere, with bears generally holding their own. Bears appear to be on the increase in southeastern, eastern and central Utah.

Archery quests — Of special interest in Utah are the archery hunts, with more sportsmen seeking to take their game as the native Americans did. Utah bowmen are doing very well. Dennis Shirly, Elk Ridge, who keeps tally of record Pope-Young world archery records, shows Utah with the number three mule deer "typical" rack, 6th best in the world for "non-typical," number one in the new typical velvet, and number four, non-typical velvet. (Note: Mule deer taken during the August bow season usually possess velvet on the antlers. The new measurement category allows measuring muley racks without the tedious task of removing velvet.) Shirley and fellow archers have re-written the state record book several times in the past few years with bow-killed elk.

Utah also allows a **muzzle-loader license** in early November to a hunter who has not killed a deer during the regular hunts. The "mountain man" permit, however, must be purchased *prior* to the regular October rifle shoot. Black powder shooting seems to be mushrooming in popularity. Since effective range is rarely beyond 100 yards, challenge is heightened.

It would be advisable in Utah for a beginner or newcomer to join an archery or muzzleloading club in order to keep up on big game regulations, to refine skills and to learn from the experts. Rifle hunters can also benefit by joining a sportsman's organization to learn more about the equipment and game they seek, as well as regulations and conservation needs.

The Big Game Proclamation includes important **application deadline information.** Starting in 1990, applications were accepted in April-May, with a consolidated lottery drawing in June to determine who receives permits on all hunts.

Hunting areas are listed by "units" with a description of various deer "herds." These terms shouldn't be taken too literally, since deer know no boundaries and they rarely remain in herds. Utah's Board of Big Game Control, which decides on hunting seasons and regulations, has two of five members representing agriculture. Heavy farm-ranch damage by game in any given year means more permits issued. The proclamation's mention of "trophy units" does not necessarily mean there are more large bucks in those units; it may mean a low population where little harvest is needed. Some areas of Utah may also be good hunting because of a higher buck-to-doe ratio than another area, albeit less total deer.

Elk are managed in units like deer, but wapiti roam widely in Utah as elsewhere and may cross boundaries frequently. Nevertheless, elk are managed on a unit concept based on where they are *expected to be* in hunting season. Weather, of course, may change that.

Residents must buy their permits for deer or elk prior to the opening day of season. Antelope can be hunted every other year, and moose and bison only once in a lifetime. All big game but deer and elk require application and lottery selection. Also on a draw basis are limited-entry, second deer permits, restricted entry elk, and other special hunts. Applications must be filled out, and submitted with proper fee, then sent via mail to UDWR headquarters.

Hunting dates remain rather stable each year, with seasons something like this: general deer, third Saturday in October plus 10 more days; archery deer, third Saturday in August to early September. Muzzleloader deer, first Saturday in November and seven more days; general elk, first Wednesday in October and 10 more days; archery elk, approximately Sept. 2-17; muzzleloader elk, about Sept. 16-24. Antelope, with local variations, around Sept. 16-24.

Utah has some special restrictions on transporting horses. Roadblocks and deer checking stations in the past have issued citations for those trailering horses without ownership papers, along with failure to tag deer, dressing out animals without leaving proof of gender, and failure to remove ammunition from a firearm while within a moving vehicle.

Utah regulations also call for hunter orange cap and coat or vest during regular rifle hunts. Interestingly, new research indicates big game may be able to detect bright colors, including hunter orange. It is not yet determined how big game animals react to these colors, but it has been proven that elk and deer can be taught to find food in different colored buckets. If so, perhaps the nimrod can wear "mottled" or "broken" orange to camouflage the human outline, a thing archers have always realized the importance of doing, along with pine scents and gum-soled sneakers. Many archers even paint the face to break up bright "fleshy" appearance. Hunters may continue to wear orange regardless, because it would seem safer with other hunters around. I've personally decided that elk don't pay much attention to the brightest red or orange if the hunter stands absolutely still. One six-point bull looked at me recently as I sat in a snowbank and then resumed nonchalantly feeding 75 yards away. Other hunters may interpret different results from mine.

Equipment — Utah law also requires a center-fire firearm of at least .23

OFFICIAL SCORING SYSTEM FOR NORTH AMERICAN BIG GAME TROPHIES

RECORDS OF NORTH AMERICAN
BIG GAME COMMITTEE   **BOONE AND CROCKETT CLUB**

Minimum Score: Deer   Boone and Crockett Club
Col. Blacktail: Typical — 130   Records of North American Big Game Committee
Mule: Typical — 195   **MULE and BLACKTAIL DEER**   c/o Carnegie Museum
                                                                    4400 Forbes Ave. Pittsburgh, Pa. 15213

KIND OF DEER: MULE

DETAIL OF POINT MEASUREMENT

SEE OTHER SIDE FOR INSTRUCTIONS	Supplementary Data		Column 1	Column 2	Column 3	Column 4
	R.	L.	Spread Credit	Right Antler	Left Antler	Difference
A. Number of Points on Each Antler	5	6				
B. Tip to Tip Spread	24 3/8					
C. Greatest Spread	30 4/8					
D. Inside Spread of MAIN BEAMS 26 5/8 Spread credit may equal but not exceed length of longer antler			26 5/8			
IF Inside Spread of Main Beams exceeds longer antler length, enter difference						
E. Total of Lengths of all Abnormal Points						2 7/8
F. Length of Main Beam				26 7/8	28	1 1/8
G-1. Length of First Point, if present				2	2 1/8	1/8
G-2. Length of Second Point				20 2/8	20 1/8	1/8
G-3. Length of Third Point, if present				10 7/8	9 6/8	1 1/8
G-4. Length of Fourth Point, if present				13 4/8	13 7/8	3/8
H-1. Circumference at Smallest Place Between Burr and First Point				5 3/8	5 3/8	
H-2. Circumference at Smallest Place Between First and Second Points				4 6/8	4 6/8	
H-3. Circumference at Smallest Place Between Main Beam and Third Point				4 2/8	4 3/8	1/8
H-4. Circumference at Smallest Place Between Second and Fourth Points				5 4/8	5	4/8
TOTALS			26 5/8	93 3/8	93 3/8	6 3/8

ADD	Column 1	26 5/8	Exact locality where killed S. Indian Canyon, Lincoln Co., Wyo.
	Column 2	93 3/8	Date killed 11-13-69 By whom killed Al Firenze, Sr.
	Column 3	93 3/8	Present owner Al Firenze, Sr.
	Total	213 3/8	Address 1001 Airport Blvd. South, San Francisco, Calif. 94080
Subtract Column 4		6 3/8	Guide's Name and Address Monty Nelson, Alpine, Wyoming
FINAL SCORE		207	Remarks: (Mention any abnormalities)

I certify that I have measured the above trophy on   *March 2*   19 *71*
at (address)   *Carnegie Museum*   City   *Pittsburgh*   State   *Pa.*
and that these measurements and data are, to the best of my knowledge and belief,
made in accordance with the instructions given.

Witness: *Peter Haupt*   Signature: *Arnold O. Haugen*
                                                    Boone and Crockett Official Measurer

Instructions

All measurements must be made with a flexible steel tape to the nearest one-eighth of an inch. Wherever it is necessary to change direction of measurement, mark a control point and swing tape at this point. To simplify addition, please enter fractional figures in *eighths*. Official measurements cannot be taken for at least sixty days after the animal was killed. *Please submit photographs.*

Supplementary Data measurements indicate conformation of the trophy, and none of the figures in Lines A, B and C are to be included in the score. Evaluation of conformation is a matter of personal preference. Excellent but nontypical Mule Deer heads with many points shall be placed and judged in a separate class.

A. Number of Points on Each Antler. To be counted a point, a projection must be at least one inch long AND its length must exceed the length of its base. All points are measured from tip of point to nearest edge of beam as illustrated. *Beam tip is counted as a point but not measured as a point.*

B. Tip to Tip Spread measured between tips of main beams.

C. Greatest Spread measured between perpendiculars at right angles to the center line of the skull at widest part whether across main beams or points.

D. Inside Spread of Main Beams measured at right angles to the center line of the skull at widest point between main beams. Enter this measurement again in "Spread Credit" column if it is less than or equal to the length of longer antler.

E. Total of Lengths of all Abnormal Points. Abnormal points are generally considered to be those nontypical in shape or location.

F. Length of Main Beam measured from lowest outside edge of burr over outer curve to the tip of the main beam. The point of beginning is that point on the burr where the center line along the outer curve of the beam intersects the burr.

G-1-2-3-4. Length of Normal Points. Normal points are the brow (or first) and the upper and lower forks as shown in illustration. They are measured from nearest edge of beam over outer curve to tip. To determine nearest edge (top edge) of beam, lay the tape along the outer curve of the beam so that the top edge of the tape coincides with the top edge of the beam on both sides of the point. Draw line along top edge of tape. This line will be base line from which point is measured.

H-1-2-3-4. Circumferences—If first point is missing, take H-1 and H-2 at smallest place between burr and second point. If third point is missing, take H-3 half way between the base and tip of second point. If the fourth point is missing, take H-4 half way between the second point and tip of main beam.

Trophies Obtained Only by Fair Chase May Be Entered in Any Boone and Crockett Club Big Game Competition

To make use of the following methods shall be deemed UNFAIR CHASE and unsportsmanlike, and any trophy obtained by use of such means is disqualified from entry in any Boone and Crockett Club big game competition:

I. Spotting or herding game from the air, followed by landing in its vicinity for pursuit;

II. Herding or pursuing game with motor-powered vehicles;

III. Use of electronic communications for attracting, locating or observing game, or guiding the hunter to such game.

I certify that the trophy scored on this chart was not taken in UNFAIR CHASE as defined above by the Boone and Crockett Club.

I certify that it was not spotted or herded by guide or hunter from the air followed by landing in its vicinity for pursuit, nor herded or pursued on the ground by motor-powered vehicles.

I further certify that no electronic communications were used to attract, locate, observe, or guide the hunter to such game; and that it was taken in full compliance with the local game laws or regulations of the state, province or territory.

Date   *February 1, 1970*   Hunter   *Al Firenze, Sr.*

caliber. Much of the state's hunting involves wide open spaces and long-distance shooting, so a *flat-trajectory* rifle like the .270 or 7mm Remington magnum or .300 Winchester is popular. It goes without saying that the right rifle is also one that the toter is familiar with on the practice range. Practice going from a safety "on" to safety "off" situation, in the same sitting or kneeling positions to be used on real game. Most shooters favor the sitting because it is the steadiest and most practical. Prone position is accurate, but it just isn't practical, even when trying to shoot over Utah's low sagebrush. Make certain that you feel confident at the maximum "efficiency range" of your rifle, probably about 325-340 yards. Shooting a 30/06 beyond 325 yards is not wise, since bullet drop at that range can be as much as 25 inches. Claims of accurate shooting at greater distances are usually exaggerated.

Much Utah hunting requires a sturdy vehicle capable of climbing steep roads, or fording streams. I would bring along a shovel and chains (with chain tighteners) anytime after early September for the possibility of snow. Be sure you have treaded tires for slippery-when-wet back roads. When steep, they can be dangerous. Road conditions, an integral part of any Utah venison quest, will likely be given in community newspapers just prior to any year's deer hunt.

Obviously a hunter needs to dress for cold weather, and at high elevations be prepared for below zero temperatures, as well as low visibility blizzards. A 17-year old youth sought deer on Mt. Nebo after school a short distance from his home in the 1989 deer hunt, and made a wrong turn near dark with a sudden snow squall coming on. Temperatures plummeted. He was rescued during the night, but hypothermia was too much. He died the next day in the hospital. While this is an unusual case, the point is there: dress warmly, keep track of directions when leaving your vehicle, and bring along the makings for a fire. Always let someone know where you are going. A stalled vehicle or a slippery patch of ice might delay you and cause problems in cold high country.

Camping in forest service improved campgrounds will usually be without running water in October. Most are closed. Many licensees hunt from campers, trailers, or vans, but "tent villages" are not uncommon. There is usually ample room on public lands to camp. Check the maps to determine access to your hunting area. When you set up camp near expected hunting terrain, don't chop wood or rev up the chain saw, yell to neighbors, or worst of all, "sight-in" your rifle. None of this bodes well for success anywhere, especially with an elk's keen ears.

Physical conditioning — In addition to the above, it is important to get in top physical condition. Utah mountains are among the steepest and most precipitous in the continental United States. Success and safety often depend on previous conditioning by exercise, jogging, or both. Your hunting competition is probably also doing it!

Scouting ahead is the key to success in Utah big game hunting. The days of easy bucks or bulls posing by the pavement are gone. I remember reading in the early 1950s about road hunters "picking up a nice forkhorn" in Mountain Dell country above Salt Lake City, or Hobble Creek Canyon above Springville in time to reach an 8 a.m. job. It could still happen in some rural areas, but probably only if the nimrod has been scouting. Opening day bucks may, for the moment be uneducated, but they learn quickly. Only hunting well back in, by horseback, fetches naive deer in these modern times. Bucks seem less skittish Tuesday through Thursday than on weekends.

There are perhaps close to a quarter million savvy mule deer surviving successive mild winters among Utah's 84,000 square miles. Deer still hang out around alfalfa fields and orchards in central and southern counties even during the hunting season. But, they are more surreptitious about how they do it. I know of one 33-inch spread which was taken by a California hunter a few years ago who didn't know any better than to scour barren slopes above a large hayfield. The monster which had been living there unnoticed for perhaps four-five years was likely bedding by daylight and foraging after dark. The non-resident scored because he tried something residents didn't.

Besides locating deer, a hunter should get a "reading" on their modus operandi. Studies in Utah show that the muley moves relatively little. Bucks may venture two miles during their entire lifetimes unless long winter migrations are required. Deer are territorial, not nomadic. Scout a big buck and it will likely be somewhere in the vicinity when you return.

How does one locate oversized antlers nowadays? A very good way in Utah, where cities often touch the mountains, is to get out looking in December after snow pushes game downhill. With the rut beginning, bucks grow foolish. From valley roads, you can observe giant racks following after the does. Mule deer shed antlers in January, elk about late March. If you want to hunt the central Utah region, check Hobble Creek Canyon for elk and nice bucks on the north side of the canyon. On the north Manti, check Starvation Canyon, Dairy Fork, Lake Fork and lower Skyline Drive. Around Salt Lake City, the biggest bucks will often show in December just above the Holladay Gun Club. Or drive to McCook Ridge in the Book Cliffs of Uintah County, or Box Elder County's Raft River Mountains. Sure, those deer won't be precisely there come the next hunting season, but you can find them a little higher. You also know they are there and such confidence helps immensely in glassing patiently during the hunting seasons. When you are certain the big ones are around, you'll do more looking and less walking. Moving without careful scrutiny of all within rifle range is probably the number one reason beginning Utah hunters do not score.

Utahns can tote a deer rifle at **minimum age 14**. But many of these new nimrods have not convinced themselves of the importance of letting their eyes do the "walking." Haste is a hunter's number one enemy. Successful hunters I have known try to scout ahead far enough to know when they are within a quarter mile of the game they seek. Then, they proceed *most cautiously* so as to pinpoint game before it pinpoints them. Caution is extremely important, for a Utah muley which isn't absolutely certain where danger is located will frequently stand statue-still until it finds out. As a youngster, I noticed that most big game ran directly away from people. Now, those animals have learned their legs can take them into as much danger as out. Deer are now so sophisticated that they refuse to be pushed for long — knowing guns wait them ahead. I have even seen Utah mule deer run *through* the first wave of drivers, curling quickly behind them, out of danger. Deer have not been hunted all these years without learning from it.

OFFICIAL SCORING SYSTEM FOR NORTH AMERICAN BIG GAME TROPHIES

RECORDS OF NORTH AMERICAN BIG GAME COMMITTEE   **BOONE AND CROCKETT CLUB**   Boone and Crockett Club
Records of North American Big Game Committee
c/o Carnegie Museum
4400 Forbes Ave.   Pittsburgh, Pa.   15213

Minimum Score: 195:45 = 240   **NON-TYPICAL MULE DEER**

ABNORMAL	
Points Line E	
R	L
3 4/8	
3 6/8	
1 2/8	8
3 6/8	6 5/8
6 2/8	7 7/8
9 2/8	5 1/8
9 5/8	1 1/8
2 6/8	2
7 7/8	4
2 3/8	5 6/8
4 2/8	2 2/8
	3 1/8
1 2/8	

Totals	57 7/8	45 7/8
To E	103 6/8	

DETAIL OF POINT MEASUREMENT

SEE OTHER SIDE FOR INSTRUCTIONS	Supplementary Data		Column 1	Column 2	Column 3	Column 4
	R.	L.	Spread Credit	Right Antler	Left Antler	Difference
A. Number of Points on Each Antler	18	15				
B. Tip to Tip Spread	19 2/8					
C. Greatest Spread	40 2/8					
Inside Spread D. of MAIN BEAMS	22 1/8	Spread credit may equal but not exceed length of longer antler	22 1/8			
IF Inside Spread of Main Beams exceeds longer antler length, enter difference						
E. Total of Lengths of all Abnormal Points	103 6/8					
F. Length of Main Beam				22 5/8	21 3/8	1 2/8
G-1. Length of First Point, if present				3	3	
G-2. Length of Second Point				14 7/8	15 2/8	3/8
G-3. Length of Third Point, if present				10 5/8	11 7/8	1 2/8
G-4. Length of Fourth Point, if present				10	9 2/8	6/8
Circumference at Smallest Place H-1. Between Burr and First Point				4 6/8	5 1/8	3/8
Circumference at Smallest Place H-2. Between First and Second Points				5 1/8	4 7/8	2/8
Circumference at Smallest Place H-3. Between Main Beam and Third Point				5 3/8	4 6/8	5/8
Circumference at Smallest Place H-4. Between Second and Fourth Points				5	4 6/8	2/8
TOTALS	103 6/8		22 1/8	81 3/8	80 2/8	5 1/8

ADD	Column 1	22 1/8	Exact locality where killed North Kaibab, Arizona
	Column 2	81 3/8	Date killed 11-23-69 By whom killed Robert C. Rantz
	Column 3	80 2/8	Present owner Robert Rantz
Total		183 6/8	Address Box 547, Williams, Arizona 86046
Subtract Column 4		5 1/8	Guide's Name and Address none
Result		178 5/8	Remarks: (Mention any abnormalities)
Add Line E Total		103 6/8	
FINAL SCORE		282 3/8	

I certify that I have measured the above trophy on   *March 1*   19 *71*
at (address)   *Carnegie Museum*   City   *Pittsburgh*   State   *Pa.*
and that these measurements and data are, to the best of my knowledge and belief, made in accordance with the instructions given.

Witness: *G. T. Church, Jr.*   Signature: *O. Uggen*

Boone and Crockett Official Measurer

One Carbon County buck was particularly elusive for hunters in our party a few years ago. It hid in a sage gully, then ran into the face of drivers, as they emerged from the forest edge. By then they had relaxed their guard, and not one rifle was ready! The incident isn't so strange when you realize the buck had been "pushed" repeatedly while in those trees. He eluded them by *departing* the cover. A bag of tricks like that may even cause a buck to die of old age. I also witnessed one great buck in Duchesne County jump from the view of a dozen onlookers to seemingly vanish into nothingness. He was located an hour later flattened against barren ground when someone happened to look closely in his direction. Even then, that high-tined four-pointer did not get up until I had walked within nine paces of him, looking him squarely in the eyes. Yes, big bucks are still there, but many have developed elusive powers that would rival Houdini. I've also witnessed elk remain hidden in stumps and fallen timber when a large hunting drive moved through a few yards away.

Off-season scouting — Most Utah game can be readily scouted in the winter. Get out and see what the hunters missed. It can amaze you. Elk will usually be a little higher than the deer, having longer legs to locate browse. Moose may not move downhill far, but they will likely be at their lowest elevations of the year in winter. Antelope bunch up and can often be spotted near roads during "scouting season." Watch game closely to determine feeding and watering routines as well as bedding and other habits. Where they go when spooked is extremely important. Watch for trails leading to bedding areas in particular. When scouting, a hunter not only learns how to see deer, an ear, leg, antler tip *et al*, but how to approach that animal. Approaching from the top down is almost always best, not only because of greater visibility, but because game expects danger from below and is more alert to sounds or scents from from that direction. Nearly every Utah buck I have ever witnessed looked up from feed or water to glance *downslope*. Bedded bucks and bulls usually faced *downhill*. The one exception to this is where most access roads are on top, as on Manti Mountain. Watch for deer and elk at the edges of forest cover. Little browse or bitterbrush or cliffrose grows inside a wall of timber, so watch for deer to move outside of it a body length or so. It is an axiom of Utah deer hunting that muleys will often be on south and west-facing slopes when feeding, but in moisture-retaining and jungled vegetation of north and east-facing slopes when hiding. If you hike into a canyon before daylight, keep track of the direction you are going. Come daylight, watch for the south slopes where game will likely feed.

A note of caution on elk: do your scouting from half a mile away if possible. Elk skitter easily and may not be there when you return. This can be a problem in Utah, for someone else may not be as careful as you . . . and send "your" elk across the county line.

Consider best access routes for your vehicle. Where can you camp without spooking the game? Where will you want to be first thing opening morning . . . and where when the surprise element of opening morning has fled? Where can you pussyfoot silently in the conifers, or check on your knees beneath high-boughed mountain mahogany? Where can you wait for deer to show by watching into the wind? Is there is a knoll where you can sit and glass dawn and dusk?

Another important thing with all game is to look for expansion room — is there ample winter range here for the animals? Foothills filled with cabins and people almost always mean fewer game animals than where they can forage for food. Good winter range usually means getting away from *Homo sapiens*, particularly his permanent abodes. Look for lonely foothills.

Scouting for the specific game you'll seek during the upcoming hunt will almost always pay off. I spent several days in September of 1989 scouting for antelope and saw none on west Parker Mountain in my first attempt. Later, Leon Bogedahl, Wayne County conservation officer in Torrey, explained the problem: a drought had moved pronghorns from the sage flats to an area of more rainfall near Boulder Mountain. Such things need to be known before the hunt begins.

Trophy buck chasing away a smaller rival during the December rut.

FIRST AID FOR BIG GAME

Sadly, some "successful" big game hunters learn to their dismay each year that they were unsuccessful in one place which will hurt for decades to come: they failed to properly skin and cape their animal for mounting.

According to veteran big game taxidermist Merlin Anderson, Sandy, the one major area of greatest concern is in leaving "enough" front shoulders when caping out head and neck. Some nimrods stop at the lower end of the neck, cut the skin there, and return with too little cape for the taxidermist to display the front shoulder. With it included, the mount will be much more for anyone to brag about on the den wall for years to come. Another problem is cutting the neck underneath, where it will be readily seen from below. **SO, HERE IS WHAT YOU DO:** Bring in the entire animal after cleaning, to the taxidermist. If you cannot for any reason, then make a cut down the BACK (not underside) of neck, beginning from top of head. Cut to the top of the shoulders, then BEHIND (not on neck side) of front shoulders. Allow plenty of cape for the taxidermist to work with. Do not attempt to make all the cuts around ears, eyes, nose etc. unless you are an expert at it. Do not cut underside of neck! Bring the entire head to taxidermist. Be certain to apply salt (ordinary table salt is fine) HEAVILY inside and outside, on every part of the skin. Salt will drive moisture away, preserve skin from spoilage.

For a list of other qualified taxidermists in your area, contact your local fish-game department, or a guide-outfitter.

Other hints for care of animal: If weather is warm, as during antelope, archery deer seasons, etc., you will have to get animal to locker in hurry. If you cannot, prop open, cool in stream, snow, and hang for maximum air circulation. Wrap in buck bags, or sheet to keep flies away. Leave hide on, unless you can bag meat and keep it away from dirt.

BEST MULE DEER RANGE

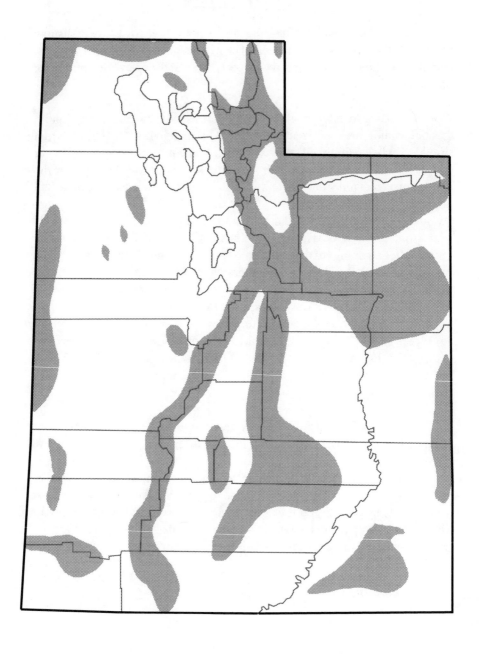

CHAPTER ELEVEN

Best Bets for Big Bucks

Secret deer hunting hot spots change from year to year, since oversized bucks seek out forgotten niches. But there are some places which consistently produce large racks. Many times this is due to limestone in the soil which is absorbed by plants eaten by mule deer. Another factor is a superior gene pool in any given region. Other factors, more variable, depend on abundance of food and water from season to season. A deer will use limited calories first to sustain life and only after survival needs are satisfied will antler growth flourish.

Thus, if a tough winter didn't kill a buck outright — estimates soared as high as a 60 per cent mule deer kill in many areas of the West due to heavy snows of the mid 1980s — lack of suitable nutrition may well curtail antler development. A drought might also stifle antler growth. Therefore, finding big bucks often depends on finding good conditions repeated several years in a row. Search for hunting grounds with adequate winter range nearby.

Let's take a close look at Utah's best big-buck regions over the years and analyze your chances of scoring in each. Little credence will be given to published "deer hunting success maps." They can lead to false conclusions. A high success rate (50 percent or above) on the Vernon unit in Tooele County doesn't mean much unless you applied early for a permit. This was limited entry and while many of the permittees did score, success was usually for locals who know the region very well. Another misguided notion might be that one should hunt anywhere in Box Elder County (the entire county is listed at 50 percent success or above); but in reality, the best bucks hail from a few small mountain ranges within the county.

From year to year some units have limited entry or differing seasons, and may be "trophy only" or at least three points per side. With that in mind, here are the author's carefully selected best bets for big bucks in the 1990s. The areas are listed alphabetically:

ABAJO (BLUE) MOUNTAINS — Whether called by the Spanish or English name this range in San Juan County looms as a bluish haze in the distance. It contains some of the state's least-pressured big deer units and traditionally produces large bucks. In the early 1990s it is probably the hottest deer unit in Utah — if you have a permit for it. In future years, however, it may be open for general license. Location is west of Monticello and Blanding and east of the Dark Canyon Wilderness Area. Deer have plenty of room to spread out between 11,360-foot high Abajo Peak and the surrounding rabbitbrush valley floor. Incidentally, places like Bears Ears and Elk Ridge in this country are wilder than they appear from U.S. 191. Dirt roads lace the southwestern sector, within the Manti-LaSal National Forest. One county road accesses directly from Blanding onto the eastern slopes.

Stop at a Blanding or Monticello service station and admire the display of muley racks, then ask the locality where they were found. Some are from the foothill cedars. Many are in steep ravine oak brush, as well as higher aspen and conifer. This is big country where a guide, a friend, some extra time, scouting ahead, and all other preparations are advised.

BEAVER MOUNTAIN — Once proudly boasting the "world's largest mule deer herd," locals will tell you that the one-time Happy Hunting Grounds have fallen on harder times. The region's fame invited heavy hunting and pretty much thinned out the easy roadside muley racks. But considerable picturesque aspen-conifer-meadow habitat remains for both deer and elk.

A few decades ago, wildlife photographer Jim Bond of Portland, gained fame by filming 400 bucks one August evening at Big Meadow in Beaver Canyon. East to Junction and north to the 12,000-foot peaks at Belknap and Delano in the Tushar Mountains, or south to Dog Valley, this country has produced many records , as attested by Robert Warren's *Utah's Biggest Bucks.*

Hunters should also be aware of deer migrations from the North Beaver's Tushar Range. By radio-marking deer, game biologist Don Beale has documented that both heavy snow and summer drought can push bucks far downslope toward the Bald Hills and Escalante Desert west of I-15. So, in a tough autumn, look for deer moving westward off the higher country.

Regional conservation officer Brent Farnsworth says he still sees many big bucks on his daily Beaver area rounds. "But I get a glimpse of them only at the earliest and latest light, usually near heavy cover. Rarely more than a leg or antler tip is plainly visible at first." This thickly-vegetated terrain is not to be hunted in a hurry. Those who search diligently can return with a 30-35 inch wide rack. Many of the best hunting possibilities require horse or backpack.

BOX ELDER COUNTY — There are many small ranges with good deer on them in this county, even though little of it is classical pine-aspen terrain. The finger ridges north of Great Salt Lake are not impressive — sage, cedar, a little oakbrush. But nearly every year nice racks are taken by the patient and persistent. Several monster racks have been bagged here, some of them in the higher sage terraces. There are more deer than humans in western Box Elder County. After the shooting begins, get high enough to locate cover and vegetation. If a drought year, check any water holes. Private ranches shut out some public hunters, with more "No Trespassing" signs possible in the future; but check the Promontory Range southwest of Corinne, Hansel Mountains northeast of Corinne, the Grouse Creek Mountains near the Nevada border. The Raft River Mountains on the Sawtooth National Forest, are reached west of Strevell, Idaho, then back into Utah via Clear Creek Canyon. The only communities in northwest Box Elder County are Park Valley south of the Raft River Mountains and Grouse Creek or Etna near the Grouse Creek Range.

Time and four-wheel drive, plus good optics, such as a 30-power spotting scope, are helpful. Take a rifle sighted in at maximum distances. This is no place to be without extra gasoline, water, food. Northwestern Utah is for those who like lonely and expansive terrain.

BOOK CLIFFS — This is one of my favorite deer regions because there is sufficient room that one orange-vester may never see another. With ridges simulating a book with the pages turned up, the Book Cliffs run from the Colorado border to the Ute Indian Reservation near the Green River and from Ouray in Uintah County to I-70 in Grand County. The best access from the north is via Ouray turning south about five miles east of Roosevelt, then through Ft. Duchesne and Randlett. From the south, stay on I-70 almost to the Colorado border, then turn north onto the Hay Canyon (gravel and dirt) road. Once on top of the plateau, you can head west or north into deer country. South of Steer Ridge, you can explore along the roadless Diamond Ridge region to East Willow and She Canyons, as wild as terrain gets in the Lower 48. You can also find rugged terrain, intertwined with ridgeline roads, southeasterly to McCook Ridge. If winter and snow have already struck with any force, this middle elevation cedar country will have deer almost everywhere. It has harbored some of the largest bucks I've seen in 35 years of deer hunting .

One four-wheel drive road climbs to the top of Sego Canyon. If you can't get up Hay Canyon, East Canyon not far away provides a more gentle route to the top of the plateau. The latter accommodates trucks serving oil wells. From these few roads, of course, it's horse or hike.

This expansive terrain courses nearly 100 miles by dirt road from Ouray to I-70 so you better come prepared. Paving the road between is now in the discussion stage, and although proponents argue that it would help Uintah Basin tourism, it would almost certainly make access to wildlife too easy. Improvement of roads for oil well services means good deer hunting for a time before the resource is harmed with the added hunting pressures.

It is true that deer numbers and giant bucks are not there in the same profusion as a few decades ago. Yet, to confirm that a few remain, scrutinize the Vernal Express one week after deer season. Big Buck Contests every year still show outsized four-pointers and/or non-typicals.

But back to the roadless Diamond Ridge country. Frankly, this is so ruggedly remote, with vast grassy meadows, that it is better for elk than deer. But of 27 deer I once saw here with Layton's Gary Egbert in a four-day, 40-mile horseback ride, 14 were mature four-pointers. All were in middle elevation oak brush, even though there is plenty of aspen and conifer on the higher ridges dividing South and North Book Cliffs. We saw elk at the higher elevations, deer in the oak. Egbert took a friend back to bag two respectable four-pointers in the oak.

I returned the last few days of that deer season and again the following year to find a startling thing: no muleys even in the oak. One 10-mile trek the length of Diamond Ridge didn't turn up a single track. I have since discovered that even with little snow in the higher Book Cliffs, extremely cold temperatures trigger a sudden and often early migration. Frozen water often pushes deer below the oak to the sage and cedar arroyos even in mid-October. Many good bucks head for 6500 to 7000 foot elevations. That would put them on middle Willow Creek, and on McCook Ridge. This is one of the longest and most unusual deer migrations in Utah. South of the highest divide, bucks often move down Nash, Cottonwood, Sego and Thompson Canyons.

Along the border northward to Bonanza, hunters will find more antelope than deer in the dry washes of Bitter Creek; but a tough winter could put deer there. Traditionally, there are many does wintering along the almost barren upper sand hills. I've seen wandering bands of elk in the cedars, too, so deer permittees have to be certain of their target at all times.

Keep a map handy along the Ute Indian boundary. There are bucks here, in pinion pine mesa terrain; but once over the boundary, only Indians are allowed to hunt. An adventurous sort can also raft down Desolation Canyon's white water rapids, then float through. Public land is on the right bank of the Green River, Ute territory on the left. The best hunting is found when heavy snow on the top of the nearby West Tavaputs Plateau (much of it on private property) pushes deer off the top into canyons entering the Green's west banks.

BOULDER MOUNTAIN — Some of the state's best deer hunting is found here, yet it is possible to see no shootable game for days by being in the wrong place. There are many miles of conifer forests interspersed with volcanic rock over the upper Boulder which has little feed and poor hunting. The deer are not found right on the table-like top, but on the arroyo edges and down into the aspen, oak and cedar. If you have a Boulder "high country" deer permit (hunt is usually in September since access is often impossible in October) check the plateau's perimeter.

The hot spots are in the south slope's aspen belts, in and along the Pleasant Creek, Oak Creek and Chokecherry drainages, plus others which drop off to the Escalante River country. If you look at the mountain from the community of Boulder, you see a moderately high quakie belt more than a dozen miles long. Utah 12 skirts the eastern edge of this terrain, with entrance trails to Pleasant, Oak and Chokecherry drainages. In most cases, terrain is steep and a back pack or horse is the best way in. Get high without spooking game, and glass carefully. Check for an elongated horizontal shape against the vertical tree trunks. The deer are there, so don't be in a hurry. Deer have a love affair with aspens, not only feeling secure there, but eating bark and wet leaves. Yet, of all cover deer enter, aspens are the easiest to locate them in. Aspen hunting is also possible on the Boulder's far northeast corner along **Parker Mountain**, best reached from the Bicknell area. This sector of Parker Mountain also has many antelope.

Much good deer country is also found below Utah 12 in the Boulder foothills which drop off southeasterly into the Escalante drainage. In a tough winter, these sprawling buttes and mesas might hide any number of deer. Descent is steep, so be sure you can get back up before going in. Horses would be needed to get deer out. There are several view points along Utah 12 north of Boulder where you can size up the trek in and find open ridgeline access.

Another excellent place to locate deer is above the Fremont River on the northwest slopes of the Boulder. Some of these bucks forage Wayne County haystacks by night, retiring to cedar and oak by day. Vegetation is thick on the mountain, but quietly check the ridgelines that are within rifle range. About two-thirds of the way up, at about 8500 feet, is a productive zone, except in tough winters when deer may go lower. An excellent technique is to gain altitude *without spooking* game, then hunt below you with maximum visibility. In good weather, take a four-wheel drive to the rim, then work off the top, possibly to be picked up at a roaded point below. There are roads over most of the Boulder save for the steepest slopes. At Hells Backbone above Escalante, roads even traverse some of the steepest slopes. Get contour maps, including "Blind Lake" from the Dixie National Forest or U.S. Geological Survey. The Boulder is not far removed from civilization as compared to the Abajo and Deep Creek Mountains, and several sizeable communities nearby offer a wide range of hunter services. While on the plateau, be prepared for cold weather, and with the first storms, wind-drifted snow.

The southern edge of Boulder Mountain extends to **Escalante Mountain** where some of the best deer populations are again found in limited aspen terrain. Little trampled highlands northeast of Widstoe Junction offer deer via horseback or pack. This is well away from the Wasatch Front, and access roads are limited in tough and steep terrain, offering many places for outsized bucks to die of old age. The western ridges all the way to Antimony and the Aquarius Plateau have produced good muley hunting. It is almost impossible to drive at night near Antimony without seeing deer. Small bucks abound in the sage draws east and west of the Otter Creek drainage north of Antimony.

Many archers and rifle-toters find go-home-happy bucks in the **Mt. Dutton** area. Access is by the road looping from Antimony toward Dutton and ending north of Widstoe Junction. Although most publicized for its elk populations, the mountain is a "sleeper" for deer hunters. Big bucks there receive far less pressure than those in central or northern Utah.

CACHE-RICH — These counties abutting Idaho have pockets of good deer hunting away from roads. Deer and elk are there, as demonstrated any December day when game inundates local orchards and haystubble fields. Access routes include the Ant Flats road in upper Blacksmith into Temple Fork above Logan; the Left Hand Fork of Blacksmith Canyon; the road from Hardware Ranch north to Rich County. I have found a poor buck-to-doe ratio in this region, especially near Randolph, but some good bucks are there for the energetic in higher and rougher terrain. Many of the highest ridges receive little hunting traffic until late in the season.

The Wellsville Mountains southwest of Logan are especially precipitous. On the east side of this mountain, above Honeyville, the number two world mule deer non-typical was taken in 1949. Its numerous tines may never be topped. Bucks that big are not taken there now, but all of the Cache roadless terrain have periodically produced respectable racks. USFS offices in Logan can provide maps. Few forests have more developed campground possibilities than in scenic Logan Canyon. Some backroads, camping space and good deer country can be found around the Beaver Mountain Ski Resort, up the upper Logan right to the Idaho border.

From the upper Blacksmith Fork, across Ant Flats and into the eastward Monte Cristo region, aspen hunting for deer and elk draws many orange-vesters. Success can depend on how far you get off the roads. This is also true in the upper Ogden River drainage, which has rich populations of elk and moose. The problem here is that private property juts fairly frequently into the forestlands all the way to Deseret Livestock's vast private holdings. Locked gates will block some canyons east of Pineview Reservoir. One way to reach public lands on the upper Blacksmith is to take Utah 39 to the Monte Cristo highlands, then take a four-wheel drive or good truck north. A road continues to the slopes northward overlooking Bear Lake. Most of this terrain is not high, but it is often steep and rough. Flying over the area in the off-season, I've looked at deer in the little side canyon breaks, some with conifers on north slope pockets. You can also find such habitat and deer on the east side of Monte Cristo in the drainages heading for Woodruff in Rich County. But again, private property limits access. Some hunters have taken good bucks by riding the sage foothills of Rich County. Sage-searching is usually most productive after hunting camps show up in the higher terrain.

CIRCLEVILLE-MARYSVALE AREA — This is the east or "back" side of Beaver Mountain. Away from I-15 and easy access, it is not hunted as heavily as the west slope. The potential for big bucks is as good here as any place in the Beehive State for the rugged and serious hunter. Horses are advisable due to distances involved, and to get through thick brush. Obviously, the wise hunter will dismount where possible to check for hidden deer. You can see some foothill roads from U.S. 89, but heavy snow can block them. Basic hunting supplies can be obtained in Circleville and Marysvale. Use Fishlake forest maps.

DEEP CREEK MOUNTAINS — This snow-crowned range rising abruptly from the desert floor in western Tooele and Juab counties is one of the state's best kept secrets, not only for hunting but for the general tourist seeking natural scenery. Haystack and Ibapah peaks tower above 12,000 feet, some 7000 feet above valley communities like Callao, Partoun and Trout Creek. Even Mt. Nebo, the highest peak in the Wasatch Range, does not jut up as high. If you have time for these massive mountains, you will have a wilderness deer hunting experience of the highest order. Come prepared. The nearest supply points, if you run out, are at Vernon, Delta, Wendover, all some 75 miles away. The same is true of vehicle repair, tires, ammo, gasoline.

The only realistic access into these steep granite and spruce-studded ridges is via horse pack. A truly hardy backpacker might succeed if not hurried. For those entering from the Goshute Indian Reservation on the southwest, a "trespass fee" would be required. Around the Deep Creeks, a visitor will find self-reliant people. I've always enjoyed stopping and talking to them. Many are willing to help you locate the few foothill access roads.

At one time, this unit was designated trophy-only (three points on one side or better) but was open to the general public for regular license in 1989. Best deer hunting is often found where upper ridgelines connect, especially in aspen, oak or cedar. Looking at it from the air, I have seen little game in the conifers. Deer have remained with the browse or brushy vegetation, often on south slopes. This is one of the few regions in Utah with little annual hunting pressure. Bucks are far less skittish than those say, on the Wasatch Front. The unroaded Deep Creeks are a place which can reward the nimrod willing to put a little extra effort into his quest for a trophy.

Nice bucks are found in the rugged Book Cliffs. These enterprising hunters rafted down the Green River.

DIAMOND MOUNTAIN — Not really a single mountain, this undulating country in northeastern Uintah County is actually a series of plateaus and ridges rarely exceeding 9000 feet elevation. Named after a diamond hoax in which raw and even polished diamonds were "salted" to attract investors, visitors now prospect for wildlife and scenery. Aspens on the western slopes along with pinion-pine and juniper are near the southeastern boundary of Dinosaur National Monument. There are many well-marked roads from U.S. 40 to the Green River. Four-wheel drive is the safest way to go. Local hunters seem to do well in this country, but visitors can get lost in a maze of back roads. Bucks are often seen in the tops of breaks and draws heading down to the Green River. Pockets of high aspen groves may also have deer. Every year, the Big Buck contests in Vernal feature admirable racks from Diamond Mountain.

DUCHESNE-CARBON COUNTRY — There is much deer terrain in both counties, especially in the Ashley National Forest south of U.S. 40. Much deer habitat north of the highway is on the Ute Reservation until one reaches the forest line. But I like the rolling aspen and pine forests from the Wild Strawberry River canyon south of Fruitland to the Sheep Creek and White River drainages. The region has good access roads in dry weather, albeit with a fair amount of opening day deer hunter traffic. Some good bucks have come from the many spur ridges east and west of U.S. 191, which links Duchesne with Helper, particularly along the divide separating the two counties. Although a car or van could negotiate off-ridgeline dirt roads for a few miles, mud means four-wheel drive. One such route branches off U.S. 191 near the divide, then runs westward down a 20-mile ridge to roads in Timber and White Canyons. I've spotted bucks here in the sage and boulder-strewn foothills, well away from both roads and timbered or "conventional" deer habitat. You'll likely have to hike down into steep canyons. The lower west end is more gently undulating, but still holds deer.

"Gabby" Hayes, an old rancher along the upper Wild Strawberry River used to boast that around Timber Canyon bucks were so so big "they couldn't get their antlers through the aspens." Hunting pressure has increased considerably since Gabby's day, so get off the main trails. There are some private ranches and Ute lands near Avintaquin and lower Currant Creek.

In the Tabiona-Hanna area along the Duchesne River, Red Creek, Tabby Mountain and the cedar forests eastward, good bucks are taken nearly every year. The expansive juniper terrain south of U.S. 40 has deer, but they are difficult to locate in the thick cover. One day, I watched a thickly-tined four-pointer moseying along an open grain field near the mouth of Rock Canyon, just off the Ute Reservation. But it seemed to know the hunting season was still a few days away.

Excellent deer hunting is found at the top of Minnie Maud, Argyle and Nine-Mile Canyons, although there is some private property. A hunter can find public lands by heading northeasterly out of Wellington. From Wellington to Myton, there is no better mule deer habitat anywhere in the world, although private property prevails on much of the West Tavaputs Plateau. If you head northward out of East Carbon, you will encounter the large and private Wilcox Ranch.

FILLMORE-RICHFIELD REGION — The mountains above these communities, including Robbins Valley country northeast of Holden (access is from Scipio off U.S. 50) have always produced some of Utah's best deer hunting. The canyons normally require four-wheel drive vehicles after first snowstorms. Terrain is aspen and conifer on the Fishlake forest. One good access road leads up Kanosh's Corn Creek Canyon over deer terrain to I-70. On the Richfield side of this range, some oak and mountain mahogany canyons hold rich feed and excellent muley populations. A friend, Rich LaRocco of Wellsville, has frequently led archery cronies to good bucks west of Richfield. A good buck-to-doe ratio of about one-in-three prevails in some canyons, while the rest of the state is probably one to 30-40. In the Cove Fort area, thick vegetation often harbors nice bucks in the cedars and mountain mahogany. One reason this region will always have good deer populations is poor visibility requiring a careful approach.

FISHLAKE FOREST — This region covers everything from Salina Canyon in Sevier County to Fish Lake and eastward to Thousand Lake Mountain. Some hunters swear by Salina Canyon, saying they would hunt deer nowhere else in the world. The terrain changes rapidly from oak and cedar above Salina to forest and meadow near Seven Mile drainage southward to Johnson Reservoir and Fish Lake. Thick conifer forests south of Mt. Hilgard and Mt. Terrel often have more elk than deer. Work the aspen slopes for best bucks. On one scouting expedition, I saw five high-tined bucks traveling together in lower aspen slopes near Sheep Valley. There is some private property in here, so check the Fishlake National Forest map.

Many California nimrods like the Mytoge Mountain ravines; access is from the pavement south of Fish Lake. Small bucks abound in the upper Fremont River drainage westward into Wayne County. This region's high country includes Last Chance, Boobe Hole and some other interestingly-named deer units between Fremont Junction and Bicknell. The heavy population of deer along Utah 72 in this region has resulted in many deer-vehicle collisions. In fact, paving was not considered prudent unless extensive signs warning of deer and elk were added. In deep snow a major migration may occur out of the higher Fishlake forest into these lower canyons. The vegetation is mountain mahogany, cedar and north slope aspen patches in the shaded ravines.

HENRY MOUNTAINS — These remote mountains appeared on no map until after Major John W. Powell reported them on his second expedition down the Colorado River in 1871. The Henrys remain something of a mystery to most Utahns, although hunters ply the volcanic slopes increasingly every year. On my first expedition to the Henrys, three veteran "deer lookers" saw only three deer from the road which cuts across the middle of this 11,500-foot high range. Later, I found good bucks to the north and south, particularly on Mt. Pennell. These deer will often be found high for the August archery season, then they migrate into the lower pinion and juniper come October's rifle hunt. Access is limited to truck or four-wheel drive, with much hiking or horsepacking necessary. Prepare well in this rugged country Butch Cassidy loved so much. You're on your own south of Hanksville. Utah 276 will access the southern Henrys. This range was closed for a time because of drought, poor feed and dwindling deer populations. The deer are now coming back and some big bucks abound in the remote ridges and ravines.

LASAL MOUNTAINS — Rising to over 12,000 feet in San Juan and Grand counties, snowy peaks here appear in sharp contrast to crimson-hued Canyonlands and Arches National Parks westward. South slope access is via LaSal Junction in San Juan County. Or from Moab, take Utah 128 north along the Colorado River, then turn south on the LaSal loop road through Castle Valley. The same Colorado River route, requiring a ford (check with hip boots first) across the Dolores River, can take a hunter over to the well-publicized **Dolores Triangle** deer hunting unit. This has excellent deer populations when heavy winter buffets Colorado's nearby high country. The Dolores can also be reached from the upper end, without a ford, out of Glade Park, Colo.

Deer can be found almost anywhere in eastern Grand and San Juan Counties. The LaSal foothills are often a source of good bucks; the higher terrain contains massive snowfields with little cover or vegetation. Monarch bucks have been taken by those willing to negotiate LaSal's steep slopes. One of the best ever was Bill Norton's number 9 world typical listed in the 1973 B-C records. Make a clean camp; this range has one of Utah's larger black bear populations.

MANTI MOUNTAIN — Pronounce it Man-Tie. This is Utah's "bread and butter" deer mountain. It is a 10,400 foot high ridge, flowing continuously for 100 miles from U.S. 6 on the north to I-70 at Salina Canyon, with access roads from a

Skyline Drive on northern Manti Mountain leads to good deer country.

dozen Sanpete and Emery County communities. A high percentage of Utah bucks come off this aspen-conifer-oak terrain. Within the Manti-LaSal National Forest, campgrounds and camping areas are numerous . . . and most will be filled on the eve of the deer opener. Skyline Drive, which runs the length of the ridgeline , is a good road for pickups when dry, but four-wheel drive when wet. Access is:

West slope: Utah 31 from Fairview to Huntington is the only paved road across the mountain and the only one consistently negotiable for passenger cars. It can be icy and slippery by mid-October. Other dirt (mud) roads connect to the mountain from Ephraim, Manti, Sterling (Six Mile Canyon), and Mayfield (Twelve Mile Canyon). Much of the best deer habitat is on the steep slopes facing Sanpete Valley.

East slope: Roads lead from Orangeville to Joe's Valley Reservoir. West from there, the mountain is suddenly steep. I've seen several pickup trucks here which slid down the mountain. I wouldn't push vehicular access in stormy weather. The roadless canyons make the best hunting.

North slope — Access is via Skyline Drive off U.S. 6 just east of Tucker. A rest stop at the Skyline Drive entrance has proven valuable to hunters with trailers and campers. Spur roads depart the main road on top of the mountain. Other access is via Lake Fork to Indianola, Dairy Fork, Starvation Canyon near the Skyline Drive entrance. A paved road (Utah 264) south of Scofield Reservoir up Eccles Canyon connects with Utah 31 on top of the mountain.

South slope — There is only one access on the south, a poor Jeep road to upper Twelve-Mile. Skyline Drive exits through Twelve Mile Canyon westerly to Mayfield, or easterly down the Ferron-Muddy River drainages to Ferron in Emery County.

The Manti top has sparse vegetation, with most camping about one-third mile below the open summit. The deer are usually about two-thirds up the mountain in aspen and conifer. With pressure from the top, the deer have found the middle-to-low oak slopes to their liking. The extreme north and south ends often receive less attention than near the middle sector's many east-west access roads. Landowners in this region know the deer are there, for orchards and hayfields swarm with them every winter and spring. Respectable bucks can be seen at such times above Indianola, Mayfield, Ferron, and almost everywhere around the Manti perimeter. The challenge on the Manti is to get where other nimrods haven't. Some do every year and return with great bucks. I accompanied a big game biologist in a helicopter one December day to look for deer on the Manti after licensees complained of seeing no antlers. We saw 87 bucks on one slope of newly-seeded bitterbrush! We counted nearly a thousand deer on the west slope of the Manti alone. A veteran hunter, O.E. Neuman, Granger, has taken many bragging-sized bucks over the years from the east slope's Trail and Wagonroad Ridges.

All of the communities mentioned are geared to deer hunters and their needs come October. Check with the Manti-LaSal USFS office in Price or other communities for additional information and maps. A tip: when hunting the Manti, check the small openings such as wind-swept ridgelines, powerline cuts, avalanche swaths, stream flood paths, etc. Much of the mountain is canopied in heavy vegetation, but fortunately, deer food is primarily in the openings. Those are the places to watch dawn and dusk. There are many small ravines tucked into these mountains which cannot be viewed from a vehicle. To fully appreciate the Manti, hike slowly away from the roads and search carefully.

MONROE MOUNTAIN — There are people in Sevier County who claim this is deer heaven. The mountain above the community of Monroe cannot be fully appreciated from the valley. You can't drive even a few miles from Koosharem after dark without encountering deer. In the winter it is advisable to drive slowly anywhere from Sigurd to Koosharem Reservoir. About the only road climbing this 11,227-foot high mountain, even for four-wheel drive, leads from the town of Monroe to Koosharem. Most of the terrain is aspen and conifer, with cedar and some oakbrush. A roadless ridgeline to the south provides excellent hunting for the energetic hiker. More good hunting can be found east of Marysvale and northeast of Junction.

The deer and elk populations have flourished because so much good hunting is found in all directions. Hunting pressure is dispersed. Feed conditions are also excellent with aspen-bitterbrush-mountain mahogany in abundance. The area is sometimes "trophy only," or three-pointers and better. Elk are on the increase here; be certain of your target.

NEBO COUNTRY — While dominated by nearly 12,000-foot high Mt. Nebo, there is much more to the Mt. Nebo Wilderness Area than a lofty, precipitous face. From the instant one enters the Nebo presence in the Uinta National Forest between Payson and Nephi, it is difficult to believe that civilization is barely five minutes away. East of the wilderness area is Mt. Loafer, nearly as steep and resplendent as Nebo in the early morning sunlight. To the east of Nebo and south of Loafer, lies an undulating "badlands" of oakbrush creek drainages with excellent deer populations almost all the way down to U.S. 89. Rough, dirt roads provide access up Nebo and Benny Creeks near Birdseye. These canyons offer a different type of hunting than the steep ledges on Nebo and Loafer. Deer are there, but you will need to watch carefully to see them in the brush. Horses are helpful in cutting through cover. Stop on knolls and higher terrain to search below. Be alert for elk in upper Nebo and Benny creeks.

Drew Dockstader, Payson, says he used to take many hefty bucks off the steep west side of Nebo. "It's tougher now, but big bucks still abide there. The savvy hunter should look in the pockets not visible from roads."

The paved Nebo Loop road connects Payson Canyon on the north with Utah 132 in Salt Creek Canyon east of Nephi. A good dirt road climbs Santaquin Canyon from the northwest to join the loop road. These roads are steep and can be slippery when wet or icy. No roads climb the precipitous west face of Nebo. You can reach it by hiking west from the designated pulloff at the summit of the loop road. Roads on the west side do not penetrate farther than the foothills. Cedar canyons on the south slope are likely to harbor deer all the way to the aspens in Gardner Canyon, but there is no vehicle access there.

Hunting the west Nebo face can pay off. A nimrod in the community of Mona, below Nebo, one day trained his spotting scope on the steep ledges and located a mammoth buck. He nailed the trophy later that day. Dockstader says it is an old trick for oversized Nebo bucks to hide out on the face because it looks steeply formidable to hunters. "But sometimes that's where you have to go to outwit the big ones." The face has many hidden terraces and ledges with feed.

I've personally seen several mosshorn bucks in Santaquin Canyon on both sides of the road. It is steep here, almost too steep for a horse, but you would need that or a good pair of lungs and legs to get up the higher ridges. Clearly, this is not a mountain for the faint of heart. Dress warmly. Early storms seem to delight in buffeting Mt. Nebo.

PARAGONAH-PAROWAN-PANGUITCH — The hunting season reaches a fever pitch in these communities every autumn. One good reason is the Dixie National Forest's excellent deer hunting opportunities between the three communities. Out of Paragonah, it's likely to be oak and sage. Higher slopes toward Parowan mean aspens, then spruce and fir. Some of the best hunting, however, is not necessarily in the "classical" upper conifers, but in the oak at about 7500-8000 feet. A local hunter, Val Robb and his family have taken many giant muley racks from Red Canyon to the edge of Cedar Breaks National Monument. In Panguitch, nearly every teen-ager will show off respectable bucks by the end of October, often taken in the hills above town. Much of the best hunting can be reached via Utah

143 from Cedar Breaks to Panguitch Lake. This region also includes Cedar Mountain above Cedar City where wide racks are taken south of Utah 14 to the slopes plummeting toward Zion National Park. Other access is via dirt road just south of Hatch in Garfield County to the upper Mammoth Creek drainage and over to Utah 14. The Markagaunt Plateau northward has produced some fine bucks over the years. More access can be gained from Utah 20 north of Panguitch. Finding deer in your rifle sights is admittedly not easy in heavy stands of mountain mahogany and oak, but they are there. Visibility is particularly poor in the cedars until you gain a little elevation. A nimrod can see into mountain mahogany, of course, by crawling through, since most boughs are about waist high to a man or higher.

PAUNSAUGUNT PLATEAU — This is loosely applied to everything east of U.S. 89 from the highlands near Bryce Canyon National Park to Kanab. It has more than its share of monster bucks. Anyone attending the 1989 Mule Deer Expo in Salt Lake City would be very quickly convinced. Many of the bucks on display came from the cedar gullies southeast of Alton and Orderville. A friend told me his hunting party only caught glimpses of mossback antlers in the sand and cedar hills, but "they were some of the largest racks we've ever seen anywhere."

There is one complication, a limited entry permit which must be applied for ahead of time. Only 300 permits are allowed. When I scouted this area west of Bryce Canyon with Dr. Jack Nelson in August, 1989, for his permit, we drove into the area off Utah 12 to Tropic Reservoir after dark, seeing five mature four-pointers in the first five miles. Afterward, we witnessed a high buck to doe ratio of about one to two. The next morning in canyons with unusual names like "Left and Right Fork of Blubber," we saw bucks everywhere simply by driving the roads. Nelson returned during the season to drop a nice buck in the same area.

Below the Bryce rim, this country descends quickly from orange cliffs to oak brush and aspen, some of it on private land, down to the community of Alton where the pavement ends. Beyond Alton, dirt roads wind through cedar-studded big buck hinterlands all the way to Cannonville on the east side of Bryce Canyon. Hunters in Alton will tell you there is no better place in America for a deer-hunting enthusiast to be. The slopes northeast of Alton were the setting for an impressive film titled "Awesome Bucks." This video, living up to its name, may someday be commercially marketed.

When heavy snows precipitate deer migrations, hunters find bucks all the way southeasterly from Johnson Wash past the White and Vermilion Cliffs to U.S. 89, near the Utah-Arizona border. Two dirt roads connect from 89 to the Dixie National Forest northward. One for four-wheel drives is is just east of the Paria River wash, the other a good gravel connection about 10 miles east of Kanab. Of hunting in lower terrain, a Kanab hunter says Utahns "would be surprised if they knew how many large muleys autumn in the cedars within sight of U.S. 89. I see them often when driving at night to Lake Powell."

In most years, you can hunt on a general license west of U.S. 89 all the way to Zions. There is some private land here. Most is rolling cedar landscape where deer can and do play hide-and-seek. Every winter, local residents of Orderville and

Glendale learn the deer are there, as bucks and does alike descend on gardens and backyard shrubs. During the hunt, these wise old cedar and rimrock bucks like to bed near a ridgeline, then with one leap, they are out of sight. Before hunting this east Zion country, practice shooting quickly and accurately on the off-season practice range. Also learn how to pussyfoot about in sneakers.

PINE VALLEY — This sector of northern Washington County in Utah's Dixie is a favorite of Californians. The access from south is up the Santa Clara Valley to the Dixie National Forest beyond the communities of Veyo, Central and Pine Valley. From the north, take Utah 18 to the same communities. Some nice bucks have been taken here on the 10,000-foot plus Pine Valley Wilderness Area. The mountainous canyons have more deer habitat than would be supposed from a view from the desert below. Deer checking stations in 1989 showed a healthy 38 percent success rate from this general region. Range conditions and fawn production was up in the late 1980s, a welcome change after drought decimated deer populations earlier in the decade. (The state's average annual hunter success rate usually runs about 30 percent.) Visit sporting goods stores in St. George. They display large racks bagged from the mountains northward.

Southern region wildlife biologist Don Beale, who has been studying mule deer migrations for several years, says deer often move west and north off the Pine Valley Mountains with either drought or heavy snows. "The deer may move as far as western Iron and Washington counties." Beale stresses that deer may migrate when a dry summer kills Gambel oak, serviceberry, mountain mahogany and other feed. "Deer on the Pine Valley Mountains may move to lower cedar canyons westward as far as Beaverdam Wash, Pinto, Enterprise and Newcastle." He concludes that there can be much good deer hunting in western Washington County, depending on where deer are or have migrated. A casual nimrod may well waste time in unproductive terrain. At the same time, an alert hunter will check for tracks and sign.

Harmony Mountain southwest of Cedar City has a high density of deer during the summer, but they move near the Nevada line to spend the winter, Beale says. Much of October's hunting hinges on migrations all across the state. A hunter not finding deer in one place needs to keep moving around.

THOUSAND LAKE MOUNTAIN — Like Boulder Mountain across the Fremont River valley, this high plateau encompasses much good-to-excellent deer habitat from 7500 to around 11,000 feet. Many of the best bucks are near the upper plateau rim and along the heads of ravines which break to the valley below. Watch in the oakbrush, mountain mahogany and aspens. Access is from Utah 72 on the gravel road leading east from the Elkhorn Ranger Station, south of Forsyth Reservoir near the Wayne-Sevier County line. This unit has been restricted entry.

THREE CORNERS-DAGGETT — This unit east of Flaming Gorge Reservoir and north of the Green River has always been prime game country. It is sometimes listed as restricted entry and one nearby sector, Baretop Mountain, was closed in 1989 for deer hunting to encourage establishment of newly-planted

Rocky Mountain sheep. To reach Three Corners, watch for signs in the Clay Basin area as you head for Ewing Canyon north of Browns Park. This is also antelope country on both the Utah and Wyoming side of the state line. This entire region was once a vast wintering grounds for mule deer moving off the Uinta Mountains, perhaps the state's longest muley migration. There are fewer deer here now, with a hunter forced to be both prepared for long distances and few services. A few years ago I saw a high-racked four-pointer in the open sage just east of Dutch John on the road to Flaming Gorge's Lucerne Valley Marina. It was two days before open season, with the buck likely taking up residence in the Green River side canyons after that.

UINTA MOUNTAINS — I've looked at many impressive muley racks in the timberline Uintas, but unless you are ready to invest in a week's looking, the best hunting in these mountains is around the perimeter aspen and pinyon belt. This is primarily below the Uinta Wilderness Area. However, the 100-mile long Uintas are really four distinctly different hunting types. Let's take them one slope at a time.

West slope — This includes the area above Kamas and Oakley in Summit County. There is also much deer habitat above Coalville, but it is mostly private ground and covered under fee hunting. There are only two access points here, Utah 150 above Kamas to Mirror Lake country and the Weber River road above Oakley to Holiday Park. The latter has private land on the north of the road, Wasatch National Forest southward. Several Boone-Crockett bucks have come from the upper Weber, but mostly on the Moffitt Canyon and private sectors. In lower elevations, much of the cover is oakbrush, with heavy conifer forest on top.

Above Smith-Morehouse Reservoir there is considerable aspen on public land, and not so coincidentally, some very respectable bucks. These wily deer have become particularly adept at eluding any normal stalk from the canyon bottom. To score, you often have to get on top and hunt down, requiring a long hike to reach the ridges at about 10,500 feet elevation. The rest of the west slope rises to that height in many areas, with thick cover. Deer may be about anywhere. I have seen some monster bucks above Trial Lake some 25 miles east of Kamas off Utah 150, but rarely in the same place twice. The problem is that the conifer forest has few openings and scattered feed. Archers find deer here on occasion, but by October's rifle season most of these deer are several thousand feet lower. This is a huge chunk of real estate, and horses would be advised. Following heavy snow, foot hiking might work east of Kamas and Marion.

One area southeast of Kamas which has given up good bucks in the past is Riley and nearby canyons from the Woodland road, Utah 35, then hunting to the north. Hunters find deer off Utah 150 east from Samak to upper Beaver Creek drainage, but competition is heavy.

South slope — The Ute Indian lands below the Ashley National Forest Service boundary are not open to non-tribal members. However, any of the canyons such as Rock, Lake Fork, Duchesne etc. have major deer populations on the public lands. A longtime favorite for me has been in the Rock Creek drainage immediately above the reservation. Access is west from Mountain Home on a good paved road leading northwest to Upper Stillwater Dam. Watch for forest service signs at McAfee Basin and northward. Rock Creek has many migrating deer in most years because it has the longest ridgeline on the south slope leading to lower winter range.

Log Hollow above Tabiona, west of Rock Creek Canyon, has healthy deer populations, although the solid wall of conifers makes hunting difficult in places. Try the timber edges near ridgelines. Some high basins also have openings and deer browse. Near the Uinta Wilderness Area, there is not enough time in one deer season to explore it all. But with any luck on the weather, most deer will be out of the highlands to spend October at about 7500-8000 feet.

Another excellent deer hot spot is on the high aspen forests on the west side of Lake Fork Canyon. Just east of Rock Creek Canyon, the map shows names like Pigeon Hollow, Bear Wallow etc. The aspen terrain on the south slope has deer in most years, so take a four-wheel drive and locate access roads. Some very large bucks are taken every year from upper Rock Creek to the Whiterocks River Canyon north of Roosevelt. If in doubt, look for major stands of aspens. After heavy snow storms, deer may be at the edge of foothill cedars, but you'll have to be certain you are off the Ute reservation. Yellowstone Creek drainage, less accessible than the other canyons, should not be overlooked. Access is from Lake Fork Canyon north of Mountain Home.

East slope — This includes much conifer forest along the road to Paradise Park Reservoir, with access from the Whiterocks area, and also north of Vernal off Utah 191 leading to Flaming Gorge. Like the west end, middle altitudes have aspens with good hunting. However, there is much pinyon pine, mountain mahogany, cedar in the remote canyons off Brush Creek and Ashley Creek which have bucks for the patiently meticulous types. It is not easy hunting because visibility is often limited. But big bucks show here on the winter foothills every year, so they are there simply a little higher in October. As with the remainder of the Uintas, deer remain off the beaten trails to fishing lakes, so glass a side canyon from the medium elevation rims. Toward Browne Lake on the high northeast, rugged pine and glacial cirque country take over, but there are also a few lonesome monster bucks.

North slope — This side of the Uintas has heavy Englemann spruce and lodgepole pine cover, with less deer feed than other sectors of the Uintas. Winter feed is extremely difficult to find, with muleys making long migrations, many toward Flaming Gorge. Hunting success can depend on weather and migrations. Resident deer are scattered, with archery questers often seeing as many elk and moose as deer. The best of the north is in oak and aspens, including the West Fork of the Bear River (west of Utah 150) but there is some private land there. The Wasatch forest encompasses the north slope, including Blacks Fork, Henrys Fork, three forks of Beaver Creek and smaller drainages. Buck Pasture on Blacks Fork has a promising name, but deer are scattered here like much of the North Slope.

I've hiked and ridden much of this country without finding many deer. But there is enough country here to hold a few big bucks, if for no other reason than people are seldom seen in any numbers. And the lush greenery, topped with perpetual snows and clear streams makes it a very nice place to be while looking.

WASATCH COUNTY — North of Strawberry Reservoir to Wolf Creek Pass and eastward to Currant Creek lies traditional deer domain. This general area rarely produces giant bucks due to quick access from U.S. 40, but it does seem to have a number of first or second year racks. For that reason, it is enjoyed by many beginners. Better antlers would likely be found north of Utah 35 to the south slope of the Uinta Mountains. Some excellent hunting is still found in Currant Creek Canyon, which puts out an amazing number of bucks each year, although obviously a growing favorite with many Wasatch Front licensees. Yet, all one has to do to verify hunter success is sit at the Daniels Canyon checking station south of Heber City and listen for a few minutes as the story repeats itself.

"Where did you take your buck," the biologist asks.

Hunter: "My usual, 23B."

The number 23B, Currant Creek drainage, shows on the Hunting Proclamation as a unit no larger than many, but it gives up a substantial percentage of the venison for eastern Utah in any given year, whatever the preceding winter or current hunting pressure. Much of it is aspen-dominated, with lower pinion and oak. A local hunter says he gets a very nice buck every year less than a dozen miles up the Currant Creek drainage from U.S. 40. This is scenic, although not particularly rugged or steep hill country with considerable deer browse and wintering range. North of Currant Creek, Wolf Creek Pass, via Utah 35, also yields many nice bucks, although attracting permittees from the Wasatch Front less than two hours away. Hunting can be very good, away from the road, from West Fork of the Duchesne River drainage nearly to Hanna and all the Uinta foothills area northward.

In Daniels Canyon and Center Creek, east of Heber City, hunting pressure has grown rapidly in the last decade with declining success. The same is true north and west of Heber City along the Wasatch Range. Nevertheless, there are a few bucks. There are many public campgrounds in this region on the Uinta National Forest.

CHAPTER TWELVE
By the Cities and Highways

What if you don't have time to hunt back in in the areas recommended in the preceding chapter. Should you give up? Definitely not! Possibilities remain near the major cities and highways in Utah. Some of my "short hunt" favorites are listed below, many within an hour from Wasatch Front cities. We'll look at the ones closest to metropolitan populations first.

WASATCH RANGE ABOVE SALT LAKE CITY — Contest-winning bucks have come from the Wasatch Mountains just east of Salt Lake Valley. Dozens of trophy racks have been taken from Parleys Canyon, Lambs Canyon above it, and from Mill Creek to Big Cottonwood Canyons. The possibility of that occurring nowadays has decreased due to loss of foothill winter range. Deer attempting to survive between the State Capitol Building and Olympus Cove just south of Mill Creek Canyon, find homeowners guarding decorative pfitzers, dogs, vehicles, and in many cases, there is just no place for winter deer to go. Starvation often results.

However, some deer terrain remains in Mill Creek and Big Cottonwood Canyons, and on the south edges. One precaution: A special (free) permit must be obtained to hunt in the canyons east of Salt Lake City. It includes instructions about safety near canyon homes.

One access is to drive 12 miles up Mill Creek Canyon to end of the road. From there, take trails southeast to the divide with Big Cottonwood Canyon. On one occasion there, despite myriad opening day orange-vesters waiting on every knob and overlooking every low saddle, I heard a large animal rustling in the dry leaves. A high-tined three-point buck emerged. He apparently eluded so many rifle-toters by keeping to small arroyos of oakbrush and aspen.

On the north end, Emigration Canyon to East Canyon at the edge of private property, still has some small bucks, even though overall hunting success has declined. Access to it and Wasatch forestland is via Utah 65 to the top of Mountain Dell Canyon. Other hunters head south of Parleys Canyon to Lambs Canyon, but the turf is pretty well trod there nowadays. A better possibility is over the ridge toward Park City and Heber City.

Those who want to see the best bucks from the south sector of the Wasatch each winter should check the foothills above the Holladay Gun Club road on the north flank of Big Cottonwood Canyon. The bucks you see there prove deer hunting is not passe east of Salt Lake City, at least for those energetic souls willing to hike into precipitous terrain. Horses are not allowed on this critical watershed above Salt Lake City.

LONE PEAK — Southeast of Salt Lake City, towering above Draper, is some of the West's best big buck habitat. The 11,400-foot high mountain, steep and rugged, was designated the Lone Peak Wilderness Area, Utah's first. It has no easy access, with motorized vehicles off-limits and no roads allowed. Horses are not allowed on the north end because it drains into a drinking water supply. I've found good bucks about halfway up, where oakbrush and mountain mahogany give way to conifers. I've also seen does and fawns very near the uppermost granite cliffs, so just hiking furiously to the summit is not necessarily the best way to hunt this mountain. Watch the upper oakbrush belt carefully. Peer down from ridgelines into ravines. On the north slopes, oak is often thick and difficult to get through. Remain out of the worst thickets in order to approach quietly, rifle or bow at the ready.

In 1962, on the last day of the season, hunter Glen Furrow hiked into some high basins in Bell's Canyon, on the north side of Lone Peak. In the shadows, he found a thick and high-tined non-typical buck which measured 266 7/8th B-C points. It won a place in the B-C world record books and the Silver Bullet award as the largest mule deer shot anywhere in the world that year. Since then, many license-holders have attempted unsuccessfully to duplicate Furrow's feat. But the Lone Peak area is so rugged and demanding that few comb it completely in any given season. Best access is above Draper or from Dry Creek above Alpine in Utah County. Private land lies between some residential area roads and the mountain south of Little Cottonwood Canyon. Climbing from the precipitous Little Cottonwood Canyon itself is not advised.

WASATCH IN DAVIS COUNTY — Old-timers say the big bucks are harder to come by now, but a few nice ones remain from Bountiful to Weber Canyon. One of the best areas has been Mueller Canyon above Bountiful, and then southward to the top of City Creek Canyon overlooking Salt Lake City. This terrain is steep and heavily-vegetated with oakbrush and chokecherry, with some aspens, and pines in the north slopes. Access is via steep dirt roads, which are slippery when wet, and then energetic hiking. The terrain is rougher than it looks from the valley floor, and grows higher as you proceed east . Go prepared for a full day's challenge. North Canyon and Mueller Park trails are open to motorcycles and ATVs but closed to vehicles over 40 inches wide. Horses are banned from the City Creek and Mountain Dell watersheds.

South of Farmington, above Layton and Kaysville, hunters like Gary Egbert of Layton ride horses, working the ravines on both sides of the divide. "There may not be a large number of deer in this region, but our party has taken respectable bucks in most years," Egbert says.

WASATCH FROM OGDEN TO LOGAN — The Wasatch has yielded some good bucks above Ogden Canyon and Pineview Reservoir. Access from Ogden is via Utah 39, and from the road east of Ben Lomond Peak eastward through the Wasatch to the hamlet of Liberty. This region also has a growing moose herd despite the absence of "classical" meadow-beaver dam habitat. Most Weber County canyons are narrow and deer skittish of any noise from bottomland trails.

North of Liberty, a good road provides access to the Cache Valley towns of Avon and Paradise. Some of the best antlers in Utah come from the Wasatch forestlands southeast of Avon. Few roads are available. It is abrupt terrain, with a horse helpful, but in some places only a person on foot can make it. There is also private property in the general area. Most of the Wasatch face in Weber County has deer, remaining high in warm weather, moving down with snow. With early blizzards, good deer could be fairly low along the entire Wasatch Front. If deer are high, they're in maple, aspens, and conifers on the north slopes. If low, deer are in mountain mahogany, and oakbrush. Try to work ravines and vegetation that others have missed. The easy spots have been worked over on opening day. Spooked bucks then tend to hide in boulders, cliffs ledges, defiles.

WASATCH, SPRINGVILLE TO PLEASANT GROVE — Best hunting in this area is in Hobble Creek Canyon above Springville, both in the Left and Right Hand Fork sectors. The Left Fork main road leads to the ridge above Wallsburg in Wasatch County, with most terrain capable of growing good bucks in the aspen terrain near the top of Daniels Canyon. This can be reached south of Heber City, but better hunting is found on the drainages leading away from U.S. 40.

Not long after taking the road up Left Fork, you'll also see a road leading to the west onto the Wasatch face overlooking Springville. Here, it becomes steep and also dangerous if wet. This route provides an excellent view of Utah Valley, but it isn't for the faint-hearted. In any event, some good racks have come from this sector. I've also seen wide-antlered bucks on the *east* side of Left Fork canyon. Summer cabins prevent access in some areas of the Left Fork, but sooner or later, you'll find Uinta forest right-of-way.

At the top of Right Hand Fork, oakbrush and heavy vegetation make hunting difficult but nice bucks are usually taken every year, especially southward to the top of Maple Mountain. Right-hand fork, a dirt road, very slick when wet, leads east to the top of Diamond Fork and on up to the divide above Strawberry Reservoir.

To see what game Hobble Creek has to offer, check the north side of the canyon mouth come December for nice bucks and scattered elk. Good deer can also be seen at the mouth of Mapleton Canyon just south of Hobble Creek in a tough winter. To find them in autumn, you'll need to get approximately a thousand vertical feet higher. Like Hobble Creek, Mapleton Canyon is fraught with thick brush on the north slopes, with more looking room on the south slopes.

Above Provo the mountains are particularly steep and precipitous, providing little road access. Lower foothills are filling in with homes, and fewer deer are seen than in times past. In Provo Canyon, some bucks may be be found off the scenic loop road past Sundance Retreat on the east side of Mt. Timpanogos over to American Fork Canyon. About the only gentle terrain is in the rolling oak hills from Cascade Springs to Heber Valley or Provo Canyon. The countryside is heavy in oak and aspens, but there are a few good bucks here for the determined.

On the valley face or "front" side of Timpanogos, enough deer spend the winter in orchards and fields to warrant issuance of extra hunting permits, albeit usually for antlerless muleys. The upper foothills have a few bucks below Timp's snowfields on a massive plateau of oak. A horse hunter would do well searching the heads of canyons in the upper oak belt. In deep snow, many bucks would be in the "toe hills" immediately above Pleasant Grove and American Fork.

DIAMOND FORK — This canyon offers excellent one-day hunting possibilities, especially with a hardy hiking effort, or horse, southeast toward the summit overlooking U.S. 6. There are a dozen roadless miles here with big buck possibilities in upper Diamond Fork from the First to Sixth-Water Creek drainages. While fishing that area, I looked at a particularly thick and high-antlered buck, a definite candidate for the Boone-Crockett book's typical rack minimum score.

Access to Diamond Fork is either from the top of Hobble Creek Canyon, or via Spanish Fork Canyon. Watch for the "Diamond Fork" sign on the east side of U.S. 6. Once in Diamond Fork Canyon, several four-wheel drive spur roads lead up canyons north and south, but the wildest and best big buck terrain is to the continuous ridges southeasterly. This region has several campgrounds alongside Diamond Fork Creek on the main road.

A road leads to Strawberry Reservoir from the end of pavement in Diamond Fork Canyon, but it is clay-based and extremely slippery when wet. The Strawberry road does allow a hunter to gain altitude, and then hike out laterally into good deer country on either side of the road. Chains would be vital for even a four-wheel drive in rain or snowstorm. Take a shovel just to be safe. Vegetation goes from oakbrush to pines near the summit. Try to gain enough altitude to allow glassing lower terrain. Sit down and take the scene apart with your binoculars or spotting scope.

For a person with only a few hours to hunt, some bucks are occasionally taken in lower Diamond Fork, out of sight but near the main road. The attraction is old, nearly-hidden alfalfa patches. They are surrounded by Uinta National Forest, so just hunt around the private property.

NEPHI AREA — Mt. Nebo has been spotlighted elsewhere, but south of Nephi (Nee-fie) many medium-elevation mountains hold good populations of deer. A casual visitor to the scattered cedars and hayfields south of Nephi will see deer often. Deer move down from the Uinta National Forest to the mouth of Chicken and Pigeon Creek Canyons east of Levan. To reach this terrain, get off the freeway to Utah 28 just south of Nephi, and watch for roads to the east. Although roads lead uphill almost everywhere, this is rough and twisting terrain, juniper and oakbrush frequently limiting visibility. With opening day shooting, the bucks usually head upward quickly.

Other access from the top can be obtained by driving through Salt Creek Canyon to a dirt road to the south which switchbacks tortuously to Log Canyon and the Moroni Ranger Station. This road takes off Utah 132 about two-thirds of the way from Nephi to Fountain Green, so if you have reached the latter town, you've driven too far. This is a route well known to locals, crowded on weekends during the season. Nonetheless, many small bucks grace camps after opening morning's first light. Best bucks would likely be found in the jumbled red cliffs at the extreme north of these mountains. The cliffs tower above Utah 132 in Salt Creek Canyon, but hunting from the canyon bottom would just drive deer higher. Best bet is to hunt from the top down. Access from the top is via the aforementioned dirt road to Moroni Ranger Station, but turn north once you've reached the summit. Once, flying over the red cliffs on the north end in a fixed-wing aircraft, I saw elk and several oversized bucks. These deer live close enough to man that they possess a magician's bag of escape tricks. The hunter in a hurry will not see them. They tend to hide, often statue-still for many minutes, rather than announce their presence by running. Like much of the Wasatch Mountains, steep terrain almost demands a horse to get a deer out.

OQUIRRH MOUNTAINS — Rising abruptly to the west of Salt Lake Valley are the Oquirrhs. Named by Ute Indians as the "shining mountains," they often appear exactly that from the valley cities, even today. The problem with the Oquirrhs, besides the huge chunk of real estate in the middle owned by the Kennecott Copper Co., is difficult access. There are almost no roads, except the private ones into the old mining town of Bingham Canyon, now part of the "world's largest open pit copper mine." Roads to ghost towns of Ophir and Mercur help a hunter gain altitude on the west slope. Hike the open ridgelines, but keep checking the oak and mountain mahogany, or aspens in upper basins.

The middle and south sectors, especially those canyons draining toward Tooele and Stockton, harbor a few cagey old bucks, along with elk. Some canyons like Rose and Butterfield are privately owned. There is no national forest on the Oquirrhs. Fortunately some of it is BLM.

STANSBURY MOUNTAINS — Westward from the Oquirrhs are the Stansbury Mountains. The east side, offering a lush mountain diversion above Grantsville, is well-trafficked at any time of year. A hunter could hike from road's end in North and South Willow, HIckman or other east side canyons, but the best access is over Johnson's Pass on Utah 199 to the "back side" of the Stansbury Range. Then, take the road through Skull Valley Indian Reservation toward Iosepa. Any canyon road to the east will take you toward the Deseret Peak Wilderness Area, with highest point at 11,030 feet. I've seen many nice four-pointers wintering along the foothill cedars here. During the venison quest, I look for them about two-thirds of the way up in oak, mountain mahogany and almost any sizeable quakie patch. Water is always scarce, so check the small streams or ponds. If driving to the Iosepa area from the north, head out of Salt Lake City toward Wendover on I-80 and then turn off at Rowley Junction, a few miles east of Delle. Note: Iosepa isn't a town anymore, but consists of a single ranch with a nearby, and most unusual cemetery of pioneer settlers from Hawaii. Look for access roads south of Iosepa. Avoid loose, soft sand. Remain on rutted tracks. Take a shovel just in case.

Southward, near Vernon, a hunter with required permit could find small bucks on the Sheeprock Mountains. They tend to gather on the west or "back" side of the mountain after opening day. Vernon is south of Rush Valley on Utah 36. Several mountains in Tooele County, like the Simpson Range, also have worthwhile bucks for those with a little exploration time.

NORTH MANTI — While Manti Mountain is listed in the preceding chapter as a major deer hunting Valhalla for those with sufficient time, there are some possible quick-access quests on the Manti off U.S 6 and U.S. 89, less than an hour south of Provo. One is into Lake Canyon, with good dirt road leaving U.S. 89 a dozen yards south of the Thistle Bridge. Watch closely for this route which winds eventually over to Indianola. Many spikes and fork-horns are taken from here every autumn. Another quick access is up Starvation Canyon from U.S. 6 east of Tucker, and from side roads above Soldier Summit, particularly following heavy snowstorms. In Spanish Fork Canyon, there are some private ranches west of the highway, but hunters hiking nearby public land also find a few muleys.

In Sanpete County, heavy winter snows force deer down to the edges of Spring City and Mt. Pleasant. From aerial surveys here in December, I have looked at monster racks in the cedar foothills which even many locals may not realize are there. Southward, then east of U.S. 89 to Mayfield, longstanding hayfields attract many deer. Some of these alfalfa patches are owned by the UDWR to provide winter range for deer. Of course, repeatedly tough weather could put deer onto foothills anywhere around the massive Manti Mountain.

DELTA-EUREKA — Some two hours south of Provo, deer are found on the Tintic Mountains surrounding the mining town of Eureka, and southward to the Fishlake National Forest. Oak Mountain is a good bet for deer east of Oak City in Millard County. Oak Mountain is an isolated mule deer range which has long been studied by the UDWR game biologists to determine response to hunting pressure, deep snow, drought, almost anything. The mountain has also given up a few worthwhile racks, many of them "street-wise" because of easy access and concentrated hunting pressure. On this popular hunting ground an occasional hunter laments that the deer are "all shot out." Then another survey by veteran biologists indicates Odocoileus was there all the time.

MORGAN COUNTY — If some of Utah's best deer hunting is on Deseret Livestock land in Morgan County, then bits and pieces of that tableland oak and aspen ought to harbor good bucks on neighboring public land. There is little public property available. You will need to chart your hunt carefully to avoid private land, but from this limestone -rich country come some of Utah's largest bucks. Some access onto the Wasatch National Forest is possible north of Devils Slide-Croydon off I-84 by hunting north of Lost Creek Reservoir. As a youngster, I enjoyed some of my first deer hunting here. The bucks were some of the biggest I'll ever see. Those were in Heiner and Hells canyons on the ranch, with cost then at $1 per gun for the season. The price is now many times greater, but a Nimrod with a good map might score here on public land.

More public forestland is available north of Mountain Green, a village which has gained fame as the world headquarters address for the Browning Company and its historical "win-the-West" firearms. With little road access above Mountain Green, take a horse if possible. Other small "swatches" of quality deer hunting might be found near private land west of Randolph in Rich County, north of the Weber River in Summit County, or east of private holdings in Chalk Creek.

BEST ELK RANGE

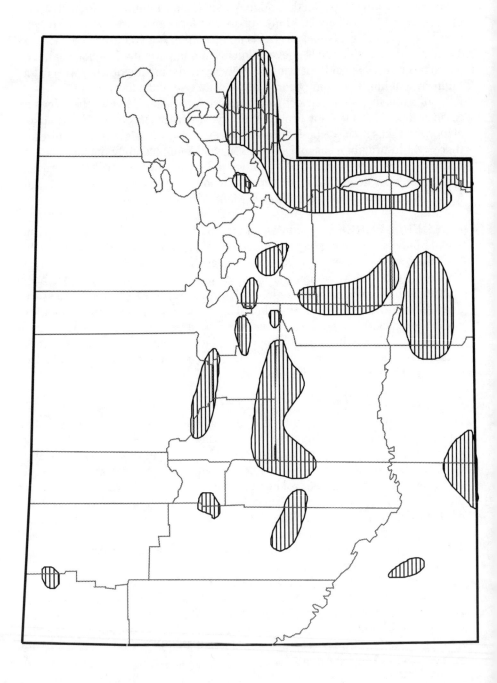

CHAPTER THIRTEEN
The Utah Elk Story

Utah has always been blessed with myriad mule deer. Such is not the case with elk. In the 1800s wapiti were found mostly in the Uinta Mountains with only a few scattered populations elsewhere. Citizens joked that a hunter might as well seek Bigfoot as an elk in Utah. This began to change in 1913 with railroad shipments of Yellowstone elk into Mt. Nebo, Fishlake National Forest, Logan Canyon, the west side of Manti Mountain, the Oquirrh Range, and Mt. Timpanogos. The transplanted elk took hold, to the delight of hunters and wildlife managers. It was 1925 before numbers were deemed as "huntable" east of Logan and on the remote flanks of Nebo. Licenses were issued later on the Fishlake and Manti.

Stocking continued in more Utah back country, including the LaSal Mountains, Mt. Dutton, Book Cliffs and the Ute Indian Reservation, Cedar Mountain, Strawberry-Diamond Fork plateaus, upper Ogden River, Boulder Mountain, and the Wasatch above Salt Lake City. Elk populations began to explode on the grass-rich Cache forestlands. Landowners complained of too many elk, and game managers agreed on a winter feeding refuge at Hardware Ranch in Blacksmith Fork Canyon. Some 500-600 elk are now wintered there. Hardware remained as the state's only elk sanctuary until recently when a benevolent and far-sighted Rocky Mountain Elk Foundation raised money for a second refuge, also in Cache County, east of Richmond.

Things progressed so well that by the 1950s Utahns could draw out for a special elk tag in many regions of the state. However, it was in about 1975 that wonderful things began to happen: transplanted elk spread more rapidly, and natural herds like those in the Uintas maintained a similar pace. Game managers kept elk in line with food-producing capacity of winter rangelands (always the key element in big game management), replaced food-poor cedar and pinyon-pine forests with bitterbrush and crested wheat grass, then introduced the state's first open bull elk season. This meant that any Utahn could now hunt elk just by putting down the money — no more draw. There were critics. They said that such a system would kill off the seed animals and that the UDWR was only interested in grabbing sportsmen's money. But one game manager told me: "It's a natural. As soon as the elk become too populous for the range, hunters will score easily. As soon as they become scarce, hunters can't find them, and so elk will increase again."

It worked out that way, although I have to list one problem. Thousands of rifle-toters scouring the hills began to make it difficult for any hunter to scout, sight and stalk a given bull, since swarming competitors often drove it away. Unfortunately for elk hunters, at least in the long run, much of Utah is well-roaded. Utah's open bull quest near access roads lacks the solitude and one-to-one challenge of a hunt in say, Idaho, Wyoming or British Columbia.

The answer for those seeking quality wapiti hunting is to put your name in a draw for one of the restricted entry units. With the average shooter willing to go for open bull in order to skip application fuss, the possibility of drawing out for a limited entry unit has been enhanced. A hunter who does not see his name on the computerized lottery list can still go for the regular hunts. But if I were to compete in the popular open bull jousts, I would avoid the easily accessible areas.

The tolerant mule deer may prefer familiarity with home range, but elk are different. That was a lesson I learned when scouting 13 nice bulls in a Fishlake National Forest meadow, then finding tents pitched in that very spot come opening morning. The elk, of course, were nowhere to be found in that entire drainage. With a wapiti's intolerance for people, all were probably in the next county before the first tent stake was pounded in on that Fishlake meadow.

Elk spread from existing populations to nearly every corner of Utah. Herds from Nebo explored out into Loafer, the Hobble Creek area, south of Nephi to the oak and cedar forests. It should be noted that while "classical" elk terrain is pictured as a green meadow rimmed with pines, Utah's elk have proven otherwise. They have adapted to pockets anywhere without permanent human habitation, even the backyard orchards of Utah County. On the other hand, those "nuisance" elk wintering in Mapleton and Spanish Fork lowlands just might be there because of the usurpation of natural winter feeding grounds on Elk Ridge between Loafer and Nebo, an area now ensconced with homeowners who have a magnificent front room view of Utah Valley. But Elk Ridge is only one of many winter ranges where elk have encountered people.

Human habitations have also taken over the Wasatch foothills east of Salt Lake City, greatly reducing elk numbers there. But, in regions where civilization is more sparse, elk have taken to many places where they have never been before. In Paragonah, Iron County, veteran hunters Val Robb and his father, Ivan, now find elk in the valley cedars and undulating sage arroyos. "We've taken some large bulls in such places," Val says. "The elk are definitely flourishing where doubters thought elk would never make it years ago."

It should be noted, of course, that elk were once a plains animal. Pioneers seeking their manifest destiny pushed elk from the prairies to the mountains, and in some parts of Utah, the flexible wapiti returned to previous habitat. Interestingly, bison did not make the transition to a new environment. I have seen Utah elk adapt to many things: oil pumps in the Book Cliffs, cattlemen on the south slope of the Uintas, train traffic on the north Manti, myriad roads on the Fishlake. In researching the book *Elk and Elk Hunting*, I also noted elk adapting well in other states, but the challenge was much greater in Utah because population has increased faster. Elk will adapt if artificial situations remain consistent; that is if the pumps, trains, roads don't change from day to day.

This is one factor in wapiti adapting to new places: onto Monroe Mountain, Heber-Red Creek, Panguitch Lake, Pilot Mountain and Indian Peaks near the water-lacking Nevada border, Pine Valley, Thousand Lake Mountain, the rolling hills of Avintaquin-White River and into rather surprisingly low terrain such as Paunsagunt, the Pahvant in Millard -Sevier-Juab Counties, northern Carbon County's Argyle-Minnie Maud drainages, *et .al.* In the meantime, the Uinta Mountains continue to "fan" elk out into Goslin-Three Corners, Kamas-Oakley,

Whiterocks, and lower Ashley Creek and into terrain possibly later designated new elk hunt units.

The wise elker will get a current Big Game proclamation and check the limited entry units before going afield. Success in the restricted entry units can run about 40 per cent ; but in general open bull it averages 10-20 percent. Some areas also have "spike only" units (working toward larger bulls for future hunting). *Note that in recent years, three units have been spike bulls only: Boulder, Fishlake and Manti.* Many antlerless permits are allocated every year. And I might add that a cow elk is a most legitimate quarry, much more challenging than the female of any other big game species. Some areas are either-sex from year to year.

The elk sleuth should check with UDWR officials for the best odds on a given unit. For instance, the Oquirrh Mountains have produced a few mammoth bulls over the past 40 years, but permits are hard to come by. Some of Utah's greatest bulls have come from the roadless Book Cliffs. I have seen several dozen bulls in a single day when scouting the upper Willow Creek drainage on the roadless sector of the Book Cliffs, and many smaller, wandering and nomadic herds south of Ouray. However, the entire Book Cliffs allow only 95 resident and nine non-resident permits each year.

Of course, elk success depends considerably on the weather. One October, hunters were stranded with three feet of snow on the Manti, spending all their efforts to merely dig out and get home. Another year, a dry one, elk deserted their normal slopes to seek more lush feed and water.

Note that the Utah elk seasons normally open the first Wednesday in October, but restricted hunts are usually held in September. Access is not guaranteed by issuance of a permit. Some units, especially those in Ogden River and Chalk Creek, require payment of a trespass fee, or written permission.

The September quests in particular offer an opportunity to bugle in a bull, although in mild weather elk may mate as late as mid-October. It has been my experience that wet weather erodes the ardor of rutting bulls, so you may have to go sans any bugling help. When deciding on a call, get a good one. Veteran hunters say some Utah elk are so sophisticated that with the first artificial note, the bull knows brand name and the year it was manufactured.

A few elk guides have done well with turkey calls. They squeal rather effectively for the practiced. Nimrods who have studied elk also use a plastic tube for amplification of a human chest-throat bugle. A call can be made from metal pipe by cutting a hole in the top and the end. Practice until you can give the low and higher shrill whistle, finished with guttural grunts. The clarion call of an in-rut bull elk cannot be fully explained here; but there is simply no more exhilarating music in the wild. Many sporting goods dealers have the sound on tape.

Artificial bugles are usually far more effective where people are rarely encountered. I once lip-whistled in an enraged six-point Utah bull from half a mile away. He answered three times, trotted across 300 yards of open sage flat, stopped at a spring 25 yards from my tent and began pawing the ground. I'm sure his lack of caution was helped by being far from any roads.

Elk are among the most challenging of Utah's (or any state's) big game animals. Study maps; include a flashlight, matches and makings of a fire. Carry fire starter or paper in case a blaze is needed when the entire world seems wet. As an elk guide often facing violent weather, I learned the value of warm clothes. You can't remain out hunting if you are not comfortable. Wear insulated Snow-packs instead of regular hiking boots; be sure gloves are waterproof; have a Scandinavian pull-down cap to keep head warm. Many veteran elkers also carry red ribbons to mark the path to downed elk, or even to mark key trails back to camp in case of inclement weather. A thousand conifers can all look very much alike when visibility is limited, especially in flat terrain.

Record wapiti — For years Utah wapiti did not show up in the Boone-Crockett record books, even with many entries in mule deer, black bear, cougar etc. However, measurements in 1988 turned up two record elk that had been hanging in obscurity for nearly half a century.

Where are the best chances for respectable Utah bulls? "Respectable" is a relative term, especially with elk; even many veteran hunters regard downing a spike as mission accomplished, since there is rarely such a thing as an "easy" elk hunt. As for precisely pin-pointing elk locations, remember that elk roam widely, with no assurance they will be in a given unit if drought or heavy snows trigger a migration. But the best bets under normal conditions year-to-year are listed below. Be sure to check with Chapter 11's "best bets for deer" for access information on each location.

ABAJO MOUNTAINS — This unit includes some of the state's better elk country, with bulls found from cedar to pine, as with deer. There is potential for even better elk hunting in the years to come because of the region's wild nature. Horses are almost imperative, since there are thousands of square miles, and four-wheel drive roads are limited. Scouting is vital to learn access into this rugged terrain. Then, hunt away from roads into the hinterlands.

BEAVER-TUSHAR MOUNTAINS—There is ample high country here for elk, particularly around 12,000-foot plus high Mt. Belknap and Delano Peak. Elk and deer are often found together, but also look for the wapiti in slightly higher terrain. The region has more elk potential in mile after mile of aspen and conifer than current harvest success statistics indicate, and could likely absorb more elk transplants in the future. Westward, beyond Minersville, the **Indian Peaks** area has taken kindly to elk. But time is needed for them to become better established.

BOOK CLIFFS—The elk living in this expansive country are not as skittish as many in Utah. Elk are farther removed from man, with normal contact limited to seeing a few ranchers putting out salt or keeping track of livestock. For that reason, it is one of my favorite hunting regions. Hunters with no idea where to go can hike miles in lower Willow Canyon and on Steer Ridge without seeing any sign at all of elk. Yet, many wapiti were and are yet found a few miles higher (south) in upper East Fork of Willow, and She canyons, as well as on slopes south of the Book Cliffs divide. The roadless area is reached from Diamond Ridge, west of Hay Canyon. Note: A hunter who goes too far west will eventually encounter the Ute Reservation, excellent elk territory but closed at this time to non-Indians.

Finding elk from say, McCook Ridge to Bitter Creek and the many undulating miles of cedar-pinyon pine southward involves more time and luck than science. Elk wander widely. Most terrain looks pretty much alike, with interlaced canyons, low ridges and sandy washes. Long-distance shooting prowess is highly recommended.

Because of the great distances involved and the difficulty in covering it, the Book Cliffs could very well produce a Boone-Crockett or Pope-Young bull of the future. The minimum score for wapiti keeps going up; so making the book now is more competitive than ever before. Still, based on what I have seen in the Book Cliffs, I predict a bull from this region (including the Ute Indian Reservation) will find its way into the records. The same is true of some other expansive wildlands such as the Uinta Mountains or Boulder-Escalante terrain.

BOULDER MOUNTAIN — While the Boulder top has some sparse grass for elk, they tend to be in rougher terrain along the perimeter. Wapiti and deer are often found together on the high aspen slopes in the Chokecherry, Oak and Pleasant Creek drainages. Much of the mountain is volcanic rock which elk avoid, so they are often bunched with deer where feed is available. Of course, elk can take advantage of meadow grass more than the deer. Elk are also found along the lower pinyon-pine and mountain mahogany canyons. An excellent place is the western flank which dumps onto lower **Parker Mountain's** aspen slopes and from the Aquarius Plateau southward to Hells Backbone and **Escalante Mountain**. Work the steep heads of ravines leading into Pine Creek and the Escalante River drainage. Escalante Mountain is often less pressured than the Boulder itself. Get away from roads and look for uneven, rough, jumbled terrain. A Boulder Mountain bull missed the Boone-Crockett world records a few years ago by one-eighth of a point. Try as they might, measurers could not squeeze out that extra credit, so it will never show in the books.

CACHE NATIONAL FOREST — Don't let the docile-looking elk on the Hardware Ranch winter feeding refuge mislead you. These bulls would not be there but for outwitting dozens of hunters a few months before. Come the hunt, they vanish into oak, aspen and conifer. I would try the terrain northward toward Bear Lake, the meadows in the northwest where the grave marker of Old Ephraim, Utah's last grizzly bear is located, and to the higher terrain toward Logan Canyon. West of Hardware, nice bulls hie to the spruce in upper Logan and Temple Fork Canyons when the shooting begins. A few elk may be taken in the Left Hand Fork of Blacksmith, but road traffic usually keeps them well away from easy access. Check the cliffs and rough canyons.

Incidentally, you may want to tour the elk displays at Hardware, and in the winter try a horse-drawn sleigh ride into the midst of the feeding elk. Just don't get off the sled, or these animals may rush off to the highlands again.

CARBON COUNTY — Elk have proliferated widely in northern Carbon, despite any truly high "classical" terrain. Most of the bulls are taken in low to middle aspen terrain from Wellington to the Duchesne County line. Check the proclamation for the Range Creek unit, open bull with some public land, plus Anthro-Argyle, a restricted unit in most years. Elk populations have mushroomed in the past decade across Argyle, Nine-mile, Minnie Maud, Soldier Creek and other drainages leading to the Green River.

CEDAR MOUNTAIN — The highlands surrounded by Cedar City, Panguitch, Parowan, Paragonah have increasing elk populations. The upper tableland is difficult to hunt because visibility is poor in the heavy conifers. Some of the steeper hillsides on the edges offer more chances. Check on the lower edges, too, as elk are taken in the oak and cedars. This area includes the Panguitch Lake unit where hunting is often in thick timber. This is expansive terrain, often relatively flat, and care must be taken to note minor landmarks in getting around.

DIAMOND FORK-STRAWBERRY-WHITE RIVER — Much of this high plateau aspen country is deer and scattered elk habitat. There is some private property. The Avintaquin area east of Strawberry Reservoir is on Ute Tribal lands. Timber Canyon to the west has public access. I've seen many White River elk on the steep upper slopes a few hundred yards below ridgelines. Elk are also taken in the upper Sheep Creek aspen slopes south of Strawberry. This highly accessible area draws many Wasatch Front hunters. Wapiti are highly intolerant of human intruders here and may run for miles if spooked. Northward, in the Heber-Red Creek unit, including upper Currant Creek toward Wolf Creek Pass, elk are also apt to be in high aspens. Some of these nomadic elk find their way into Diamond Fork and Hobble Creek Canyon. Elk are often seen wintering southeast of the Diamond Fork road. In season, check in the First to Sixth-Water Creek drainages between Diamond Fork and Strawberry. Wintering elk can often be seen in the winter on the north side of Hobble Creek Canyon. Undoubtedly, they venture much higher in fair weather. I've seen a few bands on the Wasatch face directly above Springville.

MT. DUTTON — This limited entry unit southwest of Antimony has well-established elk populations, allowing 110 permits in 1989. The land is much like that on nearby Boulder Mountain, high, steep, with thick conifers, but Dutton has less access than the Boulder. Watch for the dirt road out of Antimony, or north of Widstoe Junction. Winter range is ample and this elk herd should expand in the years to come. Far from the Wasatch Front, elk here confront hunters less often and appear less sophisticated than those farther north.

HEASTON is listed as "Oquirrh Mountains" on the deer hunt. Permits are limited, but some big bulls haunt the upper aspen basins. If I drew out here I'd want a horse and would be in no hurry, for some ridges are reached only via long and steep canyons. Heavy oak and cedar rule in lower and middle elevations. This one is for the hardy, but it can be rewarding. Private lands may be encountered but parts are BLM with public access. Access roads are limited.

FISHLAKE FOREST — Look for elk in the high conifer terrain north of

Fish Lake and Johnson Reservoir, up Seven-mile Canyon all the way to Mt. Marvine, Terrell, and Hilgard. This is some of the most productive elk habitat anywhere, a fact not lost on local licensees. Tough winters may send elk well northward to lower aspen-lined canyons draining to Salina Canyon. There are many four-wheel drive roads throughout, so hunting pressure can come from any quarter. One problem with hunting much of the Fishlake is that there is no one particularly high or rugged place to ascend; it is all equally wild, with elk apt to be almost anywhere . Don't get lost in the more level tablelands. Pick out some landmark, take a compass and remember where camp is located.

Across the valley to the northwest of Fish Lake is **Monroe Mountain**, a ridgeline above Sevier Valley with a small but mushrooming elk herd. Migrating elk may also be in the cedar country between Fish Lake and Monroe Mountain, particularly above Koosharem Reservoir. Elk are on the increase in the **Thousand Lake Mountain** area above Loa-Bicknell-Torrey. Elk hang out beneath the upper rim, or down in the steeper canyons below roads. Thousand Lake, like Monroe Mountain, has been a special permit unit. Only five permits were allocated in 1989 for Thousand Lake, with 10 for Monroe.

LASAL MOUNTAIN — Elk are found where the deer are, on the middling slopes up to snowfields capped by 12,000-foot plus peaks. Try to get on the less-visited east slope. Diligent hiking or horses are almost a must for elk on this massive mountain. Elk often reside in aspens, but there is expansive winter range in oak if elk decide to move down.

MANTI MOUNTAIN — Elk can be almost anywhere on this high plateau's many ridges and canyons. Use the roads to gain altitude, then leave them. Get where it is tough to get. This sometimes requires hiking into steep canyons and basins. The upper backbone is barren, so watch for elk moving across the top, but if unspooked, they will feed and bed in the aspens and conifers. After a few days of hunting, the pressure seems to send the bulls into thicker oak and mountain mahogany at middle elevations.

One day, Manti conservation officer Ken Tuttle showed us where many big bulls go — onto the high roadless face above Ephraim, Manti, and Spring City. I have looked at many elk in Willow Canyon which is accessed south from Ephraim Canyon. Access tends to switchback up canyon bottoms, then join the ridge-long Skyline Drive. Hunting is crowded here in October.

Best hunting is on the least-visited southeastern sector, the Ferron-Muddy drainage and from the top of Twelve-mile Canyon above Mayfield southward toward Salina Canyon. Elk can also abound on the roadless ravines above Indianola and Fairview and eastward to Upper Fish Creek. They descend on croplands above Indianola every December.

Elk populations are also good on the ridges above Joe's Valley Reservoir in Emery County. This higher elevation is a jungle of chokecherry and other underbrush and a horse is very useful. Roads can become impassable with rain or snow. At dawn and dusk look for elk in any grassy opening, however small, including pipeline or power pole cuts, upper stream flood plains, wind-swept ridges, small avalanche paths. This is one of those hunting grounds where game can be anywhere, so watch for elk spooked by other permit-holders as well as yourself. Wapiti camps are not rare on the mountain; the elk have learned to elude all but the most alert. In the summer of 1989, I watched archery deer hunters enter an aspen stand from one side and a cow elk take flight from the other. It ran past me, splashing through a long meadow and several swamps, not stopping until she reached thick timber two miles away. The hunters never knew she was there.

Across Sanpete Valley from the Manti, above Fountain Green, I've also seen hundreds of elk on both sides of Utah 132. This is relatively low, undulating oakbrush, a signal that elk anywhere utilize foothill oak — perhaps more than most orange-vesters realize. One day UDWR Conservation Officer Brad Bradley and I saw many elk in the middle of Six-mile Canyon. They were with deer where oak gives way to aspens, and interestingly enough, the elk shunned bright sunlight while deer did not. This could have been because the elks' warm coats would be uncomfortable outside the shadows. Then, again, it may have been because elk could not survive in numbers on the fairly accessible west side of the Manti if they did not possess some special savvy.

In aerial surveys of the Manti with game biologists, I've witnessed large bands of elk bedding on snowbanks at the top of Six and Twelve-mile Canyons where they could have a panoramic view of all going on below. On one occasion, I looked at two outsized bulls hiding directly below the Heliotrope, a high cliff between Twelve-mile and Ferron drainages.

MORGAN-SOUTH RICH — Much private land is found here, including Deseret Livestock Ranch. (Also see Chapter Nine on Fee Hunting.) Many of Utah's greatest elk antlers come from this high plateau, some of them by bowmen who have found a place in the Pope-Young world record archery books. Terrain is oak and aspen carved by winding canyons. Nice bulls are taken here, but a public licensee will have to figure how to bag one while remaining off private property. One route is above Causey Reservoir on the west; another, north of Lost Creek Reservoir. Utah 39 provides some opportunities all the way to Monte Cristo campground on top of the divide overlooking the Ogden River drainage. From the air, I've also seen elk in upper aspens half a mile from Utah 39.

MT. NEBO — There certainly are bulls on the flanks of this ll,877-foot high mountain, but too few orange-vesters realize how many elk remain in the lower oak and aspen where most of the feed is. One such place is the middle elevations of Benny and Nebo Creeks on the eastern slopes of Nebo. A friend, Bill George, Salt Lake City, bugled in a six-point bull in this area a few years ago on his first trip to Nebo. He was home by noon. Such rapid success on elk is rare, but it just points out how things can go when you are in the right place at the right time doing the right thing.

Other elk are taken on the south side in the Gardner Canyon area or the feeder ravines to upper Salt Creek. Every winter, bands of elk can be seen from I-15, sometimes even without binoculars. They spend the autumn hunting season on upper oakbrush ridges of Santaquin Canyon and southward about midway up

Elk have been a unique success story in Utah.

on the mountain. A large canyon just north of Nephi, and two more a little north of Mona, often hold elk. The long conifer-laden ridge from Santaquin to Payson has shown elk at times. Many elk have dwelt on the Payson Canyon ridges, invading winter orchards and old hayfields from there eastward to Elk Ridge and Mt. Loafer. Loafer is as precipitous as Nebo and will frequently have elk just because access is so difficult.

Look carefully when hunting Nebo. Elk here are well acquainted with humans and will often hole up when pressured. Once, from a helicopter, I watched a huge bull hiding beneath a rim where two hunters were eating lunch. The elk remained below a patch of oak, apparently not running because other rifle-toters were about. Doubling back later, we noted the hunters tossing snowballs. I doubt if they ever did realize a giant bull hid from them less than 300 yards away.

PAUNSAUGUNT AND CANAAN MOUNTAIN — This is widely varying terrain in and around Bryce Canyon National Park's high plateau extending southward to the cedar country near the Arizona border and toward Zions National Park. Many elk are well away from the roads in thick conifer and oak or cedars. Check waterholes in the lower elevations. If you hunt the Bryce terrain you will be at about 9,000 feet with rapidly descending arroyos, escarpments, buttes, and mesas. The units have had only 15 permits between them in recent years.

UINTA MOUNTAINS — There are many opportunities to find elk on this 100-mile long east-west backbone, with its dozens of glacially-carved basins and river canyons on both north and south sides. The range includes seven elk units. The four with names prefaced with "Ashley," are on the eastern and southeastern toe of the mountain. Some of Utah's best wapiti hunting is found here in a day's horse pack up the likes of Ashley Creek, Dry Fork, the Whiterocks River or Yellowstone Creek. However, many local elkers keep an eye on the weather, for bulls can be in the cedar-sage foothills north of Vernal and Roosevelt if snow piles up early in the 13,000-foot high peaks and environs.

The entire North Slope is classical elk country, with high emerald meadows surrounded with canyons of dark timber. This is more elk than muley terrain. Nor does one have to probe all the toughest and highest lodgepole ledges. I've seen respectable bulls less than two hours from Christmas Meadows on the Stillwater Fork of the Bear River and crept within 15 feet of one on spongy lakeshore grass. The bull was behind a clump of spruce and when he went, the whole basin seemed to rumble with fleeing elk. Bulls are often sighted high on Henrys Fork, and in the Blacks Fork drainage, particularly the out-of-way Little Left Hand Fork of Blacks.

Hunters I know have scored on big bulls on the West Fork of the Bear, but there is private property there to avoid. A favorite haunt for some is from Gilbert Meadows to Hoop Lake. Gary Egbert, Layton, has bugled in large bulls in this general region for a decade of hunting seasons.

On the west slope of the Uintas, hunting is not as fast; but there are elk here in the **Kamas** unit, as witnessed by winter elk watching. To the southwest, at Wolf Creek Pass on over to the Duchesne River and Rock Creek, nice bulls have also been taken. While most of the Uintas require a horse, there is some hope on the west and south slopes of getting into elk on foot or even four-wheel drive outside the Uinta Wilderness Area.

Another unit near the Uinta east slope with a growing elk herd is **Goslin-Three Corners** (near the Utah-Colorado-Wyoming state lines). Elk in this remote region are often found in the high sagebrush. Some 50 permits are usually allocated each year to Goslin-Three Corners.

Elk can be found over much of Daggett County. I've seen them the night before the opener camped right on the Dutch John church and residential lawns. But some hunters seem to want it too easy, patrolling in vehicles along Utah 44 from the Dutch John turnoff to the scenic overlook above Flaming Gorge's Sheep Creek Bay. If an elk was to show, these road hunters would have but a few seconds before the animal reached a solid wall of timber on the opposite side of the pavement. More elk success is found westward in the top of Sheep Creek Canyon over to Browne, Sheep Creek Reservoirs, Spirit Lake and above. That region is an open bull unit under the designation "Ashley-Daggett." Nearby is the **Chalk Creek-Mill Creek** unit, but it has so much private land that it is not recommended for anyone relying on public access.

WASATCH MOUNTAINS, CENTRAL — This includes the unit listed in the proclamation as Salt Lake-Timpanogos, along the Wasatch Front. Despite its proximity to three-quarters of a million people, this is steep and rough elk habitat. I've seen much of the so-called "Salt Lake herd" wintering in Mill Creek Canyon's south-facing oak slopes, or in autumn, at the extreme upper end of this canyon. In a tough winter, elk will be found in the first ravines both north and south of the Parleys Canyon mouth. Scouting them out here, even though out of season, seems to help a hunter *know* they are in the general vicinity and work that much harder to find them in season. Elk are also known to range over into East Canyon, but that is primarily on private property. A friend, Duane Erickson of Salt Lake City, has outwitted elk by bow and arrow in the top of Big Cottonwood Canyon. Elk and deer are often found together here.

Elk may be found on the continuous Wasatch ridgeline from Lone Peak to the top of Alpine and American Fork Canyons, and the oakbrush slopes of Mt. Timpanogos. These animals cause enough agricultural damage in an average winter that game managers sometimes issue antlerless permits, as well as open bull licenses.

WASHINGTON COUNTY — This includes the Pine Valley Mountains north of St. George, where elk are often found with deer. Terrain on these mountains includes heavy conifer, but elk may move into lower cedars, as considerable wintering room is available there. Only five permits were allocated in 1989. But the elk population is growing.

BIG GAME HABITAT

▦ Moose	(M S) Mountain Bighorn Sheep
■ Antelope	(D S) Desert Bighorn Sheep
(B) Bison or Buffalo	(M G) Mountain Goats

CHAPTER FOURTEEN

Moose, Antelope, Sheep . . . Plus Goats

Except for deer and elk, all Utah antlered or horned big game animals were on a permit drawing basis as of 1990. Check the Hunting Proclamation in any given year for application deadlines and computer drawing dates. Typical application dates are from mid-April to mid-May, with the drawing in June. Some game like moose, wild sheep, goats and buffalo are a once-in-a-lifetime hunt. Others may require waiting two or three years before drawing again.

MOOSE

Moose are fairly well scattered throughout northern Utah and hunters have relatively little trouble finding a target in Cache, Rich, Morgan, Weber and Summit Counties. It wasn't always like that. Historically, there was one sighting of a moose in Spanish Fork Canyon about 1906, one of the few outside of the Uinta North Slope. Even those animals probably migrated from southern Wyoming into the Uinta Mountains. From there, moose moved throughout the Uintas, upper Ogden River, Blacksmith Fork, and many other northern Utah stream drainages.

I recall a few decades ago going with a permittee on the Kamas unit who tracked his quarry in a foot of snow for five days without finding legal game. We did not hesitate to wade the bitter-cold Bear River sans hip boots to keep on the tracks of that moose. The hunter told me he had scouted the area for a week, and this was the first sign he'd found, so we followed faithfully. The licensee went out again with patience and dedication, but finished the season without seeing a single Alces Alces. The hunter would likely have scored in the 1990s.

Nowadays, the toughest part of bagging a moose would be getting the permit. In recent years, Utah has allocated 145 moose permits, all but five for bulls. Hunting success began to soar in 1988 with an incredible 99 per cent success that year, only one permittee failing to score. As I understand it, that person grew ill on the eve of the shoot and participated sparingly.

Since about 1985 it would be difficult to walk around even casually on the North Slope without seeing moose. On one six-day backpack from Spirit Lake to the Burnt Fork drainage, then over the Uinta backbone to the Uinta River drainage, companion Gary Webster, Salt Lake City, and I saw several massive bull moose. Fishermen also told me about seeing a giant rack near Spirit Lake. Friends and I have seen good bulls across the North Slope on Henrys Fork, Blacks Fork, Smiths Fork, Beaver Creek. A young bull on Henrys Fork stood in the road one day and refused to let my pickup truck pass. Honking put him on the sidelines, but angry eyes made it clear he had moved only for a larger foe. Henrys Fork moose have been pushed out of some winter rangeland by oil exploration and development.

It has not been surprising to me that moose have has flourished in the lush meadows and beaver dams on the Uinta North Slope. What is not as easy to explain is why moose left this lush habitat to migrate into totally different environment of Morgan and Weber Counties with its steep and semi-dry juniper-oak slopes. This is not "classical" moose country. But they are there in profusion. A Montana archer in 1988 bought the one available high bid permit for a Utah moose and told me later he had never seen as many moose in Montana as he had in Weber County. Hunting for 18 days alone and on foot above Pineview and Causey reservoirs, he "had his pick" of over 100 bulls, settling on a 48-1/2 inch monster which I helped dress out and load onto horses.

Moose have migrated to the South Slope of the Uintas, Chalk Creek, parts of the Wasatch Range, and especially the Flaming Gorge country. Biologists say the calf crop in Utah has also been very good. The animals are putting on extra size. In 1980 Utah had turned up only one Boone-Crockett moose, a 14th ranking bull from the Bear River area, Uintas North Slope. It had a spread width of 51 7/8 inches and 181 5/8 B-C points. Then, a giant bull was taken in the upper Ogden River in 181 which scored 180 2/8, with a 51 2/8 inch width, also placing high in the records. But hunters have for several years sought what may be an even larger moose occasionally sighted on the south rim of Flaming Gorge Reservoir, southwest of Dutch John. Observers say it has a rack estimated at some 55 inches width.

Moose have also been transplanted to the Uinta South Slope at Currant Creek, the north Manti's Upper Fish Creek drainage, and the Fishlake Forest, probably the southernmost range of these animals in the world. It is interesting that Colorado has many miles of potential moose environment, but had none until Utah shared some of its surplus a few years ago. The moose is a northern critter, preferring extreme cold and snowy climes. Utah's southern highlands such as Boulder, Beaver and even LaSal Mountains are likely cold enough to harbor moose, and perhaps some day they will be there in profusion.

Utah would already have huntable populations on the North Manti above Scofield Reservoir, and probably the Fishlake, were it not for illegal kills. Attempts have been made to stop moose poaching by offering rewards of $300 and up for information leading to the arrest of offenders. It would be preposterous to suppose that a hunter could sincerely and honestly mistake a coal-black animal the size of a horse for a deer or elk.

Until the problem of illegal kills is solved, most likely only with the help of alert sportsmen, moose permits will remain about as they are now. This means one permit per person per lifetime if a hunter is successful in drawing out. The application flurry is brisk among all eight units: Uinta North Slope, Daggett (Flaming Gorge), Uinta South Slope, Cache-North Rich, Kamas, Chalk Creek, Ogden River, Morgan-South Rich. The latter three units have considerable private land, so permission to trespass is needed. In many cases, Utah landowners now require payment of a trespass fee or the more expensive guide-services route.

There are several big game animals, moose certainly among them, which symbolize the wild. A trip to Yellowstone National Park was complete if I could see a bull moose. Now, if I wanted to see a moose for sure, I'd travel the road in Rich County south of Laketown to Hardware Ranch in Cache County, checking ravines along the road. A friend of mine saw 22 bull moose on one deer hunting foray above Porcupine Reservoir east of Hyrum in Cache County, and twice that many while hunting the upper Ogden River. They will likely continue to disperse, since moose are not particularly social animals and don't like crowding.

As for which rifle to tame this beast, a heavy slug of some 180 grains or more is recommended. Many a Utah moose has been dispatched with a 30/06, but more rifle might be useful as well. With moose we should realize we're talking about an animal here which can weigh half a ton, so horses and helpers are vital. Moose seasons usually open in September, with preferred elevation about 7500 to 9000 feet. I have also seen moose on high ridges away from any beaver dams or water, in heavy conifers. The thick, warm hide of a moose may require higher terrain in warm weather to find the desired comfort zone. And if weather is warm, get meat out quickly. Be especially careful of leaving the upper chest lying uncooled for long periods.

Whether hunting or otherwise, keep in mind that moose are often belligerent. I've been chased by several. They may not shy away from humans because they're not frightened by anything smaller. Watch a moose's body language. If eyes stare and glare, be cautious. While fishing, I've had several absolutely refuse to move off the trail. These animals can charge if crowded, and a cow with calf is dangerous. Take heed!

PRONGHORN ANTELOPE

While pronghorns once thronged Utah to the point of Great Salt Lake's Antelope Island being named by explorer John C. Fremont "for its many antelope," these animals declined in the late 1900s.

Yet there is good news, for the state has many more antelope now than several decades ago. Accordingly, additional permits are being allocated, with more than 1,000 available statewide in the early 1990s. When a permit is obtained, individual success is around 75-90 percent, depending on the unit, almost as high as with moose. Utah's problem has often been a clash between game animals and domestic livestock on the most desirable high plains rangelands with an adequate rainfall. Improving antelope numbers has required agreements between agricultural and government-BLM interests to make room for more pronghorns. Reseeding large plots of semi-desert terrain has helped, along with careful management. Much of Utah is prairie or treeless flatlands, including the western third of the state, but it is not always prime antelope habitat because more rainfall is needed. The best pronghorn terrain is found in the higher flatlands attracting enough rainfall to promote major plant growth. This includes Parker Mountain, Daggett County, Icelander Wash in Carbon-Emery County, Bonanza, Myton Bench, Cisco area, Rich County and similar areas. Parts of Box Elder County, San Rafael Desert, Escalante Desert west of Cedar City, Puddle, Johns or Rush valleys, and the West Desert have good rainfall areas to produce sagebrush and grass, as well as waterholes.

Of them all, I have been intrigued with Parker Mountain in Wayne County. Game managers consider it one of the state's most productive pronghorn habitats, issuing more permits here than any other single unit. Parker allows 100 hunters. Just below Boulder and Escalante Mountains, Parker gets a good dosage of rainfall, with soil and mineral conditions encouraging grass, sage and browse. Swales and arroyos on Parker have aspens, but the main requirements for *Antilocapra americana* in addition to food is there: the security of distance.

An antelope with its superior eyes can see well out there. He thus has an indication what danger lurks for a dozen miles roundabout, and the means in those powerful legs to abscond in a hurry. Best estimates say an antelope runs up to 63 miles per hour , with an ability to cruise for miles at 40 mph. So certain is a pronghorn that he can beat any pursuer, that he will prove it to you — racing with a vehicle. In many cases, he will not depart your presence until first *crossing over in front of you*. Another quirk is that although he can easily leap over a seven-foot fence, this animal prefers to crawl under it. I have seen antelope send back hair flying as they tunnel below a barbed wire fence they could have easily jumped across. I observed one large buck remain trapped along U.S. 89 in Rich County for hours because he refused to leap over a three-foot high strand of fence. Another nice buck with horns of 13-14 inches burrowed into the sand to get beneath a fence strand.

My first time attempting to find pronghorns on Parker, south of Fish Lake, ended in utter failure. Not a single sighting. Checking with UDWR Conservation Officer Leon Bogedahl, Torrey, I discovered the trouble. There had been a drought and game was higher, with more lush feed closer to Boulder Mountain. By taking the road from just east of Bicknell, up Pine Creek about 20 miles toward Escalante, we looked at antelope by the dozens. Some were in or near aspens. Pronghorns will inhabit 8000-9000-foot high terrain to find desired feed and water, of course, but another reason is to elude lowland hunting traffic. A friend of mine, Dee Smith of Salt Lake City, took a nice pronghorn buck on west Parker near the Antimony side. More dirt road access is available for lower Parker directly out of Antimony in Garfield County, connecting to Loa in Wayne County. This is also excellent deer country, so be sure of your target. A motorist is likely to see antelope south of Parker Mountain past Antimony and Widtsoe Junction almost to Bryce Canyon National Park.

In addition to Parker, I have witnessed many antelope in the Flaming Gorge-Three Corners region, great game country whatever the species. Pronghorn bucks in this remote terrain are not as sophisticated as in many parts of Utah; in fact, I've seen good bucks alongside back roads in Daggett County, northeast of Dutch John, especially from Clay Basin and Browns Park to the Wyoming line. Forty permits were allowed here in 1989 at the edge of heavy cedar forests.

Well to the south, open terrain in the likes of Bonanza's lower Bitter Creek provides more "classical" hunting possibilities. Bonanza is located southeast of Ouray in Uintah County, east of the Book Cliffs and south of the White River. This is desolately beautiful butte-mesa country along the Colorado border. Despite oil development and gilsonite mining traffic, I've seen many nice antelope here. Don't go unprepared or in a hurry. Extra water is a must, and extra gasoline is advised.

The vast West Desert could require many hours and searching west of Vernon, but that is part of the lore of antelope hunting. Pronghorns in western Tooele and Millard County move around, so keep looking.

Icelander Wash is more than a single gully. The Hunting Proclamation shows it as running east from Helper in Carbon County to the Book Cliffs and southeast to Emery and Grand counties. It has one of the state's fastest growing herds, partly due to habitat plus transplants from overcrowded antelope on Parker Mountain. In a typical year, Icelander will issue about 50 permits.

Many doe-fawn permits are available for those who like antelope venison. For example, 100 in Rich County's Crawford Mountains along the Wyoming boundary, with 250 permits for Parker Mountain. Check the proclamation each year for details. Seasons vary for each unit, but are generally in early September.

Utah, for many years with a low pronghorn population, has no Boone-Crockett or Pope-Young antelope entries. If it is to happen in the future, look for such a trophy in those units farther from the roads, perhaps a West Desert, Three Corners or Bonanza buck. Utahns have not been as trophy-conscious about this animal as those in say, Wyoming or Arizona. But the pronghorn is gaining more recognition and respect as more Utahns are able to gain a permit and become familiar with the sleek animal. It will take some special practice for those who have only hunted Utah's main passion, the mule deer. An antelope moves as smoothly as if on roller skates, with little deer-like bouncing, but its speed makes hitting the target tougher than other game. So be sure to practice first on moving targets like jack rabbits or cardboard-filled tires.

In my opinion, antelope or "prairie goats" have long been underrated throughout the West as a game animal. They offer a worthy challenge to a hunter who can frequently see the quarry, but is unable to outwit a creature with the best pair of legs and lungs on the North American continent. Some hunting tales tell of tricks appealing to an antelope's curiosity, such as holding a hat on a stick to bring it closer. But Utah's more sophisticated antelope do not always succumb to such trickery. All it takes for a nimrod to gain respect for this animal is to hunt it once. I recall some quests with lengthy vigils on a 30-power spotting scope, then a two-hour stalk. After that, super accuracy is required to 300 yards or more. The latter encourages familiarity with a flat trajectory firearm, like the 7 mm R. Magnum, or .270. Hopefully, more sportsmen will gain an opportunity to give this game animal their best shot through Utah's permit-draw approach.

DESERT BIGHORN SHEEP

Indian petroglyphs along the Colorado River and in Canyonlands National Park, indicate that Utah has long held desert bighorns. Sheep were also sighted by the Mormon Hole-in-the Rock Expedition of 1879 in Garfield and San Juan counties. It has been said that the expedition made it across the treacherous Colorado River by following the path of a desert sheep.

But the sheep lived in such rough terrain that it was 1967 before game managers could ascertain the animals were there in huntable numbers. Nine of nine first-year permittees met success with desert sheep. On the next quest, only three of 10 scored. In the 1972 hunt, only one of eight succeeded. By then, sheep began to hole up in the wilds of the Colorado River's east bank in such places as Cataract Canyon. In addition, several more areas such as the Escalante River drainage and Kaiparowits Plateau were discovered to have sheep. Hunters learned they were challenged as much by the precipitous cliffs and formidable terrain as by the wary sheep themselves.

Nimrods who have spent weeks nailing trophies to complete a Grand Slam for the other three sheep species have learned that their Utah ram may be tougher to reach than the others. One hunter said he got his Dall ram in Alaska, his Stone trophy in British Columbia, his Rocky Mountain bighorn in Montana. Requiring most time was his Utah desert ram.

Other than the one opportunity at a permit via highest bid — with the minimum set at $20,000 — there were 11 licenses allowed in 1989. Units with two resident permits each were listed as South San Juan, Potash on the Colorado River north of Moab, Escalante River, North San Rafael, Kaiparowits, and one non-resident allowed in any unit. To learn about current requirements, sheep permit-holders must attend a special hunter-orientation course before going afield. In Utah, it is also important to do it right the first time since permits are once-in-a-lifetime.

Initially, Utah-taken rams had to be three-quarters curl, but now regulations simply *recommend* such a goal. The farther south a person hunts in North America, the greater the chance of bagging a 38-to 40-inch trophy head. Mexico, Arizona and California have produced most of the top rams in world record books. Utah has none. To rectify this, Utah desert sheep need to maintain long lives free of disease. Numbers are growing in the San Rafael and Potash units, but sheep maladies, including lungworm, were reducing populations in 1989 in the San Juan area. Presence of domestic sheep almost always signals lungworm trouble for wild sheep, and the state will have to make some decisions which species they want in a given region. If the problem isn't fully resolved, Utahns will hunt fewer desert sheep in the future.

NOTE: Utah does not at present have a hunt on **Rocky Mountain sheep**. However, successful sheep transplants have been made to augment natural sheep found in the Uinta Mountains during pioneer times. Such plantings are taking hold in many places, including Mt. Timpanogos, Nebo, Wellsville Mountain, Tushar Mountains, Flaming Gorge area. UDWR biologists are asking for the public's help in reporting sheep sightings; note color of ear tags. In 1989, I looked at a band of 14 near U.S. 44 south of Flaming Gorge Reservoir, coincidentally above Sheep Creek Bay. Respectable rams have been sighted for several years on the north side of Flaming Gorge, and in the nearby Baretop Mountain area which was stocked several years ago. Things look favorable, according to UDWR big game biologists, but only time will tell if self-propagation swells numbers to huntable populations.

ROCKY MOUNTAIN GOAT

This is another Beehive State success story, for a few decades ago anyone contemplating a local goat hunt would be hauled away to a team of psychiatrists. Now goat hunting is a reality because transplants from Olympic National Park in the state of Washington have adapted to a "vacant niche" in Utah. Goats were brought in during the late 1970s. In 1989, five goat permits were allocated, four on Lone Peak and one on Timpanogos. A few years ago, I looked at several dozen goats on the north-facing granite ledges of Little Cottonwood Canyon. The goats can often be seen by driving a mile up the canyon, then hiking a few hundred yards up the left or north side, and glassing to the south. With the number of ewes and kids to be seen, it is obvious this is a healthy herd on its way. Even though the unit is labeled "Lone Peak," most of the best goat populations are in one place: the approximately 5000-foot high cliffs in Little Cottonwood Canyon. Classical goat terrain, it is also tough on humans.

Utah goats are also an unpredictable lot. A 100-mile migration has been documented for a lonesome billy who vacated his release site on Bald Mountain in the western Uintas to somehow make its way past freeways and to Provo Peak in the Wasatch Mountains. The tagged goat was found when game managers released more of the species in 1989. Both the vertical Provo Peak and Timpanogos highlands just east of Provo are classical goat terrain. The animals have been sighted on occasion by alpine climbers at 9000-11,000 feet. It is likely more permits will be allocated on both Timp and Provo Peak in the future.

Nine goats were released into Whiterocks Canyon on the southeastern Uintas in July, 1989. There are other Uinta crags and peaks which could likely receive goats if the Whiterocks infusion works out. A few are Mt. Emmons, Gilbert Peak and Kings Peak, all well over 13,000 feet high. These rugged mountains are expected to show more goats in the future from Hayden Peak above Utah 150 to the Flaming Gorge area 100 miles eastward. Peaks in the Tushar Range rise to well over 12,000 feet and should provide viable habitat for future hunts. But biologists are looking for more evidence that the Tushar transplant is self-propagating. Anyone hiking the north Beaver country near Mt. Belknap and Delano Peak should report goat sightings particularly if kids are identified.

BUFFALO OR BISON

Utah has one of the nation's few freely-roaming bison herds. Located south of Hanksville and southwest of the rugged Henry Mountains, these animals wander widely. Two veteran hunters looked for nearly 10 days before homing in on the herd in rugged juniper foothills. Forty resident and four non-resident bull permits were allowed in 1989, with 20 and two, respectively, cow permits. The season on bulls is in November, earlier in October for cows. Buffalo meat is considered as good as beef by many people, making this an in-demand event, with far more applications in a given year than actual hunting opportunities. Those drawing out need a four-wheel drive, a large ration of water, and plenty of time. This is a tougher quest than many hunters realize.

Another buffalo hunting possibility has arisen on Antelope Island on Great Salt Lake, where a private herd grew to 417 animals in the 1980s. Since this resource is now owned by Utah in a state park, five annual permits are typically allocated. One should not suppose this restricted island to be an easy shoot. I was allowed to shoot two bison on Antelope a few decades ago. Covering some 18 miles of undulating junipers on poor four-wheel drive roads, no game was sighted for the first 13 hours of diligent searching. Such conditions can make for an intriguing quest.

COUGAR AND BEAR HABITAT

Cougar (Mountain Lion) Habitat

Black Bear and Cougar Habitat

These animals are widely scattered over their extensive range.

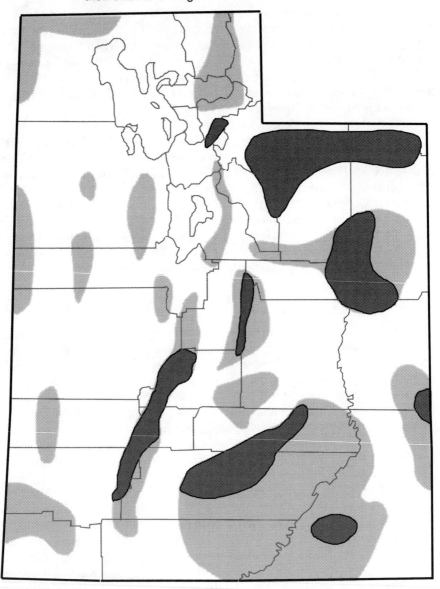

CHAPTER FIFTEEN

Cougars, Bears, Bobcats, Coyotes

Note: For other viewpoints on these animals, please see Chapter 18,
"Our Wildlife Future."

MOUNTAIN LIONS

Utah has one of the nation's largest mountain lion populations. It also has some of the largest lions. With a good guide you can put a puma at bay on Manti Mountain, Boulder, LaSal, Deep Creeks, Uintas, Book Cliffs, Flaming Gorge, Box Elder and Tooele counties' remote mountains. Ditto for Wasatch, Oquirrh and Nebo ranges, plus Strawberry-Diamond Fork country, near major human population centers. The large cedar forests in Duchesne and Carbon counties, as well as those bordering the west desert, have both cougars as well as bobcats. Lions are often found wherever deer are permanent residents and Homo sapiens is not.

Being nocturnal animals, lions are rarely seen even when their tracks and kills are abundant. Mountain lions are often stereotyped as a mountain-only animal. In truth, the undulating semi-desert terrain of the Escalante Desert in Iron County or the criss-crossing canyons of Garfield County are sometimes more to their liking. Cougars have been sighted relatively often by river runners along the Green River. They are found throughout the Ute Indian lands in the Book Cliffs, northward to Diamond Mountain, and, southward into the San Rafael Swell-Robber's Roost country east of Hanksville and through southern Utah's rimrock canyonlands country. A young cougar was even captured hiding in a southeast Salt Lake City window well in 1988. It was tranquilized and returned to the Wasatch Range. If deer are not available, the cats can subsist on squirrels and rabbits. In the Flaming Gorge region, lions have been known to kill mountain sheep. Ranchers have historically accused them of killing chickens, sheep and in pioneer times, even cattle around the Boulder and other wildlands.

Unfortunately, cougars were considered "kill on sight" predators until the 1960s. Nowadays, both hunters and guides must be licensed. To avoid the old unethical "canned" hunts of yesteryear, where a cougar was released for dogs to chase just ahead of an unsuspecting client, rules were established for cougars to be reported to the UDWR within 48 hours of the kill. Additional information, including names of guides, can be obtained from a wildlife resources office.

The Boone and Crockett record books show the greatest cougars come from Utah, Arizona and New Mexico. For years the number one world lion came from Garfield County, a 16-inch skull from a male killed in 1964. It reigned as the world's largest until a 4/8 inch larger cougar skull was presented from British Columbia in 1979. As of 1989, Utah had the number two lion in the B-C books and two tied for 14th, both from Carbon County. Other lions in the world records have come from Spanish Fork Canyon (2), Parowan area, Iron County, Hanksville. Commercial movies have been made of cougar hunts near Parowan and on Manti Mountain. Rex Peterson, Sandy, has a room full of cougar trophies taken with his Plott hounds, including a pack leader fondly named "Lugnut." The value of a good dog when chasing lions cannot be underestimated. Peterson never would sell "Lugnut" for any amount of money, and I'm sure that's the way veteran cougar guide Val Robb, Paragonah, Iron County, felt about his specially-trained hounds. Other guides like Gordon Pace of Bountiful have taken many large lions from the Deep Creek Mountains on the Nevada border by using the right breed of dog.

The best time to go after pumas, the experts emphasize, is when fresh tracks appear after a new storm. I remember one hunt in the Book Cliffs when a guide and I found tracks quickly one morning after a skiff of overnight snow. We followed the sound of the pack through rimrock and pinyon pine until we were nearly exhausted. That is one of the challenges in lion hunting: keeping up with the dogs. We found a two-point buck which had been downed by the cougar, partially eaten, then covered with sticks and leaves. We spent all day zeroing in on baying dogs, but several steep-walled gorges prevented hunters from reaching the pack and their treed quarry. Finally, the guide declared the terrain too rough for humans and called it quits for the week.

Although opposed by some, Utah law provides a permit for simply chasing lions with dogs. Lion hunting regulations change based on populations. Some areas, such as central Garfield-Kane counties, are occasionally closed to any lion hunting in order to facilitate research. For both lion and bear hunts, a mother with young cannot be legally killed, nor the kittens and/or cubs.

Livestockmen have been allowed under Utah law to take marauding lions. However, in most cases only a weak or senile cat is apt to attack livestock. Stockmen might profit from a "molesting" lion by contacting a permit-holder and charging him a trespass fee; this seems better than landowners killing a lion themselves just because it ranges near cattle or sheep. Research shows that cougars, particularly healthy toms, patrol a wide territory perhaps walking 10-12 miles in a night. The toms, display little tolerance toward other lions, sometimes causing competitors to migrate. Because of that, new hunting units may open in the future. Utah's lion populations have pretty well held their own or increased slightly since gaining game animal status, according to UDWR biologists. One reason for a previous decline is that deer hunters were allowed to shoot a lion on sight. Utah may now have as many or more cougars as during pioneer times.

BLACK BEARS

Utah has no grizzly bears. The last one was killed in 1923. There is quite a story about how the silvertip nicknamed "Old Ephraim" plagued local ranchers. The grizz, trapped with logs and chains, dragged himself about and growled in pain all night before a predator hunter finished him off with his trusty rifle. That's the way the story goes on the grave marker northwest of Hardware Ranch in Blacksmith Fork Canyon, Cache County. A plaque on the marker says it is over 11 feet tall because it represents the grizzly's height when standing on hind legs.

In any event, since there are none of these hunchbacks left in Utah, all bear hunting is for the black bear. As many visitors to Yellowstone have learned over the years, the black bear species may be almost any color, cinnamon, brown, or other, but still are "black" bears.

Generally, they are found in Utah where cougars are, and the proclamation often includes both animals in bear-lion management units. Bears are less numerous in Utah, but being slower and more hunger-prone, are seen more often. I have seen bruins in Utah in the Book Cliffs, the Ute Indian Reservation, and the Flaming Gorge terrain, the latter along U.S. 191. I've looked at the carcasses of domestic cows dragged through the snow by bears in the Book Cliffs, and marveled at their brute strength. Claw marks high on nearby aspens indicated a reach well over six feet high. Friends I have talked with have sighted many bears in the LaSal Mountains, outsized ones in Carbon County's mule deer country, others in Strawberry-Diamond Fork. A bear was killed in 1987 while raiding a corn patch near Springville in Utah County. Sightings in Spanish Fork Canyon indicated two-year old bruins ousted by a mother sow to make room for the next brood, born as usual near the end of spring hibernation. These young bears are often "kicked out" of the home to forage for food with few developed skills, getting into trouble by raiding garbage cans at the edges of civilization. A large bear smelling food in a Ute Indian deer hunting camp barracks broke through a wooden panel, took what he wanted, couldn't find his way out, and nearly destroyed the barracks before finally escaping, according to a Ute guide. Such hungry bruins are apt to be easy prey for a baiting hunter. But in Utah, only archery-wielders are still allowed to bait for bears.

Utah's bear population began to increase when indiscriminate "predator" shooting was halted. Many bears were taken by rifle-toters during the annual deer hunt. On one of my first deer hunts back in 1950, near Wolf Creek Pass on the Uinta South Slope, two big bruins hung in nearby camps, and only one small buck.

Utah has some big blacks as measured by skull size. The world record for years hailed from Manti Mountain's Pleasant Creek drainage, taken by Rex Peterson and Richard Hardy in 1970. It was a dramatic conquest, as these veteran hunters told me in a story I did for *Field and Stream*. The beast had the pair's lead dog "Lugnut" in its massive paws when the hunters shot five times, as much to save the dog as to dispatch the bear. The hide I looked at was enough to fill an average-sized bedroom. That bruin was topped by several entries, but the Beehive State took it over again when a giant bear skull was picked up on the Manti. Cause of death was not known, but it may have been natural causes. Federal government trappers protecting sheep long ago removed some big bears from the Manti. Fewer remain nowadays, but they do attain monster skull size.

In addition to the new number one bear as of 1989, Utah also has the numbers four, five and nine. They were taken, respectively, from Sevier County, Sanpete County, Uintah County. In Sevier, there is much Fishlake National Forest for bears to roam over; in Uintah, the Book Cliffs. The latter probably contain the state's largest bear populations. I have seen many large bear tracks in the remote upper Willow and She Canyons over to upper Hill Creek. In addition to B-C records, I looked at a huge bruin in 1989 which was taken by an archer from Carbon County's Minnie Maud-Argyle canyons. It is expected to make the Pope-Young book.

Bears do, on occasion, molest livestock. However, since bears can subsist on such a wide variety of vegetation and carrion, stock kills are not common. A sheepherder friend, George Chournous, has documented bear-killed sheep in Cache and Box Elder Counties, although he personally shot or trapped only a few problem bruins in a lifetime. He actually tried to protect bears on occasion by carrying orphan cubs well away from sheep. He once took considerable pains to pack a wounded cub away from his sheep herd using a sling apparatus on a very nervous horse.

Utah bears rarely attack a human being. An attack might occur when a bear feels cornered or a sow is protecting cubs.

BOBCATS

This animal can be found almost any place in Utah. I have taken two bobcats, which had been stalking chukar partridges, in the sage terrain of the Book Cliffs. The pelts were made into rugs by a taxidermist who offered to pay over $100 per cat. The price has gone up since then.

In totally different terrain, the spruce and aspen forests of the northeastern Uinta Mountains, I have also found bobcats. One had been dragging a dead beaver across a back road at night. As the cat vanished from my truck headlights, I shined a flashlight out my left window. The cat was sitting on a log two feet away glaring at me. Reluctant to leave its kill, the bobcat remained in the vicinity for another hour, allowing my young son and me to study its beautiful markings and determined spirit. When we finally drove away to camp at Browne Lake for the next day's fishing, I suspect the bobcat continued working on that beaver.

Bobcats are likely to inhabit the wide, open sage expanses. Trappers seek them particularly in the western semi-desert counties. Here cats subsist on jack rabbits, and other small animals. Weighing only 20-25 lbs. they can inconspicuously dwell near man and get along on much smaller fare than lion or bear.

In 1977 a hunting moratorium was placed on bobcats, partly due to heavy poaching and illegal trapping, including over-limits. The high price for a pelt has kept them in demand. Studies are conducted frequently in some areas to determine huntable-trappable numbers. Not covered in the lion-bear proclamation, the bobcat is listed in the annual furbearers regulations.

Utah's Uinta Mountains are reported by backpackers to harbor the secretive **lynx**. Resembling bobcats, they are a heavier breed with tufted ears, found more abundantly in Canada than in the Lower 48. There are no open seasons on the lynx in Utah.

COYOTES

There is no game status in Utah for the coyote. It is so widely distributed and so sought by agriculturalists, particularly sheepmen, that it is considered a predator to be shot on sight. Perhaps it should be added to the list of game animals, although sheep interests have always opposed it.

I have used the distressed rabbit call to bring in coyotes on the west desert country of Tooele and Juab counties, have seen many more in Emery and Garfield counties, and have heard their hunting cry in the Book Cliffs of Uintah and Grand counties. From a motel room in Green River, Emery County, I have heard coyote families communicating with one another barely outside the town limits. Another morning while deer hunting in the Book's McCook Ridge area, companions and I were awakened by coyotes calling one another to join the hunt. It was as wild a shrieking and yelping as I've ever heard. On another occasion, I was awakened one night 20 miles from the nearest Book Cliffs road by a distant howl. The answer came less than three feet from my head, just outside the tent. After that, I lay awake wide-eyed for over an hour trying to figure out the critter's audacity. He must have known I was there. Another time, in the Uinta Mountains I saw a male-female duo which seemed more interested in playing a mating game than in my presence. One shot and they were a blur of gold and grey fur. Few animals can run faster than a spooked coyote

Some of the state's heaviest coyote populations are along Utah's four borders, possibly due to agricultural activities in remote regions. But with such an increase of coyotes following the banning of poisoned baits, it is possible a beleaguered rancher anywhere might invite a careful and responsible shooter in to help him control coyote numbers.

One Utahn experienced at bringing in coyotes with rabbit calls is Bob Templeton, Fruit Heights, Davis County. Templeton says "to blow or squeal as if a wounded rabbit once or twice. Don't overdo it. Remain absolutely quiet and sit where you are camouflaged, waiting quietly for the slightest movement. Any unnatural noise will send them skittering. Keep a vigil on the shadows. Windless days are best for obvious reasons, since these little wolves have a keen nose." Templeton suggests you shoot accurately, "because you will probably only get one shot." In winter, Templeton dresses in white, even wrapping his rifle in white cloth.

Spotlighting coyotes or jack rabbits in Utah has not been illegal in the past, but pointing a spotlight at game animals like deer is illegal when firearms are nearby. So, some good advice is to notify a local conservation officer what you are doing, likewise a sheriff who might patrol the area. Generally, you won't be bothered much in the sagebrush, but may in mountainous terrain. If spotlighting, watch out for other animals, including kit fox, raccoon etc. and know what the proclamations say about them.

Officially, Utah has no documented sightings of **timber or other wolves**. However, seasoned coyote hunters I know say they have definitely seen timber wolves on the Uinta North Slope near the rugged, remote Kabell Meadows region. Probably only time will tell.

National legislators have debated whether to allow the timber wolf re-introduction into Yellowstone National Park. Stockmen argue that the villain of Little Red Riding Hood stories would cause sheep and cattle deaths. However, any wolves on the spacious and remote Uinta North Slope would probably not cause confrontation problems with mankind.

The Book Cliffs are a prime area for bobcats and other predators.

OTHER SPECIES

Utah's furbearer proclamation lists **red and kit foxes, badgers, mink, weasel or ermine**, and many other species.They are found in such abundance that hunting or trapping limits are usually open. Kit foxes are fairly common on the western sage flats. The red fox, once rare in Utah, is making a comeback. I saw several in 1989 near farmlands in Rich County. Beautiful animals and the main fare on hunts in other parts of the world, they are often considered predators in the Beehive State. Yet, I know of one farmer who never bothers the foxes who follow him during spring plowing. "They eat far more rodents than the occasional chicken," he says. "I don't treat them as a problem at all."

Other animals rightfully protected in Utah include the secretive **pine marten.** True, one will eat a fisherman's catch at any opportunity. But I still remember the thrill of seeing a marten near Notch Mountain in the Uintas' Provo River drainage. A few other rare sightings have been made of **wolverines**, perhaps the wildest and toughest little critter left anywhere in the world. Most are relegated these days to Alaska and Canada. To me, such a sighting in Utah reminds us that nature still has meaning in our lives close to home.Hopefully, hunters or landowners will also recognize that these creatures provide one more symbol of the frontier wild, enriching our quality of life. Who can say they have not marveled at the single sighting of an ermine, or white weasel?

One traditional native of Utah seems to have disappeared. It is the **black-footed ferret**, that masked and relentless raider of prairie dog colonies. The latter's demise in Utah probably helped precipitate the extinction of ferrets in Utah. Nevertheless, the possibility of seeing one was raised during the 1980s by confirmed observations in Wyoming. If anyone can confirm a black-footed ferret in the Beehive State, contact the UDWR. Rewards are often offered for ferret sightings.

PHEASANTS — PARTRIDGES

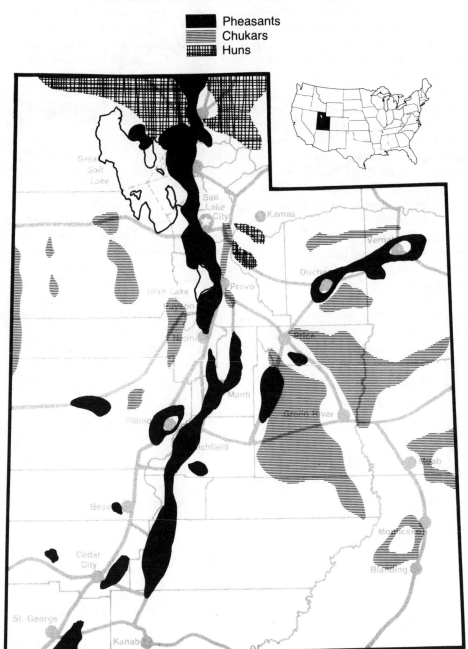

CHAPTER SIXTEEN
Upland Birds and Bunnies Too

In Utah, upland birds include ring-necked pheasant, two types of quail, three species of "forest grouse," plus sage grouse, chukar and Hungarian partridges, mourning doves, white-tailed ptarmigan, wild turkeys and a new bird on the block, the sandhill crane. Cottontail rabbits and hares are also discussed here because they are included with birds on Utah's small game license and in the Upland Bird Proclamation. Jack rabbits are considered predators (no hunting license required) in Utah, but worthy opponent that they are, will be covered here.

PHEASANTS — In Utah, the "Chinese" pheasant, faces an uphill battle. Little of the state can be honestly called "pheasant habitat." Only 2-3 percent of Utah is cultivated in crops like corn and alfalfa which pheasants favor. Agricultural areas are also being managed more "effectively" nowadays, at least for landowners. For ringnecks, it means less "wild" corner cover, fewer brambled ditch rows, and less habitat. The number of guns has increased on every available cropland acre until there may now well be more hunters than pheasants. Some wags along the Wasatch Front even complain that the pheasant is a "rare and endangered species."

The pheasant is too wily to ever be eradicated by hunting pressure, but there is concern about habitat. The pheasant is not exactly a hardy creature in cold weather. Some studies show it surviving only about two average Utah winters. Right now, ideal habitat runs in a Y shape from Washington County northward along the strip of civilization to about Utah County. Then, it branches off easterly into the Uintah Basin. The main stem reaches to northern Cache and Box Elder Counties. The best counties carry lowland agricultural real estate: Millard, Iron, Sevier, Sanpete, Emery, Piute, Duchesne, Uintah, parts of Juab, Utah, Weber, Cache, Box Elder. Counties with spotty populations of *Phasianus colchicus* are Washington, Kane, Garfield, Grand, Morgan Tooele, and the Jordan River Valley in southern Salt Lake County. Most of it is on private land, and more of that than ever before is posted "No Trespassing."

Some of the traditional hotspots, north to south, are: western Cache County, Tremonton-Howell Valley in Box Elder County, western Weber County from Plain City to the Farmington Bay Wildlife Management area, Utah County along the shoreline and croplands adjoining Utah Lake, Duchesne River bottoms and nearby farms, including Ute tribal lands to Randlett (Indian license required). Ditto the Vernal area in Uintah County, farming acreage in Juab County, the entire Delta-Lyndyll lowlands to Fillmore area in Millard County, the farming strip from Emery County's Castle Dale to Elmo, all of Sanpete Valley, Gunnison area to Salina, the Richfield area, and Beryl farmlands in western Iron County.

Already one of nature's most savvy critters, pheasants grow even more elusive where hunted as much as in Utah. Generally, these birds will be in the croplands opening morning and then hide out in stream bottoms and marshes. On a second weekend quest in Sanpete Valley, I found pheasants had moved into sage and oak-strewn foothills above Ephraim and Manti. Southwest of Gunnison, I bagged rooster limits on consecutive days along the brambled edges of the Sevier River. One opener on the northeast banks of Utah Lake, I watched as birds hid from gunners following the 8 a.m. inaugural by flattening down in beet and potato fields. When pressured, they hurried to shoreline tamarisk and swamps. I watched one rooster fly to a mat of cattails just out of shotgun range and stay there all day. I had neither boat or chest waders to reach him. But the smartest cockerel I ever met was just east of Duchesne. It crawled into one side of a short culvert where I thought my friend and I had him cornered. Yet, we could never flush him out. Finally, realizing we couldn't remain forever, we left him to his smug escape.

A favorite strategem is running through cover rather than flying above it. Birds may become airborne once, but learn quickly, and then it is difficult to get them off the ground. Because of it, a good dog is a asset, particularly after the first 20 minutes of opening morning. Best method is to walk about in half circles and halt as if you have spotted a bird. Sometimes, you must nearly step on one before he will show. The hunter in a hurry is apt to find no shooting at all. Stopping occasionally gives game a chance to grow nervous and suspect that they have possibly been seen.

Toughest to flush out are those wily birds ensconced in the thick tules around water. Utah has allowed for this by providing a longer season in the waterfowl management areas. Armed with licenses for upland and waterfowl game, the gunner can legally take geese, ducks, and pheasants in the same place. I've also seen male pheasants as high as 7,000 feet in the mouth of Rock Canyon on the Uinta South Slope. This is strictly an escape plot, for the birds would find the winter too cold there for survival in most years.

One answer to few pheasants and crowded hunting in Utah has been the "hunting unit." To date, they easily comprise the best shooting in Utah's annual rooster roundup. Most of these units are well advertised ahead of the hunt, scheduled for the first Saturday in November. These posted units raise a few dollars for local farming co-ops, and help maintain quality control. Only so many gunners are allowed on a farmer's "Back 40." The landowner also feels better about allowing trespass when he can harvest some of the "grain-eaters." Check with the UDWR, Utah Farm Bureau, or local landowner associations for a list of units and how to apply.

Neighborhood "Triangle Committees" composed of owners, hunters and UDWR officials evaluate each unit following the "pheasant follies" and determine how many guns can be allowed in next time. They are first-come, first-served in most areas. If you do fail to garner a permit, best hunting is likely to be on the wildlife management units, or the unposted periphery in stream bottoms and semi-wild foothills. Know the boundaries well.

Then, too, Utah's sportsmen's clubs and other entities offer preserve shooting. If this is not on public land, shooting may be allowed much of the year. Since these preserves must be commercially licensed, a list can be obtained from the UDWR.

Good outdoor manners will aid in keeping private lands open to pheasant hunters.

QUAIL — These birds are not widely hunted in Utah, but they could be since the bird is fairly well spread along the Wasatch Front. The two quail species are the top-knotted valley and Gambel's. The latter is found almost entirely in Washington County's semi-desert terrain. Bobwhite, so popular in the mid-West and South, have not taken hold in Utah, although stocking attempts have been been made in the past.

Valley quail are found primarily in the Wasatch foothills, often close to residential areas. in Salt Lake City, Ogden, Provo, that they are thought of as more "decorative" than huntable. For one thing, it is illegal in the state to discharge a firearm within 600 feet of any residential dwelling. The best places to find quail in a more wild setting are the canyon stream bottomlands, especially those with oak brush. This would include the brush-laden foothills in Morgan County, or sectors of the Sevier in central Utah. The quail may be slow to spook, but can move quickly when taking to the wing. Traveling in coveys of 5-15, the birds are not considered as tough to take as doves.

The Gambel's quail in Utah's "Dixie" is a favorite target in a warm climate among cactus and mesquite. Water is vital, so look for seeps and waterholes. Like the valley quail, Gambel's can explode suddenly in front of you, frequently in all directions. Quail seasons usually open with pheasants in early November. The Gambel's season runs to December, generally a little longer than the statewide quail quest.

CHUKARS — The chukar partridge, so named because of its propensity to keep calling "chukar, chukar" even when pursued, is a popular game bird in Utah.

I have personally enjoyed trying to get uphill of this energetic creature, knowing that it will not likely fly if encountered from below. Approach from below and it will simply run ahead like a rabbit. Flushing it can mean steep and tough hiking. When it does take wing, there are few faster flyers. And when alighting in some crag or rocky knoll, it will probably hit the decks running.

Some of my best shooting has been in the foothills of the Wasatch Range, right above Salt Lake City, Springville, Ogden and other populous areas. One morning, southeast of Salt Lake City near the mouth of Big Cottonwood Canyon, our hunting party heard chukars calling before dawn, hiked above them, and found excellent shooting. Unfortunately, some foothill suburb construction has now ruled out chukar hunting along the Wasatch Front.

The bird has taken root in nearly every steep, semi-arid mountain range in Utah, including the Oquirrhs, Box Elder County, Uintas, Book Cliffs. Another region I've liked is in southern Uintah County from Floy Wash to the Hays Canyon Road, and in the Deep Creek and other west desert ranges of Tooele and Juab counties. In remote areas, like the Book Cliffs, chukars are often fond of taking a "dust" bath on back roads.

These Asian imports have done very well outside agricultural areas, thus filling a gap left by pheasants. These heartily welcomed exotics have flourished because of similar habitat to their native semi-desert terrain. The longest seasons and best shooting are in Beaver, Carbon, Emery, Garfield, Grand, Iron, Kane, Piute, Tooele, Washington and Wayne Counties, parts of San Juan County, and west of I-15 in Juab, Millard, Salt Lake, and Utah counties. Box Elder County has a good population west of Snowville southward to Locomotive Springs. Hunting has been closed at times in northwestern San Juan, northern Duchesne, Uintah, and Daggett counties.

The season runs in best shooting areas from about the second Saturday in September to January of the following year. Seasons usually close early in Cache, Morgan, Rich, Sanpete, Summit, Wasatch, Weber Counties. Limits are usually five daily, and 10 in possession.

If winter snows begin to pile up, these birds will often take to wind-swept ridgelines and plateaus, just as elk do. It's a strange reverse migration for the birds, going uphill instead of down. It means that if you can't find chukars where they used to be in milder weather, they may have gone above foothill ledges and normal habitat.

Utah has a unique way of raising chukars for stocking from game farms. Thousands of birds are hatched at the Springville unit, then "farmed" out to volunteer sportsmen to raise. In good years, some 17,000 day-old chicks might go out to be raised, then released in the wild. Brightly colored, energetic, and good eating, these are all reasons to attempt outwitting a chukar.

HUNGARIAN PARTRIDGES — While chukars are fairly widely distributed in Utah, their slightly larger cousins, the Huns, are restricted primarily to northern counties. In Cache, Box Elder and Rich, check the grainfields and nearby sage or other brushy cover. For a decade following introduction, that was their home territory. I've also seen the round-winged, grayish-hued Huns in Wasatch

County. The proclamation now lists them as fair game in Davis, Morgan Summit, Tooele and Weber Counties, an indication they are expanding their range in this state. With short, stubby wings, Hungarians rarely fly far. However, they are nomadic, not necessarily found today where they were 48 hours ago. A local farmer may be a big help in locating the wandering birds. Their habitat and food supply coincide heavily with grainfields, so many farmers are willing to assist a careful hunter in locating the birds on private land. Seasons usually run September to late November, five daily limit, 10 in possession.

FOREST GROUSE — Utah has three legal targets, blue, ruffed, and an increasing number of sharp-tailed grouse. Hunters should study the bird books to make certain they are not looking down the muzzle at a Franklins or other grouse. The ruffed is a citizen of aspen slopes, with blues often frequenting higher conifers. The blue is also a staple of arid west desert ranges. Sharp-tails, like Hungarian partridges, tend to haunt the northern county grasslands and brushy foothills.

The nice thing about forest grouse is that they are open season during the deer hunt and often located in muley terrain. The "mountain chickens" also make for good camp meat. I've seen many ruffeds in the Uintas, Boulder, Manti Mountain, Wasatch, Fishlake forestlands. I've found blues in the Abajos and Stansburys. Both grouse species, especially the strutting ruffeds, are called "fool hens" in Utah, but that label ends quickly with the first fired shell. Grouse startle you by "blowing up" at your feet, sail downhill 200 yards, then become extremely difficult to locate.

Searching for Hungarian Partridges in typical northern Utah habitat.

Ruffeds may be within a few minutes of pavement at the top of Daniels Canyon, south of Strawberry Reservoir, or in high aspen terrain almost anywhere in the Wasatch. A hunter can connect on a bird or two and be home for a luncheon appointment. That is one of the main attractions of the forest grouse in Utah, a major reason why many in Utah take up the fine art of scattergunning.

SAGE GROUSE — I've taken sage grouse in Utah on the high sage slopes above Scofield Reservoir in Carbon County, and I've seen others do it south of Strawberry Reservoir. Some good populations can be found in Rich County and other high plateau sage country. Ditto in western Box Elder County, plus eastern and southern sage expanses.

Generally, the Wasatch Front counties have few sage grouse. There are some birds in southeastern Tooele County, but cold winters and dry summers can adversely affect sage grouse. With few large populations, the seasons are short, with limits of only two-three birds. Concentrate on 6000 to 8000 foot high elevations. Scout ahead as you would for deer hunting.

MOURNING DOVE — Utah's dove opener is usually Sept. 1 each year to provide shooting before cool nights send the birds south. Doves are frequently found near sunflower patches, water holes or taking foothill dust baths. When nights cool, shooting is better in the valleys. When nights become cold, shooting is better in the southern counties. If frost and plummeting temperatures invade the state, they're gone completely.

Note: Since the dove is a migratory bird, it is not listed with the upland bird proclamation but included with sandhill cranes, subject to federal guidelines. Shooting hours are regulated closely. Limits are usually a generous 10, with 20 after the first day.

Probably no bird in Utah requires more quick and accurate shooting than the mourning dove. Gun manufacturers love the many loads of No. 9 and 10s expended on these rapid flyers. As many as 30,000 licensees go after these birds on the opener. A drill at clay birds first helps.

I'd also scout (no hunting in summer) for dove populations in the summer. You can often hear their low "coo coo," and see their colorful salmon pink and pastel blue form in the fork of a cottonwood tree. When nesting, they rarely bother to put more than a few straws together for a nest. Doves remain near civilization to take advantage of grain crops. Watch for their distinctive sharp tail and zig-zag flight near benchland farms. Concentrate on water after a dry summer, especially in the west desert.

Band-tailed pigeons are listed in the proclamation with doves. They are found almost exclusively in the southern climes, mostly Washington County.

WHITE-TAILED PTARMIGAN — This species is an alpine bird of the high tundra. In Utah it is found only in the Uinta Mountains, and there mostly in the upper Uinta River drainage within sight of 13,528 foot high Kings Peak. Counties open for hunting are Summit, Duchesne, and Uintah. Only the hardy need attempt this one, since it requires horse or foot pack into terrain above 10,000 feet altitude in September-October. Utah ptarmigan were transplanted from Colorado a decade or so ago, but have taken a liking to their new home, UDWR biologists report.

SANDHILL CRANES — The first attempt to hold a crane hunt in Utah, despite many cranes in neighboring states, was a failure. Several bands of anti-hunters banding together in 1988 complained to the governor that these "spiral dancers" were "too scarce to kill." The hunt was finally held in 1989 after northern Utah landowners had a complaint of their own: the sandhillers were eating their grain as fast as they could drop the seeds. In the Rich County area, a rancher told me that he couldn't continue to harvest a crop if the state didn't begin to harvest sandhill cranes. The state finally declared a shoot. Anti-crane groups bought up nearly half the permits. So, perhaps some 20 cranes were harvested among the issued 100 permits in that first year.

In the meantime, these migratory birds were harvested in other states along the Rocky Mountain Flyway, including Wyoming and Idaho. Estimates given by biologists were that some 18,000 cranes had to be thinned out or birds would out-number food supply. Migrating sandhills are so numerous along the Bear River in Rich and Cache Counties and into Wyoming that I've seen them in great numbers during mid-September. In middle March, they may return to grain stubble fields covered with a foot of snow on top. I once maintained a crane checking station, with hunters saying they had never seen a smarter bird. One gunner said he hunted for three days before getting close enough to launch a shot of No. 4s. An old bird book says, "It is easier to catch a fox asleep than a crane unawares." There is a temptation to begin shooting a quarter mile away, one gunner told me, "yet I know my No. 4s will not carry more than 45-50 yards. " As for eating cranes, one successful permittee said, "The bird tastes like turkey."

It is also true that the rare and endangered whooping crane often flies with sandhills. I photographed two whoopers one afternoon which feasted on just-planted grain fields. A federal biologist monitored the white whoopers. The next fall, the vigilant marshal was back, prohibiting any hunting in the region where the whoopers flew. There was no way a gun-toter could get near that rare and endangered whooping crane. With such careful monitoring, attempts to halt a sandhill hunt based on "saving" whooping cranes carries no validity that I can see.

Sandhills are worth watching year-round. They have a unique spring "mating dance" ritual. Their call is a loudly grinding "garooo, garooo." Their giant wing span makes you think you are much closer than you are.

WILD TURKEY — This is a specialized hunt in Utah's warmer southern climates. Basically, the wild turkey inhabits lower conifer forests, particularly Ponderosa pine on warmest south-facing slopes. It is a paradox perhaps, that the smartest bird anywhere may be a wild turkey (with apologies to sandhill cranes) and the dumbest, an oft self-destructing domestic turkey. In any event, a friend who hunted turkeys on the south side of Boulder Mountain said he had to camouflage from head to toe, sneak about on his hands and knees for several days, and remain absolutely quiet before getting a single shot at one old tom.

Utah's diligent turkey-stocking program is paying off. Populations are on the increase. Season is in May for one male turkey. Hunting grounds are in Wayne, Garfield, Kane, and parts of Washington and Iron counties.

RABBITS AND HARES — Utah has four species of rabbits or hares: the common jackrabbit, cottontail, snowshoe, and the infrequently-seen varying hare. The latter two are forest animals found in mule deer and grouse habitat. The youngster with the .22 or shotgun is most likely to go after cottontails; many deer hunters have focused on the jacks via high-powered rifles in order to gain practice on a running targets come the deer quest. If you can hit a running jack, you can probably connect with a running muley. It was also on a jack expedition in the west desert that I learned the tremendous advantage of hand-loaded cartridges. I'd been slightly off target at the longer distances in the past but with the closer tolerances required for hand-loads, precise accuracy was greatly improved. Other deer hunters will use GI ammo on the rabbits at far less expense than factory loads. It is nothing in the far-flung west desert counties to shoot a hundred rounds a day. But military ammunition can only occasionally be purchased at the army-navy surplus stores nowadays. Incidentally, deer loads of 150 grains and up will weigh more and shoot lower than GI ammo, so be sure to sight in again just before switching from rabbits to larger game.

Of course, rabbits are a worthwhile target in their own right. In fact, hunters in every western state probably spend more time and money annually on the so-called lowly rabbit than any other game. At the same time, landowners and livestockers are benefitted. As the phrase goes, "Sixteen rabbits will eat as much as one cow." The jack is considered a pest by most ranchers who share their public land grazing rights with this ubiquitous rabbit.

Jacks and cottontails run in cycles, with an up-cycle in the late 1980s. Much depends on weather and food, and that nemesis of both jacks and sage grouse, aerial spraying to kill sagebrush. It is still done in Utah, although the practice seems to have abated to some extent.

I have found good jack shooting on the west desert counties such as Box Elder, Tooele, Juab, Millard, Beaver. I've found fast cottontail shooting in the Uintah Basin, and Wasatch Front near rocky foothills. On one shoot east of Salina near Fremont Junction, it seemed the world was made of cottontails. Ditto on the Book Cliffs, including the Ute Indian Reservation. Try the foothills as high as 8000-9000 feet, especially rock outcroppings. Cottontails also reside within a quarter mile of farms and civilization, say in Emery, Carbon, Sanpete, Sevier, Piute, Beaver, Iron, Washington and Kane counties. When these bunnies are spooked, they move quickly enough to prove a difficult target for anyone. In all rabbit hunting, hesitate often enough to let the animals think you have seen them. Otherwise, they'll let you walk right by.

No attempt should be made to handle a jack, dead or alive, without wearing gloves. Tularemia, a highly infectious disease which can painfully swell human lymph nodes, is found in Utah jacks and can get into open sores or cuts on any human hand. Utahns eat cottontails and snowshoes, but should skip the jackrabbits.

If you are going after jacks by spotlight, check the laws. Deer and big game cannot be legally spotlighted with uncased guns about, so if the ungulates show, turn the light off and move on. Some counties also have local laws, so it is a good idea to check with the county sheriff's office. If private land is involved, permission can oft be granted for the careful rabbit hunter.

Snowshoes are found anywhere in Utah where deer are. I'd concentrate on the higher conifer slopes in the Uintas or other high mountains. Mother Nature may err in turning these rabbits white before snow falls. Afterward, they're difficult to see. Look carefully for the black ear tips. Expect a quick exit when discovered, for padded feet give snowshoes cushioned traction across snow.

Another critter Utahns hunt along with rabbits is the **ground squirrel,** numerous in and around farmlands, as well as flatlands and foothills. Farmers like to keep their numbers down, so permission may be granted for an accurate .22 shooter to help out. Utah has no open season on tree squirrels. Ground squirrels require no license.

One final thought on rabbit and ground squirrel shooting. Most Utah gun accidents occur while hunting them. Rabbits in particular can pop up almost anywhere, often on two sides of a car. Be especially careful. And don't put a live round in the firing chamber while in a moving vehicle. It's the law in Utah, and a good one.

MAJOR WATERFOWL AREAS

Best Duck — Goose Hunting

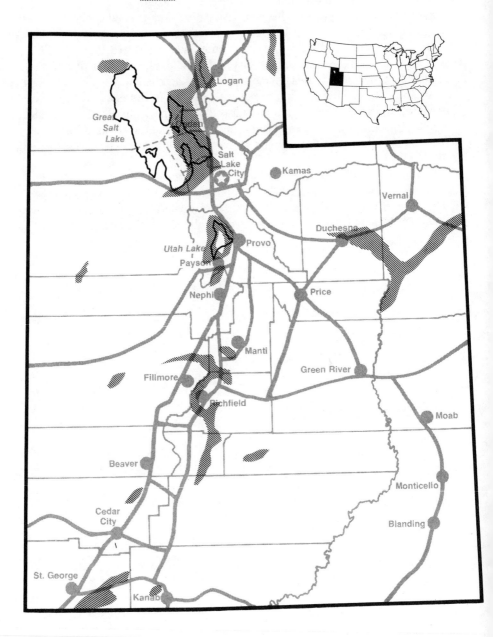

CHAPTER SEVENTEEN

Waterfowl In Abundance

Probably no major cities in America have quality waterfowl shooting so near their doorsteps as Utah's Wasatch Front communities. Fifteen minutes west of Salt Lake City and Ogden, a duck hunter could be sitting in a blind alongside Great Salt Lake looking at pintails, mallards, shovelers, gadwalls, teal, and perhaps Canada geese. For those who have a whistling swan permit, that could be a legal target as well. A bonus outing might include viewing many shore and wading birds: great blue and black-crowned night herons, bitterns, avocets, sandpipers and killdeers, snowy egrets, black-legged stilts, marsh hawks, and the state bird, the protected California gull. Some of the best waterfowl property is admittedly taken up with private duck clubs, but there is also public shooting throughout the state.

One past problem, heavy flooding in the mid 1980s, is correcting itself. Great Salt Lake rose so high that dikes were inundated, nesting was impossible, and highways around the lake, including I-15 to Wendover, were threatened with lapping water. A huge and expensive pumping project to transfer water from Great Salt Lake Lake was undertaken. Especially hard hit were the private duck clubs. One problem was in rebuilding access roads and dikes. Bear River Bay was inundated and even the headquarters were abandoned. The refuges are now rebuilding.

The private clubs have helped public shooters by thinning out competition on places like Farmington Bay, Ogden Bay, and Turpin Marsh. The duck opener is usually one of heavy competition along all Great Salt Lake dikes and roads, especially on weekends. Many serious duck hunters I know make arrangements to hunt midweek, avoiding the weekend crowds on public marshes. In addition, many Utahns get out only on opening day, then retire to the fireplace. Some of the best duck hunting may come after early October. Pick a windy day, as birds stay on the wing to find a quiet bay, and you could be alone with excellent shooting. Ditto on large, deep lakes, like Flaming Gorge and Fish Lake, that freeze slowly. Shallow Utah Lake ices quickly, but it has some fair to good late shooting at the inlets. Access is via county roads west of Provo, American Fork, Lehi, and north of Benjamin and Payson. A good road leads west of Lincoln Beach to Goshen Bay, although such easy access from there southward makes meadowlarks easier to find than ducks. A boat is a definite advantage on Utah Lake.

Although ducks are harvested from public dikes and roads in Utah, the best method is to find a quiet place where blinds and decoys can work their magic. A good retriever breed is a decided asset. Airboats or other means of departing the easy access also helps. But let's take a look at a the many diversified waterfowling opportunities around Utah.

In addition to the many marshes around Great Salt Lake, there are from north to south: Bear River through Cache County to Cutler Reservoir, Bear River Bay; 10-mile long Bear Lake in Rich County and the upper Bear River; Locomotive

Springs in western Box Elder County; the west desert's Fish Springs and scattered ponds to Rush Lake and Vernon Reservoir; Pineview and Mantua Reservoirs east of Ogden and Brigham City, respectively; Utah Lake with Powell Slough, Goshen, Provo and Mud bays, plus marshes around this 20-mile long lake; Sevier River bottomlands and reservoirs such as Yuba, Gunnison Bend, and Piute; Scipio Reservoir westerly to DMAD through Millard County to Clear Lake; eastern Utah's Strawberry -Soldier Creek Reservoir, Flaming Gorge, and the Green River with tributaries, along with Pelican Lake; all of the many lakes mentioned in the fishing sections through the central sector to Beaver, Iron and Washington counties. An isolated duck marsh is Bicknell Bottoms in Wayne County. I have seen ducks and geese there in profusion, spring and fall. Then, there are the many creeks and ponds such as the lower Duchesne and East Fork-Sevier rivers which offer jump shooting along unfrozen current far into the season when much flat water has frozen over. Late in the season, upper Lake Powell, and Santa Clara River drainage in Washington County can offer waterfowl opportunities. Other public waterfowl marshes include: Howard Slough north of Provo on Utah Lake; Harold Crane marshes west of Plain City; Public Shooting Grounds west of Ogden; Promontory on the northeast end of Great Salt Lake; Clear Lake in Millard County south of Delta; Desert Lake in the same vicinity.

But the one habitat which yields by far the most ducks and geese to Utah licensees is the east shoreline of Great Salt Lake. By the early 1990s, this resource should be back doing what it has always done best: providing nesting, food and shelter for waterfowl. The entire 50-mile long shoreline provides resident ducks until wet and cold autumn weather pushes the northern flights in. This infusion from Canada and Montana is not always what some gunners expect, but it can mean birds today where they were not yesterday. Great Salt Lake also has many mallards and pintails remaining well after ice is too thick to take a regular boat onto the lake. I've also seen decoys on a foot of ice lure the real thing in. Besides these hardy types, many blue- and green-winged teal will migrate in, along with shovelers, gadwalls, scaup and an occasional redhead, cinnamon teal, or goldeneye.

Access to Great Salt Lake marshes is west of such communities as Salt Lake City, Farmington, Sunset, Roy, Ogden, Brigham City. Most public marshes such as Farmington,Turpin, etc. are marked. North and south banks of Great Salt Lake have less tule marsh than the near-city eastern side, but offer shooting wherever there is vegetation and cover. The remote west side of the lake has more rocky-sandy shoreline with less duck habitat than that along the Wasatch Front. Islands and estuaries in the lake have ducks and geese for the adventurous boater, although many colonies of pelicans, terns, gulls and other birds may prevail.

The colorful harlequin duck species can show in the river systems like the Green below Flaming Gorge Dam. Utah has few if any black ducks and no wood ducks. Canvasbacks are becoming rare. A gunner must work with a federally-controlled point system and know his ducks if he is to take a redhead, baldpate or other less-than-common breeds. Of course, the ubiquitous coots or "mudhens" offer a liberal limit anytime. Wilson's snipes and mergansers or fish ducks can be be taken legally in most years, but offer little in the edibility department.

The warmly-dressed hunter waiting patiently in a secluded blind has the best chance among all waterfowlers. This presupposes, of course, that you have the decoys in a natural setting, with shine of your shotgun muzzle out of the sunlight, boat or canoe camouflaged. Ducks have some of the best eyes in the bird kingdom, almost on a par with antelope among game animals. One way to lure in birds, as longtime Salt Lake City duck hunter Douglas Schilling proved to me, is placing decoys in a "social" setting. He arranges them to face several directions, in unequal-sized groupings which appear randomly natural. The best way to learn is to watch ducks in the off-season to see how they rest and/or feed in the water. Duck calls may bring them in a little closer, but I've found these work best in the lips of a consummate veteran. The main thing is to offer a scenario which sends wary birds a signal of utmost security. Also be patient. As a drake pintail circles in for a watery landing 60 yards away, a special perseverance is needed to let it wing in another 20 or yards or more. More patience may be required in following a speck from the distant horizon to determine if it is incoming flock of teal, or just a flurry of gnats 10 feet away.

The dike-walker must have keen eyes to keep out of sight when a duck moves in, although some other less alert soul may suddenly veer a flock off out of range in the final seconds of truth. The beginner or young gunner will likely try this approach a few times before learning of the value of all hunters remaining concealed.

Good places for jump shooting include the Sevier in the sage country below Yuba Dam. Another might be the Beaver River from the marshes just west of Beaver community to Minersville Reservoir and the meadows below down to the town of Minersville. There is some private land here. However, habitat and birds are often on a quilt-work of private and public land, with the enterprising license-holder able to locate the latter.

Waterfowl seasons on these migratory birds usually run, within the U.S. Fish and Wildlife Service guidelines, from first Saturday in October to late December. Opening day trend the past few seasons has a noon start. In some years, a split season occurs. The duck limit is often four a day, including no more than one hen mallard, no more than one pintail, and no more than two redheads or one canvasbacks, or one of each. On geese it is usually five, limit of two Canada or dark species

Federal and state marshals patrol Great Salt Lake on a regular basis. One frequent arrest is shooting after hours. Be prudent how you transport waterfowl. If you carry birds for a friend, better include the license and stamp(s) with you. One duck hunter took three limits by himself to the poultry shop for plucking and when he could not produce three licenses, he was arrested. Also, be sure your own stamp is signed and affixed properly to your license.

GEESE TECHNIQUES

Random hunting for geese rarely works in Utah. The consistently successful shooter will study morning flights from resting areas to feeding grounds, likely a grain field a few miles from water. Around Great Salt Lake, this usually means a

Davis or Weber county grain field. The birds may circle several times to check out the landscape before moving in. If anything is out of kilter, they will not land. Your warning they are coming is often a loud "barking." Proper camouflage is a must. Use sheets as camouflage on snow. You will need to scout them to find feeding patterns. Another method, as in duck hunting, is to know where geese hang out on river bars and banks. The birds will usually be in groups of 10 or more, but on one cold November day along the Bear River I bagged a lone Canadian. I believe a band of geese, with all of their alert sensory systems, are tougher to stalk than a single or even a few. Tread softly, and don't talk. Again, don't wear bright clothing and don't let gun muzzle reflect sunlight. Creep around bends with eyes and gun ready. I like to keep my finger on the safety latch at all times. Generally, geese will flush from much farther away than ducks. Where running water is making noise and pounding the nearby ground, you may have a better chance than where water runs slowly. It is not always necessary to do a lot of walking. Find a vantage point come sundown and glass where geese are bedding for the night. In the morning, check on where flights are going. A friend, Rob Crooks, formerly of Provo, used to take geese consistently by looking as closely for geese as some hunters seek out elk. He took many of his Canadians around Utah Lake. Other goose specialists I have hunted with can hear a gander honking or yelping high in the sky miles away, so tuned in to them are they.

If permission can be gained to private property, the Bear River bottomlands east of Woodruff and Randolph in Rich County can mean good goose shooting. Ditto on the Green River in eastern Daggett County. Other hot spots fluctuate with grain production and hunting pressure.

SWAN TECHNIQUES

Utah issues up to 2500 swan permits a year, with applications taken in late August. The permits, undersubscribed in the lottery draw, are then sold first-come, first-served. Swans are a worthy waterfowl challenge and make for some 12 lbs. of good eating.

Hunt whistling swans as you would geese. The bird is seldom taken by pure luck. Another important thing to remember is that swans are big. "When flying low," one gunner told me who hunts north of the Salt Lake Airport, "swans can seem to resemble a large jet." Be certain your target is in range before wasting shells and spooking the creature away forever. Utah has a large population of whistling swans moving through the Great Salt Lake area in an average year. The larger trumpeters are rather rare in Utah, but check the bird books to learn the difference. Swans may also be confused with snow geese. Swans are all-white; snow geese have black wing tips.

Searching for birds in the marshes of an inlet stream on the Great Salt Lake.

CHAPTER EIGHTEEN

Utah's Wildlife Future

Strange it is that those who strive to protect wildlife by curtailing hunting fail to realize the far greater importance of protecting wildlife *habitat*. All of the rifles and guns in all of the West will not do so much to decimate game populations as will loss of habitat.

The most important factor for big game is *winter* habitat. Deer, for example, have no trouble finding food in the summer. Range is plentiful. But when winter snow and cold seal off higher terrain, the animals have no choice but to move into foothill and valley areas. Fine, if they can. But more and more housing subdivisions, roads, pavement and human traffic are usurping this critical winter range for which there is no substitute. If a road or housing project blocks off winter migration of deer herds then thousands of animals can starve to death.

Artificial feeding? It has been used in dire emergencies, but there are three problems: (1) deer stomachs are not designed by nature to digest hay as a sudden diet; (2) animals gathered closely together transmit diseases; (3) worst of all, crowded animals destroy the range and no food may be available for years. That's what happened on Arizona's Kaibab National Forest when hunting was banned, a herd of 10,000 deer grew to some 100,000, and before hunting was continued, there was no range remaining even for the 10,000. Things become considerably worsened with people taking over deer winter range. Then, if hunting is not allowed to reduce game to the carrying capacity of the winter range, nature will kill in a much less humane way than the hunter's bullets.

I've seen this happen in a wholesale way in Salt Lake County after lax zoning ordinances allowed building homes all along the East Bench foothills. Deer starved, not a pretty sight at all. The only answer is to prevent loss of winter range or get the money to purchase it. Without that, Utah will not manage to keep deer populations at present levels, let alone increase them.

Elk and other game get along much better than deer, mostly because elk can subsist on hay, whereas deer may die while *bedded* in haystacks, as I've witnessed in Rich County. However, in Utah County, elk are in serious trouble because human housing has taken over what was once the winter range on the foothills of Mt. Nebo, Loafer, Hobble Creek. Those elk move down in winter to raid orchards and croplands. Special "depredation" hunts have tried to remove problem animals, but this has turned out to be a conflict with riflemen chasing elk between valley homes. Transplanting has been attempted, with some success; but that too requires chasing wapiti at a time when fat reserves are low, possibly stressing animals to death. The only permanent solution is to purchase winter range where the elk can gain the greater number of calories needed in winter cold while avoiding human conflicts. One organization trying to buy up such winter habitat is the Rocky Mountain Elk Foundation and its Utah Valley Chapter. Their goal is a most valid one. It could use help from all sportsmen.

Another problem in Utah is roads. Not only do they usurp vital winter range, but they inhibit deer and elk migrations. One of the more difficult deer-highway problems in Utah is the freeway from Payson to Nephi. Whenever deer range is on terrain as steep as that on Mt. Nebo, and a roadway is constructed almost directly below, deer will "pile" onto it. This herd will undoubtedly continue to come in conflict with vehicles on the road, as well as being denied winter migration. Thus, this herd must be sharply curtailed in number to provide sufficient space and food. Which is more important, roads precisely where they are . . . or more big game? Hunters, who are probably also motorists, must help in such decisions.

Another problem with roads, research indicates, is that elk won't tolerate them, at least if they mean much human traffic. Studies show some elk won't even cross them. Yet, one entity who should be concerned about outdoor recreation, the U.S. Forest Service, keeps building them into new timber sales. Ironically, they do this road-building at taxpayer expense, so hunters lose in both ways when elk are skittered away. Sportsmen should check into roads in their area, and prevent any further loss of wapiti habitat. Many other proposed roads into Utah backcountry, including one the length of the Book Cliffs from Ouray to U.S. 6, and another north of Strawberry Reservoir to Utah 150 in the western Uintas can only lessen future elk hunting possibilities.

Another habitat problem is oil industry usurpation of elk and moose calving areas, like those on the Uinta North Slope. Oil wells are already pumping on Henrys Fork and East Fork of the Bear, with more exploration sought right up to the boundary of the Uinta Wilderness Area. This is not only a violation of the spirit of the wilderness concept, but a threat to valuable big game habitat. A prospective oil exploration on the Stillwater Fork of the Bear, near Christmas Meadows, is a direct threat to scenic meadow habitat heavily utilized by elk and moose. Hunters should learn about the facts and write to their government officials and legislators. Sometimes, the developers express surprise that anyone objects to "progress." Let them know how you feel about protecting game habitat.

Deer habitat is reviewed each spring in what is known in Utah as the "range ride." Running from February in lower areas into April, the range ride allows conservation officers and sportsmen to look together at what is happening to big game habitat. If browse plants happen to be severely depleted, then deer may well exceed food supply. If deer appear too numerous for available food, the state may as well as let hunters harvest them with extra permits rather than let nature waste them. When that happens, license money, outdoor recreation and venison are all lost.

Utah should reassess the policy on making payments for deer damage to agricultural crops. These payments should be provided only on private land where hunting to control game population is allowed. The Utah Division of Wildlife Resources can continue to stock the Wasatch and other suitable mountain ranges, such as Nebo and Uintas, with mountain sheep and goats. More desert sheep could be planted in most of southern Utah if they can be purchased or traded with Nevada or Arizona. It does not appear to me that the exotics transplanted in New Mexico, including African ibex or antelope, would work out in Utah. The range can only support so many game animals, and it might as well be more deer, elk, moose, and antelope.

When it comes to waterfowl, some Utahns figure any water which winds up "unused" in marshlands and lower lakes is wasted. That is not true. Water must be used wisely, but water in swamplands is not "unused." Turpin Marsh and Farmington Bay are "million dollar marshes" dependent upon this water being allowed to flow west of Salt Lake City. The same is true on the Weber and Bear Rivers. The bird refuges, sanctuaries and hunting areas there would be non-existent if all water was consumed upslope by growing communities.

Another factor affecting future waterfowl shooting is quality of water. Oil wastes from the refineries north of Salt Lake City have threatened Farmington Bay's entire bird population more than once. Much has been done in the way of treatment lagoons, however, and the possibility of oil getting into Great Salt Lake is now much less likely. Unfortunately, one refinery had to be taken into court to end this problem. Much of the oil and slaughterhouse blood wastes from the packing houses west of Ogden have been cleaned up, improving water conditions for both fisheries and downstream waterfowl marshes. Another threat faced by Great Salt Lake waterfowl marshes is the creation of a proposed all fresh-water diking to create "Lake Wasatch." The idea has some possible merit for a fresh-water playground and fishery, but it should be thought through carefully for one good reason: under present planning, duck hunting as Utahns now know it would be flooded and destroyed.

Pheasant, quail, etc. are primarily up to state and county management. But it should be said that one of the major strongholds of the ringneck in Utah is the state-federal duck marsh. After opening day pushes pheasants out of the corn and grain fields, many of them also find suitable cover in lowland swamps and river bottoms. If wetlands are removed, both waterfowl and pheasants suffer. Pheasant habitat would also be benefitted if farmers could be persuaded to leave a little of their terrain wild or just not cut that final swatch of alfalfa . . . or even leave ditchbank cover.

Planting of chukar partridges should be increased. Fish and game departments the world over, including South Dakota and Nebraska, complain bitterly about the costs of pen-raising pheasants for stocking in the wild. But since the Asian chukar is accustomed to an arid climate, it is likely the bird will continue to do well throughout most of Utah's many uncultivated acres.

Hopefully, Utah will make up for past mistakes where the lion and bear are concerned. Once treated as predators, they were shot at year-around by anyone. Cougar numbers dropped off rapidly as non-resident guides moved in with clients, and took dozens, even hundreds of animals. Now, there is control over lion and bear hunting. Money derived from licenses should also be utilized to educate the public about the habitat requirements. Surveys should be conducted often enough to "keep a handle" on populations to prevent them from ever dipping again to the low levels of the early 1970s. Many Utahns would also like a review of laws which allow chasing of bears with hounds, a thing practiced by many hunters. In a democracy, the majority is supposed to rule, so everyone with a strong feeling on the subject should make them known.

Coyotes are often treated like vermin, but I hope the day never comes I can't hear or see that wonderful symbol of the wild. Fortunately, coyotes are probably moxy enough to never be placed on a rare or endangered list, but the state needs to maintain a healthy population balance. While sheepmen may justifiably worry about these predators, sportsmen must maintain vigil to see that coyotes are not again removed with poisonous baiting on public lands — which also kills indiscriminately anything which gets in the way. Shooting from airplanes is also questioned, especially in areas where coyotes are not specifically bothering livestock.

One thing which will make a difference is the hunter himself. If he treats private land as some hunters have done, with a wake of broken fences, open gates, dead livestock, and litter, then hunting in the future will continue to trend from private to public land, only, and/or "club" hunting. Another thing is indiscriminate shooting: songbirds, anything which gets in the way. There is no reason to kill something just because it is seen while carrying a gun.

That brings up a major problem in Utah, poaching. The latter is not always due to unlicensed nimrods. Some carry a license for deer, but shoot an elk or moose instead. It is no secret that Utahns could likely hunt moose now on the north Manti and Fishlake Forests if most of the moose introduced there had not been killed illegally. It is strange that Utah's scrupulous sportsmen allow this to happen. Conservation officers can't be everywhere. The only way this unethical practice can be curtailed is for honest sportsmen to help out by calling the "poaching hotline," 662-3337. Write down information about anyone suspicious and call it in. In most cases, you can remain anonymous. Rewards are offered for elk and moose kills up to and beyond $300 per call if resulting in successful prosecution of guilty individuals.

The state must also continue its current trend of managing for sport hunting rather than meat. Research should determine the success of quality hunting, legal taking of spike-only bulls etc. Are the three-point only deer hunts working out? Every effort must be made to obtain the answers and manage where a quality experience can be enhanced.

There is a definite trend in Utah toward "wildlife watching." Surveys indicate some 87 percent of all Utahns "enjoy just looking" at wildlife like peregrine falcons, songbirds etc. Some provision must be made for these people. At this writing, there is little funding for such interests, although public education, law enforcement, research and field work rarely come cheap. Utahns can help at income tax time by checking the entry "Do Something Wild." Simply indicate how much of the income tax return is allocated for this purpose.

Approximately 85 percent of Utah is in federal (public) ownership. So, much public hunting, primarily for big game, is assured. But many more hunting grounds would be possible for sportsman who respect private land. Every hunter needs to treat private land with the same respect he would his own. It is the only way those lands will remain open, or re-open, to the public in the future. The trend in trespass laws is to get tougher on non-owners. A convicted trespasser faces a fine up to $299 and loss of fishing-hunting license privileges. But, more important is another much heavier price which all must pay for the careless: "No Trespass" signs. It depends on us.

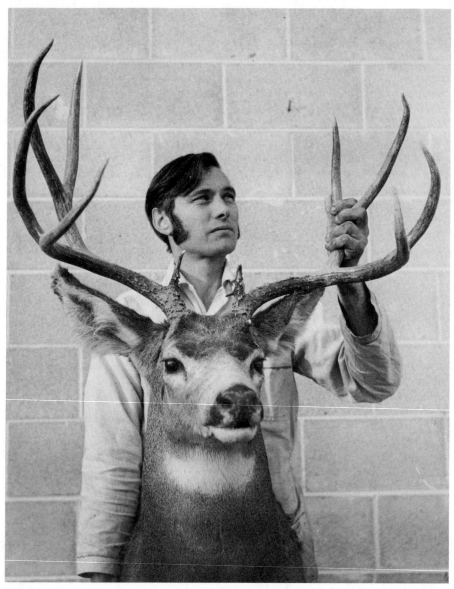

Having more trophy bucks like this one depends on preservation of critical winter range.

Utah's big game herds are of special worth to the state and should come under special scrutiny. Most sportsmen are naive on the reasons for dwindling deer populations. In addition to less winter range, the reason for fewer deer in many areas is that agricultural interests don't want more competition to livestock and crops. And in Utah they usually get what they want. The Board of Big Game Control has one representative for cattle and one for sheep, and the forest service representative frequently votes with agriculture. There is one person representing sportsmen's interests and the UDWR director in case of a tie. It would be well to change this arrangement considering it is after all, a board of *big game* control.

Too often, deer and elk have no one speaking up for them — until it is too late. In one instance, where a Rich County landowner shot 139 deer in a single late autumn period, he got away with it. He should be protected in some way. But think about the value of those deer (even does would bear many young bucks) in the coming hunting seasons!

Right now, agriculture pretty well runs the show. Stockmen are allowed to run cattle and sheep on public lands and in most cases, wherever there is conflict (especially on a poor range) wildlife suffers. The UDWR must also pay for coyote and predator controls that agriculture wants.

Why should wildlife take a second seat? It's time to balance the books. Sportsmen must work with the legislature and public officials and point out the value of wildlife to the vast majority of Utahns.

Utahns must leap into the voting process. We must determine who is acting in behalf of sportsmen's interests. I personally believe one legislator of the early 1990's who is greatly assisting fish and wildlife has been Rep. Wayne Owens. He stepped in to prevent loss of vital big game habitat in the Central Utah Project. He prevented loss of waterfowl habitat when major wetlands were to be removed in Cache County's Cutler Reservoir. We need more like him, from both parties. But he also needs more sportsmen speaking up for what he is trying to accomplish.

Far too often in the past, judgment decisions by lawmakers and politicians have neglected any course favoring fish or wildlife. Developers put forth the argument, "There are plenty more deer, or elk, or fish. They'll come back." Such argument today is irresponsible. There is no longer "plenty left over." What is left is a last frontier. Every decision adversely affecting wildlife must now be affixed with an asterisk which says: "Note: If this wildlife habitat is lost, it will never be replaced. Let's think before we act."

What can we do about it all as sportsmen? Join a sportsman's group and campaign for responsible legislation. Do not just talk about it. Act. Before it's too late.

CHAPTER NINETEEN

Gaining the Extra Edge

Serious hunters or anglers will utilize every means possible to learn more about the location of the fish and game they seek. There are a number of excellent sources which can help anyone find up-to-the-minute information. State and federal agencies can supply maps, weather and road information, new proclamations, and regulations, tips, and often, much advice. They have many answers for the courteous sportsman.

Many state conservation officers welcome the public going along with them on their daily rounds. In this way the public learns more about the world of the fish-game officer.

I once accompanied a conservation officer for several days in Utah County. We looked at apple saplings killed by antlered deer rubbing against the bark. This occurred not near Timpanogos or Payson Canyon, but at the south shore of Utah Lake. Apparently, deer were coming down at night off the low hills westward. Checking things out, it was found a small population of deer, with several nice bucks, was wintering there. When the state called a "depredation" hunt, permits went begging. Sportsmen didn't even know the deer were there.

Another conservation officer I contacted showed me giant bucks on the northern ridges of Manti Mountain. This was, admittedly, after the hunting season had concluded. But it was obvious that a good many nice bucks were somehow eluding the hunter. How they could do it with all the hunting pressure in that canyon was difficult to comprehend. But I learned to look more carefully for wise old bucks. To find deer, you sometimes have to be an orange-vested Sherlock Holmes. Bucks depend on careless hunters. I determined from that time on not to be one of them.

There was the day in Howell Valley where I followed a tip to find thousands of pheasants picking up mid-morning weed seeds and gravel. It was clear that a prolonged winter here could take a heavy toll of birds. Flocked together like that, they were easy prey even for nearby house cats gone wild, of which there were many. A local CO agreed with me that a larger harvest was needed, considering statistics indicating the average pheasant only lives 1.7 years. Here were too many pheasants. I lobbied for more permits to be sold by landowners there the following year. It was the best pheasant hunting in the state, and relatively few knew about it.

There have been many days of deep outdoor enjoyment with professional outdoorspeople. For instance, during one conversation with Tedd Tuttle, a Utah State Parks employee, he said, "Boaters are hanging things up too early. The fish are hitting out there on Scofield and Echo, and and lakes like them, all through October. Too few are benefitting from the best fishing of the year." When asked "to prove that statement," Tuttle arranged a morning in his boat on Scofield. The day was typically October-cold, but the blustery weather was scarcely noticed. In less than two hours we caught many rainbows and cutthroats. Fishing was not only good, it was ridiculously easy. The cool water had brought trout up to the surface. A flatfish didn't need wobble more than 30 seconds before a fish belted it. Fly fishing was as good as it gets.

Then, there was the time the U.S. Forest Service showed us the "South Horn" near Joe's Valley on the eastern Manti. USFS personnel showed me giant bucks in the cedars where I had suspected none. A sheepherder also told me of a monster buck like that. No one ever realized that this mosshorn was living for years in a narrow gap in the mountain very near civilization. "If hunters approached," the sheepherder told me, "that monarch would lie down with his antlers flattened against the earth."

"Why didn't you tell a hunter about it?" I asked.

"No one ever asked," he answered.

I resolved to be among the askers next time.

Once, with Bates Wilson, who more than anyone else was responsible for the establishment of Canyonlands National Park, I marveled at the magnificent color combinations. I also saw desert sheep terrain near Canyonlands. Ever since that expedition, I can understand why a sheep hunter must be in good condition and have plenty of time available. If I ever draw a permit, I will be much better qualified to make a quest for desert sheep.

It helps to ask many questions. There was the fishing expedition to the Uintah River. I explained to Ute Tribe fish-game warden Tom Chapoose I was taking "only small brook trout" in the ponds alongside the river. I wondered out loud if he had any "with larger fish." He told me to climb in his truck, and hang on. We took a bumpy road for several miles, and forded a good-sized stream before he stopped. "Those ponds over there are tough to reach," he said. "But give them a try." There, I caught large brookies. I found large cutthroats in Towave Reservoir the next day by asking similar questions. At other times, conservation officers have shown me, via electro-shocking, oversized brown trout where anglers complained "it was all fished out."

There just isn't room in all of the maps, books, proclamations, and chamber of commerce publications to write down all of the productive fishing and hunting hot spots everywhere. You'll just have to be friendly, admit you don't know it all, and cultivate the friendship of the people everywhere. It isn't so much a case of them "holding back" so much as it is them not knowing how much it means to you to know. There's no reason they should pass along a secret to someone who doesn't fully appreciate it!

In addition, it pays to always have a healthy curiosity. In February, 1990, I decided to check up on a tip about big bucks in the Wasatch foothills above the Holladay Gun Club southeast of Salt Lake City. I hadn't left the I-215 connector freeway near the mouth of Big Cottonwood Canyon for more than three minutes when I looked at a high and very respectable four-tined muley. This buck and others like him wintered near three-quarters of a million people. It was with deep satisfaction that I attempted to visualize how many hunters that muley had eluded the previous October. No big bucks left anymore above Salt Lake City? Nope. I know better!

Several government agencies like the U.S. Fish and Wildlife Service can help you locate major predator "problem areas." They will be happy to assist you in going where the coyotes are, say near Green River, Hanksville, or Delta. The various state and federal agencies are paid to serve the public. If you proceed courteously (sometime patiently, as they serve others) these professionals can likely guide your steps to the resources. They have helped many others.

Lastly, one word about gaining an extra edge on the fish and wildlife. You seek them on their terms, in their domain. They know the area better than you. They should. They've had to rely on these ravines, peaks, streams, logs, rock slides, and natural terrain for a long time in order to reach trophy proportions. They have natural instincts and insights which may not derive from what scientists call "an ability to think in abstract terms," but they sure can find a thousand ways of eluding you. You have to learn about *their* habitat, and *their* habits to outsmart them. After all, if that big trout or buck were easy, they wouldn't be special. Remember, trophies rarely come cheap, or they wouldn't be trophies.

As Teddy Roosevelt said, no one can learn it all by himself. Share what you have on occasion. Others will probably do likewise in your behalf.

The pages ahead will help. If your inquiry concerns policy making, environmental procedure, legislative matters, etc., contact the Department of Natural Resources, 1596 W. No. Temple, Salt Lake City, 84116, or phone 328-5356. Other contact sources to help you gain that extra edge are as follows:

DIVISION OF WILDLIFE RESOURCES

Headquarters: 1596 West North Temple, Salt Lake City, Phone 533-9333.

Regional Offices:
    Northern: 515 E. 5300 So., Ogden, 84405, ph. 479-5143.
    Northeastern: 152 E. 100 North, Vernal, 84078, ph. 789-3103.
    Central: 1115 No. Main St., Springville, 84663, ph.489-5678.
    Southeastern: 455 W. Railroad Ave., Price, 637-3310, ph. 637-3310.
    Southern: 622 No. Main St., Box 666, Cedar City, 84720, ph. 586-2455.

WILDLIFE BOARD

723-3334 863-3239	Valentine, Robert G. (Joan) 520 East 100 North, Brigham City 84302
789-0240 789-1165	Stringham, Paul (Dr.) (Jean) 1775 South 2935 West, Box 668, Vernal 84078
583-1735 220-2851	Jody Williams (Dave Mortensen) Room 336 1407 West North Temple, Salt Lake City 84116
896-4239 529-7430	Harward, Warren T. (Mary Lou) 800 North Third West, Richfield 84701
586-3050 586-4456	Corry, Robert (Dr.) (Barbara) 1022 So. Cedar Knolls, Cedar City 84720

BOARD OF BIG GAME CONTROL

Home Office	467-4032 748 East Parker Lane 486-0161 Salt Lake City, 84106	Miller, Merrell R. Sportsmen's Representative
Home	225-3082 4575 North Canyon Rd. Provo 84601	Johnson, Newell A. Woolgrower's Representative
Home	(303) 858-0343 1897 L Road Fruita, CO 81521	Cunningham, Greg A. Cattlemen's Representative
Office	625-5669 324-25th Street Ogden 84401	Burbridge, William R. Forest Service Representative
Office	533-9333 1596 West No. Temple Salt Lake City 84116	Provan, Timothy H. Director Wildlife Resources

WILDLIFE RESOURCE
INSTALLATIONS

Bear Lake Station   946-8501
P.O. Box 231
Garden City 84028

Beaver Hatchery   438-2619
Box 366
Beaver 84713

Brown's Park Waterfowl   885-3306
Management Area
Maybell, Colorado 81640

Central Utah Project —
Bonneville Unit
1115 No. Main St.
Springville 84633

Clear Lake Waterfowl   (Radio) 619
Management Area
P.O. Box 254
Hinckley 84635

J. Perry Egan Hatchery   425-3547
P.O. Box 85
Bicknell 84715

Farmington Bay   451-2121
Waterfowl Management Area
P.O. Box 28
Farmington 84025

Fishlake Cabin   836-2721

Fisheries Experimental Station   752-1066
1465 West 2nd North
Logan 84321

Flaming Gorge   885-3164
P.O. Box 158
Dutch John 84023

Forest Service Shrub   377-5717
and Science Lab
735 North 500 East
Provo 84601

Fountain Green Hatchery   445-3472
P.O. Box 188
Fountain Green 84632

Glenwood Hatchery   896-5218
P.O. Box 536
Glenwood 84730

Great Basin Research Center   283-4441
15 South Main Street
Ephraim 84627

Hardware Ranch   245-3131
Box 301
Hyrum 84319

Lee Kay Center for   972-1326
Hunter Education
6000 West 2100 South
Salt Lake City 84120

Lee Kay Trap & Skeet   972-9853
6000 West 2100 South
Salt Lake City 84120

Kamas Hatchery   783-4883
2722 E. Mirror Lake Hwy
Kamas 84036

Lake Powell   (602) 645-2392
Wahweap Installation
P.O. Box 1446
Page, AZ 86040

Loa Hatchery   836-2858
HC Box 20
Loa 84747

Mammoth Creek Hatchery   735-4200
P.O. Box 456
Hatch 84735

Mantua Fish Hatchery   723-6579
555 East Fish Hatchery Road
Mantua 84324

Midway Hatchery   654-0282
P.O. Box 7
Midway 84049

Ogden Bay Waterfowl   773-1398
Management Area
Hooper 84315

WILDLIFE RESOURCE
INSTALLATIONS (Cont.)

Panguitch Cabin   676-2600
Panguitch Lake

Public Shooting   854-3610
Grounds-Salt Creek
Rt. 2 Box 133
Tremonton 84337

Springville Hatchery   489-4421
1000 North Main Street
Springville 84663

Springville Game Farm   489-8053
1000 North Main Street
Springville 84663

Strawberry Project Office   654-4542
1074 South Main
Heber City 84032

Whiterocks Hatchery   353-4855
Route 1 Box 10
Whiterocks 84085

Warehouse (Ogden)   479-9719

Note: For angling regulations on Flaming Gorge, Lake Powell, Bear Lake, see current Angling Proclamation.

STATE PARKS WITH
BOAT LAUNCHING FACILITIES

Bear Lake — One of largest marinas in Mountain West. Capable of handling in-boards, cabin cruisers, etc. Located one mile south of Idaho border on U.S. 89, west side.

Big Sand Lake — Eleven miles north of Bridgeland, just off U-86.

East Canyon Lake — Beautiful mountain reservoir, ramp from U-65.

Green River — Town of Green River, east side, south of U.S. 50-6.

Gunlock Lake — Northwest of Santa Clara, three miles south of Gunlock, small lake.

Huntington — One mile north of Huntington, just off U-10.

Hyrum Reservoir — Large ramp, north shore, near town of Hyrum.

Lost Creek Lake — Fifteen miles north of Croydon, east of Morgan; last four miles not paved. Ramp, over dam on east side arm.

Minersville Reservoir — South shore, just off U-21. Twelve miles west of Beaver.

Otter Creek Reservoir — Just off junction of U-22 and U-62, 26 miles south of Koosharem.

Palisade Lake — Small lake, small ramp, one mile off U.S. 89, five miles south of Manti.

Piute Lake — One half mile east of U.S. 89, 12 miles south of Marysvale.

Rockport Lake — Just off I-80, five miles south of Wanship.

Scofield Reservoir-Between Soldier Summit, Price, 14 miles south west of Colton Junction; via U-96 from U.S. 50-6.

Starvation Lake — Along U.S. 40, just west of Duchesne.

Steinaker Reservoir — West shore, six miles north of Vernal, U-44.

Utah Lake — Large harbor and marina, two miles west of I-15, four miles west of Provo.

Willard Bay — large fresh-water reservoir near Great Salt Lake, 15 miles north of Ogden, two miles west of I-15.

Yuba Lake — East of U.S. 91, 23 miles southwest of Nephi.

Deer Creek — 8 miles west of Heber on US 189 or 17 miles northwest of Provo on U.S. 189.

Great Salt Lake — Interstate 80 milepost 104.

Millsite — 4 miles west of Ferron on Ferron Canyon Road.

Quail Creek — 3 miles east of I-15, Hurricane Exit

Red Fleet Reservoir — 12 miles north of Vernal on Hwy 191.

U.S FOREST SERVICE
OFFICES IN UTAH

Note: Where no street address is listed, simply write "U.S. Forest Service Office," and add name of town, Utah. (There are no Utah offices for Caribou and Sawtooth National Forests, which extend from Idaho into northern Utah.)

Ashley
> Headquarters: Vernal, 355 N. Vernal Ave Vernal. District offices:
> Duchesne; Roosevelt;
> Dutch John and Manila (for Flaming Gorge National Recreational Area); Vernal

Cache — see Wasatch.

Dixie
> Headquarters: 82 N. 100 E. Cedar City. District offices: Cedar City (in addition to Headquarters office), Pine Valley, St. George; Powell; Panguitch; Escalante; Teasdale.

Fishlake
> Headquarters: 115 E.900 N. Richfield. District offices: Richfield; Fillmore; Loa; Beaver.

Manti-LaSal
> Headquarters: 599 W. Price River Dr., Price. District offices: Price; Sanpete, Ephriam; Ferron; Moab for LaSal Mountains; Monticello for Abajo Mountains.

Uinta
> Headquarters: 88 W 100 N. Provo. District offices: Pleasant Grove; Spanish Fork; Heber.

Wasatch -Cache (combined)
> Headquarters: Salt Lake City, 125 South State, Room 8230, Federal Building. District offices: Salt Lake, Kamas; Logan; Ogden; Evanston; Mountain View; for north slope of Uintas, Mt. View and Evanston, Wyoming.

BUREAU OF LAND MANAGEMENT
Main Utah Office

OFFICE AND ADDRESS

Utah State Office
324 South State Street, Suite 301
Coordinated Financial Services Bldg.
Salt Lake City, Utah 84111-2303

TELEPHONE

524 + extension

INDIAN TRIBAL OFFICES

Ute Tribe (northeastern counties): Ft. Duchesne, Bottle Hollow office; 84026; ph. 722-5141. Licenses also available in Uintah Basin sporting goods stores.

Navajo Tribe (in San Juan County): Navajo Tribal Headquarters in Window Rock, Ariz.

Goshute Tribe (Deep Creek Mountains): Ibapah, Tooele County, 84034.

For general information, contact U.S. Bureau of Indian Affairs, Wash. D.C., or BIA offices in Utah

The High Uintas Wilderness Area. Fish abound in the lakes; deer, moose, and elk inhabit the forest, and Rocky Mountain bighorn sheep are gaining ground in the high country.

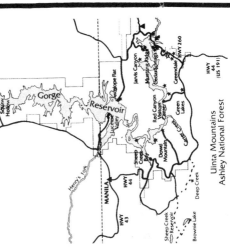

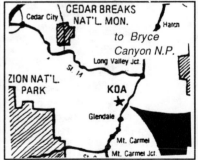

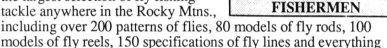

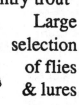

Don J. Sampson
Certified Camp Director
Owner

Navajo Trails
Rocky Mountain Ranch
& Adventure Camp
Box 886
Los Altos, CA 94022
Phone (408) 245-6789

Established 1965

LEARNING CHALLENGE FRIENDSHIP

WAIC & ACA ACCREDITED

SPECIAL FEATURES of the NAVAJO TRAILS PROGRAM

In addition to the many skillbuilding activities of the typical summer camp such as riding, crafts, swimming, waterskiing, archery, riflery, campfire programs, etc., the program at NAVAJO TRAILS provides the following special features:

- A small, family-type camp atmosphere. Enrollment is limited to fifty campers at any one time in order to insure the close, personal attention of the directors and staff to the individual needs and interests of each camper. Weekly program activity groups number 4-8 campers.

- A senior staff of dedicated, mature adults who have proven records of success (effectiveness) in working with youth. Each of these "Program Specialists" is backed up by an experienced college-aged "Program Counselor" and a trained high school graduated "Program Aide." Three such staff work within each camper's weekly program group of 4 to 8 campers.

- A truly "different" program orientation emphasizing challenging adventure and "learning by doing." Unregimented, nonactivity-period structure of program activity.

- Opportunity to develop close life-long friendships with fun-loving youngsters from all parts of the United States and some foreign countries.

A weekly concentration in a variety of genuinely challenging (physically and mentally) program activities:
- Horse and backpacking excursions into Rocky Mountain wilderness areas.
- Lake Powell (on the Colorado River) waterskiing, sailing, and skin diving.
- White-water river kayaking.
- ATC-Honda 3 wheeler wilderness excursions.
- "Mountain-bike" trekking.
- Technical rock climbing.

Travel to and throughout a colorful Western America area:

Salt Lake City	Bryce National Park
Grand Canyon	Capital Reef National Park
Zion National Park	Green River
Colorado River	Canyonlands National Park

Our campers experience personal growth through learning:
(1) to overcome fear with knowledge
(2) to confront uncertainty with confidence and
(3) to develop a sense of self-reliance by doing.

The skilled staff, the program design, and the ranch setting unite to aid the searching youth in his/her quest

- to understand and appreciate himself/herself,

- to develop enjoyable working relationships with others,

- to identify himself/herself with the natural and social forces which combine to provide opportunity for "The Good Life."

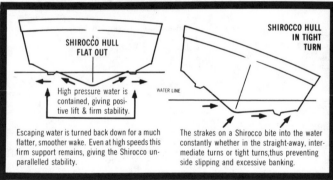

Other Books by Hartt Wixom

Utah, Belding Publishing, 1971

Hunting & Fishing Guide to Utah (First Edition),
Plaza Publishers, 1976

Richard L. Evans, The Man & the Message,
(Co-Author), Bookcraft, 1976

Penny Pincher's Guide to Better Fishing & Hunting,
(Co-Author), Winchester Press, 1978

Elk and Elk Hunting, Stackpole Books, 1986

Trial by Terror, Horizon Publishers, 1987